AGONY AND ECSTASY

AGONY AND ECSTASY

My Diary of an Amazing Rugby Season

Martin Johnson

First published 2001 by Big Four Media

ISBN 0 9541006 0 3

Typeset by Avon Dataset Ltd, Bidford-on-Avon, Warks
www.avondataset.com

Printed and bound in Great Britain by
Omnia Books Limited, Glasgow

Big Four Media
Somerset House
Clarendon Place
Leamington Spa
Warwickshire
CV32 5QN

Contents

Beginnings

I AWOKE feeling utterly knackered. It was a May Monday morning. On the previous Saturday, I had been in Paris, part of a Leicester Tigers side which had won the European Cup. Six days before that, we had beaten Bath on a hot, strength-sapping day at Twickenham in the Zurich Premiership play-off final. It had been a hell of a long season, stretching back to the previous August and full of hard matches for club and country. That is enough to knacker anyone. When you throw in two days of celebrations, first in a riverboat on the Seine and then in a Leicester bar, there can only be one result.

For some of my fellow Tigers, a few well-earned weeks of rest and relaxation beckoned. For others, the final chapter in an outstanding season was about to be written. In a day or two, many of my team-mates would meet up with England for their summer tour of North America, with Test matches against Canada and the USA awaiting them.

For myself, Neil Back and Austin Healey, a different tour heading in a different direction entirely. It would take us first to the leafy, stockbroker-belt of Hampshire, and the magnificent Tylney Hall hotel, and later to the other side of the world.

Four years ago, give or take a week or so, I had had the

privilege of leading men from Scotland, Ireland, Wales and England to an unexpected victory in South Africa against the World Champion Springboks.

Now I had been given the honour once more: this time, though, the British and Irish Lions would face the mighty Australians.

Could we pull it off again?

Early Days

IT HAD all started on another Monday, a couple of days before the Lions touring party was due to be announced. I was sitting at a table in my conservatory filling in the census form that comes round every ten years. It was a very domestic scene and my thoughts were far from rugby as I worked my way through the various questions. The phone rang and I nipped out into the other room to answer it.

Donal Lenihan, tour manager and a former Lions lock himself, was on the other end.

'Hello Martin,' he said. 'I'd like to offer you the captaincy of the Lions.'

'Thank you very much, Donal,' I replied. 'I'd love to accept.'

'I won't go into it too much now,' he continued. 'I know you're busy at the moment' – Leicester still had the European Cup and the Premiership to win – 'but I'll speak to you in the next couple of weeks and let you know a little bit more.'

'OK, Donal. Look forward to hearing from you,' I said, putting the phone down and returning to my chair and the census form. my wife, Kay, did not even look up. Eventually she murmured: 'Who was that?'

*

THERE WAS a lot of talk about me being given the captaincy. I had, after all, been lucky enough to lead the Lions on the last tour, our victorious trip to South Africa. I was also captaining an England side which was playing very well. But I tried not to think about it too much.

There were a number of other excellent candidates named in the final party.

Keith Wood would have been a good captain. He has the respect of all players, for his ability, guts and personality. The only question there was whether he would stay in one piece on an arduous tour, given the way he plays the game. Woody has a massive amount of bottle, he is fairly reckless with his body, he takes and gives a lot of big hits, and that inevitably can lead to injury. He has had a number of shoulder operations and I thought he was doing well still to be playing at his very high level in 2001.

Lawrence Dallaglio would certainly have been in the frame, and would have been another excellent choice, but his problems with the press in recent years might have brought controversy the tour did not need.

Matt Dawson had been appointed England captain for the 2000 Six Nations after I was injured and was another possible option. But I think the fact that he was going to be in a tough competition for his place, with Rob Howley and Austin Healey, mitigated against him.

Dai Young – the most experienced player on the tour, having first played for the Lions in 1989 – was in a similar position, since Phil Vickery was likely to claim the Test tight-head place. Instead, Dai looked a strong candidate to skipper the midweek side.

I was just delighted to be the ultimate choice. Despite my outwardly relaxed attitude, Donal's call had given me a tremendous buzz and a tingle down my spine. The Lions are special, there is no doubt about that.

All my games with Leicester and England have their own little flavour of history to them: Tigers matches against Bath, for instance, or Calcutta Cup matches with the international side. But when you are doing it day in, day out you tend not to think about that side of things; you live in a practical world of tactics and training and winning or losing. There is always a game next week, or next month, to concentrate on. Sometimes you even have to remind yourself what a huge honour it is to play for England. That can get lost in all the hard work, the slog and the training in the week before a game. With the intensity of the sport and the expectations on players growing each year, you can occasionally forget the bigger picture.

The Lions is different. You cannot help but be aware of the history, of the momentous nature of a Lions tour in sport and in your life. They only happen every four years now and most guys' careers will only last long enough to allow them to go on two or three tours. That is assuming they are selected: plenty of tremendous players have been overlooked.

I was acutely aware of the honour of being the only man to have captained the Lions twice but I was also very aware that everyone else would be talking about that. I did not want to talk it up, I just wanted to get on with it and try to make a success of it. I have always been a fairly practical bloke; when I was handed the Lions leadership in 1997 I did not go out and have a celebration drink. I said to myself 'Right, I need to do a good job of this and keep my feet on the ground.' It was a similar approach this time around.

I did not attend the selection announcement press conference that Wednesday. I was not desperate for the limelight and I had an important team training session with the club, with our Premiership play-off quarter-final match at home to London Irish coming up at the weekend. If it had been Thursday, my day off, or a weights session, which I could do in my own time, it would have been different. I just could not miss a team session. I am sure

Dean Richards would have allowed me to go if I had requested it but I didn't even ask.

A lot was made of this in the press: most of it was along the lines of 'no-nonsense Johnson stays with his club'. I suppose that was better than suggesting I was showing disrespect. That certainly was not the case. I am a rugby player and I have to train. That is what makes me a reasonably good player, not attending press conferences.

And, to be honest, what was I going to be asked? Either bland questions like 'How does it feel to be captain?' or interesting ones like 'What do you think of the squad?'

Both lead to bland answers: It feels great to be captain and I am happy with the squad.

I cannot say 'Well, actually, I thought so-and-so should have been picked,' because that will cause controversy, and possibly rifts within the squad, before you have even started. If a reporter had asked me straight out: 'Do you think Martin Corry should have been in the 37?' I would have wanted to give the obvious answer: 'Yes.' But that would have created headlines and hassle so I would have had to prevaricate.

Additionally, going down to London, motorway traffic, a couple of hours with the press – it all adds up to a long day and you need to be concentrating on work or relaxation at that time in the season.

My only concern was whether the coach, Graham Henry, or Donal Lenihan might think I was being disrespectful. But Donal soon laid my fears to rest. He appreciated that my first loyalty at the point in the season was to Leicester.

*

THE SQUAD announcement caused some raised eyebrows, and two of them were on my forehead.

There were a surprisingly high number of Welsh guys chosen

from what was by no means the strongest side they have had in recent years. After our Six Nations game at the Millennium Stadium, the consensus was that the Welsh players who should be on the trip were Scott Quinnell, Colin Charvis, Rob Howley, Dafydd James and Scott Gibbs. And that was how it turned out, apart from Gibbsy. A 1997 Lions talisman, he was left behind in favour of Mark Taylor and Rob Henderson, who grabbed the centre spots behind the likely Test contenders, O'Driscoll, Catt and Greenwood.

But as it turned out, a further five Welshmen were also selected: Neil Jenkins, Darren Morris, Martyn Williams, Robin McBryde and Dai Young.

I love Jenks. He has been a magnificent servant to the game, to Wales and to the Lions. He is also one of my favourite tourists. But problems with his knee meant he should probably have stayed at home. I would have taken Gregor Townsend instead – in fact, I would have taken Gregor ahead of Ronan O'Gara, too. Townsend has his critics and they had been quick to point out that he had not been playing well since coming back from injury and that he can be as mad and bad as he is brilliant, at times. My argument is that he has that class that very few people possess. He can open teams up, which is always much needed. He is also adaptable, having the ability to play centre as well as 10 – not that with a squad of 37 that is a prerequisite.

I did not really have a view on Darren Morris; he could clearly scrummage – Wales probably out-scrummaged England at the Millennium Stadium in the Six Nations – and was an either-or sort of selection who could have been replaced by David Flatman or Trevor Woodman from England.

Martyn Williams was a surprise. I thought the opensides would be Neil Back and Scotland's Budge Pountney, with Richard Hill more than capable of playing there too, if needed. Budge is a good player with a lot of skill and a lot of bottle and could have challenged for a Test place. Another 7 I would probably have taken ahead of Martyn was David Wallace, of Ireland. None of this is to say Martyn Williams is a bad player. He has played international rugby, he never let himself or us down and he was a good bloke who showed the right attitude throughout the tour.

Robin McBryde was another interesting call for the third hooker, behind Keith Wood and Phil Greening. I would have taken Dorian West or Gordon Bulloch ahead of him. Robin is a very strong scrummager and a very dedicated player – until recently he was still working for an electricity company and training in his spare time, so to have got to the level he has speaks volumes for his character. But Nobby West has better hands and is a similarly beefy scrummager. Gordon Bulloch is a very solid player and was another alternative.

The fifth unexpected Welsh selection was that of Dai Young. Dai has given a lot to rugby, both union and league, and has been a world-class player in his time, but he was a little past his peak by the time the 2001 Lions tour came around. I would still have taken him, for his experience, his nous and his leadership qualities, but he would have been the last of three tight-heads behind Phil Vickery and Julian White. White, the strongest prop around at the moment, would have offered more at 3. He is the type of player you can use at the start to try to dominate when the scrummaging is really intense, before bringing on Vickery, another strong lad but one with a better ball-in-hand game, when the match loosens up. Instead, they left White behind and planned to use Jason Leonard, who can play on both sides of the pack, as tight-head cover.

There were one or two other surprise selections. The Scot Simon Taylor was the obvious one. A young lad with hardly any international experience, he clearly has massive potential. However, I felt it was very harsh on Martin Corry. He is not just a back row; he showed during the last England vs France fixture that he can come off the bench and play brilliantly in the second row, as he did for 60 minutes, and he gives a side extra line-out options. Simon showed enough in his first and only appearance to suggest he had what it took and he could have gone on to become a star of the tour. Even so, we should have taken Corry too.

Jason Robinson's was an interesting inclusion. Jason had yet to start an international for England and the selectors had included plenty of wingers, Luger, Cohen, James, Healey and Balshaw being the other wide men. I thought he would be a star for the midweek side, terrifying the opposition teams. The worst that could happen was he might come home and have people say 'He's not quite good enough for rugby union at the top level yet.'

I might have tweaked the final 37 in other ways, too.

Geordan Murphy, I felt, could have made the cut. He is a utility player, covering wing and full-back and he is also one of the most talented footballers I have ever seen.

Denis Hickie was another winger who might have been disappointed – I know the England backs rate him – though I was not sure who you would leave out for him.

Another contentious aspect of the selection was the inclusion of players who were already carrying injuries, Lawrence Dallaglio and Mike Catt among them.

Lawrence, who had injured his knee playing for Wasps, and Mike, who had a back spasm, were potentially so valuable to the cause that I felt it was worth the risk that they might be unable to make a major contribution. At that stage, the advice from the experts was that they would recover and the selectors had followed that advice.

One other controversial issue had arisen some months earlier. Our coach was to be Graham Henry, a New Zealander. A number of commentators had been scathing of this appointment. How could a Kiwi understand the significance of the Lions, or really appreciate the history and the drama? How could he be as passionate about it as a British or Irish coach?

My view was simple: I could not care less what nationality

Graham Henry was as long as he did a good job. In an ideal world we would have had lots of excellent British and Irish coaches knocking on the door for the job. Sadly, there are not that many around. Ireland were being coached by another Kiwi, Warren Gatland. Scotland's Ian McGeechan had turned the job down. England's Clive Woodward, a manager with vision rather than an out-and-out coach, might have been a good bet but with so many English players in the group it might have been difficult, politically, to have him heading the operation. You are then down to club or provincial coaches and not too many of them could realistically be entrusted with the task, which would have been an enormous step up.

That left Henry. I had met him some months before, when he had come up to Leicester to watch us train and to have a chat with me.

He struck me as a level-headed, shrewd, honest bloke with a good understanding of modern rugby.

He would do for me – as would the squad. It would be an honour to lead them.

*

IT IS not an easy thing to bring together 37 men from four different countries and mould them into a team prepared to fight for each other on and off the pitch. We have just spent the last 10 or 11 months battering each other for club or country and now we are supposed to be on the same side. But it is a problem the Lions have to overcome and, once again, we turned to the Impact team builders. They had worked with us in 1997, ahead of the South Africa tour, and I thought they did an even better job this time around.

It is easy to be cynical about team-bonding activity – and I am more cynical than the next man – but some of it definitely works. On one level it is all very simple: playing tambourines and beating drums together, all making fools of yourselves and all joining in to break down barriers. Or building a tower of milk crates and relying on your team-mates not to let go of the safety ropes. On another level, though, a lot of what we did was quite deep: we got together in small groups and talked about things – often private, painful things, your hopes and your fears – in front of guys we hardly knew. We were going deeper than I would with my friends, which was quite strange. Martyn Williams, the Welsh flanker, told us about the death of his brother. You sit there thinking 'Jeez, that's a big thing to happen in someone's life.' Matt Dawson talked about the break-up of a relationship. These are not things guys often chat to other guys about and, in a way, it was quite moving. I think the theory behind it is that once you have opened yourself up like that you are somehow closer to them and I certainly felt closer to the members of my group afterwards. I was impressed by it and it helped people come out of their shell a little.

A few of the English lads who were new to the Lions had been anticipating a frosty reception from the others. After all, everyone hates the English, don't they? It was not like that at all, and it never is in my experience. Most guys see themselves as rugby players, first and foremost, and they will respect you for your ability and your attitude. They might love to see England stuffed at sport, they may even be fervent nationalists who hate the concept of England, but once you are in a Lions party that goes by the by.

Young guys who were new to the Lions were naturally keeping their heads down. I was like that in 1993. You look around at some of the blokes you are now mixing with and think: 'Hang on, I'm an international player, and everyone knows I can play, but I have to prove myself all over again here with these guys.' So you keep quiet and try to see how the land lies. You do not want to be seen as a big mouth. Others, like Keith Wood and Austin Healey, who had been there and done it before and are gregarious blokes by nature, were more outgoing.

The training, at the Army's physical education centre in nearby Aldershot, was hard and draining. As well as building our team spirit, it was vital that we built up understanding on the pitch. Defence was a key area. England, through the former rugby league coach Phil Larder, had built up a formidable defence over the past two or three seasons and Phil had been recruited to instil the same patterns and organisation into the Lions. It is not rocket science but it does take time and concentration and the early signs were not hugely encouraging, as one or two players struggled to come to terms with the system. On the Wednesday, for instance, what was scheduled as a 75 minute session ended after almost three hours.

I had never known a busier week. We would start around 8am and not finish until half nine, ten o'clock each evening. In between we would have crammed in two rugby sessions, two by Impact, and dealing with tour issues which arose or trying to locate kit. On top of that, I had press work, too. I always seemed to be running late. In 1997, I had thought the pre-tour week was mayhem; now I revised my opinions. In the evenings, guys would occasionally meet up for a chat or a game of cards but we were all so tired that there was precious little time for that sort of thing. Most nights, I was happy to get to my bed as soon as I could. There were certainly no trips to the pub for Johnson.

Our base, Tylney Hall, a marvellous old country house set in acres of landscaped grounds, was a superb hotel where the 'civilian' guests seemed fairly well-heeled. If anything, it was a little too upmarket; players like to feel they can relax and be themselves, wandering round in shorts and flip-flops, swearing liberally and dishing out occasional physical punishments to piss-takers. The mentality of rugby players involves a lot of banter. We are comfortable with it: I will walk into a room and someone will accost me with the words 'Oi! Johnno, you big-foreheaded tosser!' On occasion, I might have cause to lift Austin Healey off the floor by holding him around the throat. The average Tylney Hall guest might not appreciate that. Fortunately, we had a large team room where, within reason we could behave how we liked without worrying about offending anyone. The staff and those guests were all great, though. I would often be wished good luck as I walked down a corridor, sometimes by people who actually had a vague idea of who I was.

There were the usual pre-tour irritations. Take our kit. There were real problems with the formal wear, supplied by a London firm called Eden Park. Three or four items supplied to me, for instance, did not fit. It did not really make any difference to my playing because they were things I could do without. But it did not feel right. Other guys had trousers arrive late and shoes which were the wrong size. The response was: 'Oh, it is really hard to get lots of pairs of size 13 shoes.' Which is rather pathetic. It does not take a genius to work out that rugby players are often big guys with big feet. Donal Lenihan didn't get his official blazer for the send-off dinner until he arrived at the venue. Bearing in mind the tour had been planned for four years, and Donal had been appointed manager months before, I thought that was very poor. This sort of little thing can tell you a lot about the attention to detail of the organisers. We are probably spoiled with England, where absolutely everything is spot-on. The kit looks good, it all fits and it all arrives when and where it should. It may sound vaguely 'girly' but good kit makes players feel good about themselves and their team. I do not know where the blame lay – whether it was Eden Park's fault, or whether they were not supplied with the right information in the first place – but somewhere along the line the people tasked with sorting out our kit failed to do so effectively. At a time when the players were being asked to approach their work with ever increasing professionalism and organisation on the field, this did not smack of professionalism off it.

A senior players' committee had been set up, comprising myself, Dai Young, Lawrence Dallaglio, Rob Howley, Keith Wood and

Jonny Wilkinson. In turn, we organised committees to look after various elements of the tour – an indoors entertainment committee, for things like music, films and video games, and a social committee for trips out of the hotel . . . a team meal, a golf day, go-karting or whatever. More mundane questions, like team dress and ticketing policy, were also handled by players' committees.

We all had to fill out little press questionnaires which were supposed to give insights into us as people. A few of the guys were a bit highbrow; my responses were rather tongue-in-cheek:

'What would you be if you had not been a professional rugby player?' *An amateur rugby player.*

'How do you prepare for a rugby match?' *Get changed into my rugby kit.*

'How would you describe your character?' *Very dull.*

And suddenly, the week was over and we were boarding a coach to take us to Heathrow and a Singapore Airlines jumbo. A few fans had turned up to wave us off, so there were autographs to sign and snaps to pose for. When I have travelled on big tours for England, and indeed on the 1997 Lions tour to South Africa, airline staff and baggage handlers have come to the team hotel to check and secure our cases – team kit and so on – away for us, which makes the players' lives a lot easier. For some reason this had not happened so we had to wait what seemed like ages for the luggage to be unloaded from the bus before we carried it through to check-in ourselves. The media were there in force, too, and we were collared as we hung around.

All our boots had gone separately, having been scrubbed spotless because of the foot-and-mouth outbreak. We had been told that anything arriving in Perth with mud on it would be confiscated so I had taken only one pair of old boots and several pairs of new. Modern footwear does not take any wearing in.

Once the bags were through we were fast-tracked through departures and into the Singapore Airlines Business Class Lounge. We took the place over for a couple of hours and guys changed out of their No1s – formal kit – into track suits and polo shirts for the flight. One or two pulled on the support stockings reputed to prevent deep vein thrombosis, which led to predictable mockery.

It is always a pain flying to Australia because of the sheer distance, though going business class makes it better because of the extra leg room, especially for the taller guys like myself. Our itinerary took us first to Singapore, a 12- or 13-hour flight. We left around midday and most of the party immediately tried to sleep, hoping to avoid jetlag the other end. We touched down at around 1am UK time and had a couple of hours in the airport to stretch the legs. A few of the squad took the opportunity to wander round the duty free shops and bought digital cameras before heading back on board for the hop to Perth. The jetlag strategy involved staying awake for that final four hours so we had a little food and I caught a film – *American Beauty*, with Kevin Spacey. I had started watching it on the way back from England's South Africa tour the summer before but the on-board videos had broken down. Now I know what happened in the end!

Welcome to Oz

WE LANDED in Australia at around 2.30pm local time. Customs men were everywhere and they pulled random squad members to one side to rifle through their kit, checking for signs of mud. Some players had food supplements confiscated because they contained egg or milk proteins, which seemed a little over the top. I was fortunate – I was waved straight through. As at Heathrow, there was a strong media presence and Donal and I were grabbed for TV interviews.

Then we headed to our team coach for the 45-minute drive past row upon row of neat, suburban Aussie bungalows to the Esplanade Hotel in the port of Fremantle, a nice little town with some interesting old Colonial buildings, half an hour from downtown Perth. The restaurants and our team room, a place set aside for players and staff only, where we store day-to-day kit and hang out to get some privacy, were off a big, central lobby and our bedroom doors opened onto a first-floor balcony which overlooked it. That meant it was very open; you could sit in the lobby and watch all the players come and go from the bedrooms, the restaurants and team room. We were all on the same floor, which is always good. We had an open door policy so guys could pop in and have a chat if they felt like it. This was a good way to build team spirit with a bunch of blokes who were still almost strangers to each other.

We had arrived about 4.30pm and after an hour to clean up we met up again down in the team room. We met up with our baggage officer, a cheerful Maori called Anton Toia. He was known to a few of the players from previous national tours to Australia and seemed a decent bloke. Then Donal gave us a little pep talk – 'Right guys, we've arrived and the Australia tour starts here, today' – before we walked to a local Aussie Rules stadium, five minutes away, for a bit of a loosener.

I was pretty whacked – I always feel rotten after a long flight – and I was desperate to get my head down. But we needed to stay awake to enable us click onto local time so I joined the boys, jogging for five or ten minutes, stretching and then getting a game of touch going. They were obviously feeling a buzz because they were quite enthusiastic and I had to call a halt to the session. We were all wearing trainers and the surface was pretty slippery and wet. All we needed was someone to slip or fall awkwardly. Flying leaves you dehydrated and more susceptible to injury and we hoped to keep injuries to a minimum.

Back at the hotel for something to eat, the guys were extremely tired. We had been advised to stay awake until at least 10.30pm to try to get into local time as quickly as possible. In the event I got my head down at around 11.30pm, after a phone call home. The next day we were up before 7am for breakfast and a 7.30am meeting with Graham Henry. He chatted about technical matters and our training plans and off we went for our first day – the 1989 tourist Dai Young apart – as Lions in Australia.

*

TRAINING WAS 15 or 20 minutes down the road at the Palmyra Rugby Club on the banks of the Swan River. It was pretty and picturesque, with great views of the skyscrapers in the centre of

Perth. It also had fantastic facilities for what is essentially a junior rugby club: a number of excellent pitches and a modern, glass-fronted club house that looked more like a high-tech industrial building. The rain started bucketing down shortly after we arrived. And Henry was already pulling no punches with his training. It was tough and intensive, majoring on defence, and was headed up by Phil Larder, England's defensive supremo.

I already knew that I would not be appearing in either of the first two games, for which teams had been pencilled in some time previously, so, along with players carrying injuries, I did not take so full a part as most of the guys. Instead, I watched a lot from the sidelines, going on to replace people to give them a breather or just to get involved. I was not too disappointed. I had had a long season and, like all the English players, I was also up to speed with what Phil was trying to do. Many of the non-English blokes were not and were starting with the basics. Larder had guys banging into each other pretty hard for two hours as he worked on them but the gap we had noticed back at Tylney Hall had to be closed.

Eventually, soaking wet and knackered, with Phil still not satisfied and Neil Jenkins nursing 10 stitches after a clash of heads with Jeremy Davidson, the guys headed back to the hotel. Jerry soon earned the nickname of 'Dangerous Brian' for his uncanny ability to injure team-mates in training, something I had actually noticed in South Africa. The 'Dangerous' part is self-explanatory. I never found out where the 'Brian' part came from.

We had been instructed not to sleep but I grabbed 40 minutes just to keep myself going for the afternoon. It must have been really deep sleep because when I awoke I had that groggy feeling you sometimes get but I made it down for the meeting prior to the 3pm session. Again, it was a fairly long series of drills, this time working on scrummaging and playing off the scrum. A few players were a bit disgruntled. One of them complained that with meetings, training and travelling time we had been seven hours doing rugby that day. That is a long time, far longer than most England days. I felt, though, that we needed the work. Players were obviously used to different systems and it was particularly evident defensively.

Another sound night's sleep was followed by another long day on the training field. The management had listened to complaints about the previous day's 7.30am start, however, so we began at 9am. In the morning we concentrated on lineouts and followed that with some contact work and defence. The afternoon was a shorter session where I worked with the back rows. Jason Robinson took a knock on the ankle in the backs' session, which caused butterflies; after his England showings, Jason looked the perfect impact replacement and the medical team were quick to check him over and pronounce him OK.

Things were still not going spectacularly well. Apart from the problems with our defence, we had been too casual in training generally on both days so far. Possibly the length of the sessions was one factor: it is always best, if possible, to keep it short and sharp. Training for a long time sometimes leads to slackness. But principally it was down to a lack of concentration by some players. Balls were dropped, inaccurate passes thrown and teething troubles were evident. And already the complaints about the workload from one or two members of the party were getting louder, which I found a little irritating. We were not training for the sake of it – it was obviously necessary. We had arrived on the Saturday and had only six days to get ourselves sorted out before the first game, against Western Australia. They would not be testing opposition but it was important that we treated them seriously.

Tuesday was the first day that the squad split in training, with the 22 who would play Western Australia meeting an hour before the rest of us. Again, it was a very long day, with the match side out for four hours in the morning, but the afternoon was free and

I took the opportunity to snatch an hour's sleep after lunch. Later, I met up with the Geordie fitness advisor Steve Black at the nearby ground of the Aussie Rules side the Fremantle Dockers. They have a marvellous facility there with a superb gym. Blacky, a former weightlifting champion who works with the Newcastle Falcons, is a top bloke with amazing energy and a great sense of humour. I had the first of a series of very interesting workouts with him. He trains differently to other experts. Most are regimented and will give you a set number of weights to lift and a certain number of exercises to carry out; normally we do three sets of eight or four sets of six. Steve just seems to make it up as he goes along, keeping you going as long as he thinks he needs to, often to failure. He is very 'up' all the time and his style is not everyone's cup of tea. But if you have trained twice a day it can be very hard to motivate yourself for a weights session and I found Steve had the knack of encouraging me. We spent a good hour together and by the end I felt great. We did a bit of boxing, too, him with a bag and me with the gloves, which was hard work. Later we made our way down to the pool, which was full of the Aussie Rules players. Most of them were pretty young, which made me feel old. They had been having a bad season – I think they had lost 10 matches on the trot – and it was interesting chatting to them. I talked with their fitness coach, comparing notes about the games and the different training routines, salaries and salary caps, and how long guys went on for. Aussie Rules is big business Down Under and their top players earn more that a Premiership club rugby player would in the UK. They do not have an international scene though – apart from a few cross-code games against Irish Gaelic footballers – so they miss out on that side. They are different athletes to rugby players: there is less physical contact and their games go on for longer, with a lot of running on the huge fields – the game, originally designed to keep cricketers fit in winter, is played on cricket grounds – so they are lighter and leaner. There is a lot of leaping and rugby union has learned from Rules: restart jumps are one area which has been influenced by their techniques.

That evening we had our first team dinner out together at a pleasant, busy little Italian restaurant where we destroyed mountains of pasta, steak and pizza. Normally on tour, bills for these meals just go back to the hotel and are picked up there. But the 50-strong party had each been given a $35 dollar-a-day food allowance and although only 37 of us were out we had all the cash. Some of the guys were ordering four courses and it looked like even the $1750 would not be enough but it just covered the final bill. Someone at another table had a birthday cake delivered to them. Austin Healey saw this and, as he would, called a waitress over.

'We've got someone with a birthday,' he says, pointing out Simon Taylor, who was sitting there quietly minding his own business.

Out came a birthday cake for Simon, who was a little bit embarrassed but took it in good part. Of course, it was not his birthday at all. Austin announced he was planning to do this at every meal on the trip, which would have been utterly hilarious in Austin's little world.

It was an enjoyable evening but one disturbing aspect was the presence of a TV crew from sponsors ntl. They had been with us right from Day One at Tylney Hall and were to be with us all the way through, producing footage for an end-of-tour video. The idea was to capitalize on the undoubted thirst among fans for Lions product in general and fly-on-the-wall film in particular. *Living With Lions*, the coverage of the 1997 South African tour, is apparently the UK's biggest-selling sports video ever and the producers obviously hoped to repeat that success. In South Africa the camera crews had been with us, too, but they had kept their distance, filming without trying to interview. They were so unobtrusive that, by the end, you did not notice them. In Australia, the cameraman was accompanied by a guy with a microphone and he rarely missed an opportunity to jam the mike in front of people and fire inane questions at them, no matter how sensitive the situation. Many of the players did not like that; it made them feel as though they were in a permanent media interview and stopped them relaxing.

I was not slow to ask them to leave on occasions and I encouraged the other boys to do the same. There is a saying in sport: 'What goes on tour, stays on tour.' It means that, after a hard game or a day on the training pitch, when players get the chance to relax and be themselves, they expect privacy. ntl had made their intentions quite clear with an advert for the video.

'What goes on tour,' it read, 'now goes on TV.'

Guys had to be careful what they did and said because the things we do not want them to film are exactly the things they want. I am not asking for *carte blanche* to behave like hooligans. I simply wanted that space.

Donal Lenihan, a real players' manager and a modest guy who did not seek out the limelight, would not have allowed the cameras the access they had but, with pound signs dancing in front of people's eyes, the decision was taken out of his hands.

They were not the only film crew we had to worry about. At one early training session someone spotted another guy with a camera. Apparently, he turned out to be an assistant coach from the Wallaby camp, obviously trying to get a look at some of our planned moves. The danger would be that the enemy camp could see both specifics of your moves and also gain an idea of your game plan by observing the things you are concentrating on. This sort of thing goes on and is obviously very hard to stop in a massive stadium. We would have loved to watch the Wallabies in training, though it would have taken some doing because they were very guarded, and no-one blamed them for trying. Having said that, I think people sometimes exaggerate the value of seeing the opposition in training. Yes, it may give you an idea as to what they are hoping to do but the important thing in a match is how well they will do things, rather than what those things are.

Like meals, days off were organised by the social committee. There were usually a number of choices to get guys away from the hotel and the Wednesday of our first week the options were a game of golf, a fishing trip, or pistol shooting. Some of the players preferred to do nothing and just chill out in bed but I chose the firearms, as did a lot of the Welsh boys – Colin Charvis, Martyn Williams, Scott Quinnell, Rob Howley, Dafydd James. Danny Grewcock and Scott Murray were there too. We had a very in-depth safety briefing on firing guns before we were let near anything. Then we got our chance. Rob McBryde and I, starting with the little .22s, were locked away in our cubicles, concentrating hard on trying to hit the bullseyes. Suddenly there's this huge boom and a compression wave you could actually feel. We leapt out of our skins. The whole place was vibrating. A cackling Scotty Quinnell was next door blazing away with a Magnum rifle.

In that first week, we were also sorting out communications. Modern Lions tours are not as long as they used to be but it is still tough being away from your family for six weeks or more. It was not so bad for me: my wife, Kay, was flying out with friends for the Test matches and we do not have children. But for the guys who have little ones it was hard. We were supplied by ntl with laptop computers so we could keep in touch via email and there were also occasional video conferencing opportunities to enable dads to see their kids and speak to them almost live. The team doc, James Robson, was away while his daughter was celebrating her third birthday. James had bought her a cake with candles on it so he could share the day with her from thousands of miles away. He was very emotional as he chatted to her, which was moving to see. I did not use this facility myself and the chance to do so was very rare. But it is clearly the next big thing in communications and I am sure the 2005 Lions Tour to New Zealand will be fully equipped with such gadgets.

On the Thursday, the guys playing against Western Australia trained in the morning and the rest of us were given the morning off. Most guys, myself included, decided to sleep in before tackling practice in the afternoon. The way this works, you line up opposite your tacklers and run at them in a direction shouted out by Phil Larder.

I do not want to sound wise after the event but I have always been wary of this session. It is fine as long as everyone follows the direction they should. Problems occur if someone goes the wrong way. You end up running into each other, going low, and guys' knees can be hit from the side. Phil always emphasises the need to concentrate on going in the direction he indicates.

He made his call and, for some reason, Matt Dawson and Matt Perry – ironically, given that they were both well-versed in what we were doing – got tangled up and ended up hitting Phil Greening. His knee took the impact and he went down instantly, clearly in a lot of pain. My immediate thought was that he had ruptured a knee ligament, which is a very serious injury and would have put him out for months. He was unable to get to his feet unaided and had to be helped to a vehicle and taken off to hospital for a scan.

It was very upsetting and put a dampener on the whole session. We were all very sorry for Phil. On a relatively short tour you do not have the luxury of time to heal and at the very least it put him out of the early games. Later, we got some preliminary noises from the experts which were better than I had feared but not exactly encouraging. He had damaged his medial collateral ligament and it would take two to four weeks to get right. The management thought that he should be sent home straight away but we sought a second opinion from James Robson. You cannot judge an injury straightaway and James felt Phil should be given at least a couple of days to see how it went. If he could recover within two weeks he could still play a part in the tour.

I did not want 'Phyllis' to miss out if he did not have to. He would be a big loss to the group. In a playing sense, Phil is a strong, dynamic runner and probably the only hooker who would really push Keith Wood for a Test spot given the way we wanted to play. Off the field he is a top bloke, very lively and full of fun – just the sort of person you need on tour.

Faced with this argument, Donal agreed he could remain with the party for the following two weeks. Scotland hooker Gordon Bulloch was sent for as his replacement. I was surprised not to be consulted on this decision. I believe Dorian West would have been the better bet. Gordon is a steady bloke and a good player but Nobby likes to get his hands on the ball more and is more talkative on the pitch, which is a good thing. Additionally, at that point he would have been in better shape as he was still playing, out in North America with England, whereas Gordon had been on a family holiday in Colorado. This was proved when the Nob eventually joined us and leapfrogged Gordon onto the bench for the last two Tests.

The irony was that the session had been good apart from that incident – and the fact that we had no hooker for scrummaging or lineout practice – though we were struggling to come to grips with Graham Henry's way of playing. Like Larder, he had definite ideas of how he wanted us to operate. In his case, it involved a very structured approach which laid down detailed plans for multiple phases of play.

The first three phases are always fairly organised anyway. Everyone knows what they should do off first phase, from the scrum, the lineout or the kick-off. The team will look to act in a particular way – maybe the ball will be taken into midfield, maybe wide, maybe it will be kicked. When a breakdown occurs, you are in a ruck situation. Everyone ought to know who should hit that first ruck, the second phase. They should also know who will then be available either to take the ball up or to clean out and win the ball at the second ruck, the third phase. After that, most teams play 'heads up', with guys reading the game as it unfolds and reacting accordingly, using their rugby knowledge and experience. That is when high class fly-halves and scrum-halves can take charge of a game, directing the play as you look to attack. However, it is important that the organisation of those attacks is spot on. Defences are now so organised that if guys get isolated you will lose the ball. Graham was trying to guard against this by orchestrating the fifth, sixth, seventh phases of our attacks. Individual players were instructed which rucks they would go into and which rucks they would not. A lot of us, myself included, were not used to our play being so defined and pre-determined. We are more 'heads up' and we were finding it difficult both to carry so complex a gameplan in our heads and also to execute it. As with the defensive work, we just had to hope it would come with practice.

That evening, the mood was obviously a little flat. We were gutted for Phil Greening though, at the same time, philosophical: we knew there would be injuries, we had all suffered them and 'There but for the grace of God go I', was the general feeling. I spent a little while with him, trying to console him and keep his spirits up. I thought it was less than 50-50 that he would recover in time but obviously I did not say that to him. With a number of players already carrying niggles, I hoped his would be the first and last injury we would suffer but I knew this was likely to be a forlorn hope. It had been a long season for the guys, they were tired in body and mind and training was intense. In those circumstance, injuries are going to happen. Little did I know how many.

Skirmishing

FRIDAY, AND match day. Four years, give or take, from the last time a Lions match shirt had been worn, 22 new red jerseys sat in a pile on a table in our team room at the Esplanade Hotel, ready to be handed out.

Western Australia awaited.

Donal Lenihan made a speech, telling the boys: 'For every one of us there is a special feeling when you see the Lions team running out onto the field...22 guys will have that honour today.'

Graham Henry stood up and walked to the front. With characteristic bluntness, he outlined the point of the tour, telling the boys: 'What it means, guys, is winning. There's nothing else, is there? It means individuals fighting tooth and nail to be in the Test team. If you're just pleased to be here we don't want you, do we really?'

He ended: 'These people down here in the Southern Hemisphere doubt your skills. I know. I'm one of them.' It was an odd thing to say and one or two of the guys later commented on it. I think he was probably trying to be funny. He is witty but so dry that his humour was lost on many of the players, who often could not tell whether he was joking or not. It is just the way Kiwis are. I am married to one and Graham reminded me strongly of my father-in-law – they have this knack of sounding and looking very serious even when they're kidding.

One by one, the selected boys came forward and collected their shirts, some clearly very emotional, and were clapped by the rest of us. I sat at the back with the rest of the non-selected guys, watching them step up to receive the coveted prize, and felt weird because I was not involved; I was sort of on tour, but not. The main sensation, though, was of an adrenalin-fuelled buzz. The hairs stood up on the back of my neck. I could not wait for kick-off.

The tour had finally started and the fun had begun.

I had not had much to do with selection for the first couple of games. They were really about giving as many people as possible a start, and had been all-but drawn up before we left the UK. The main talking point was the introduction of Brian O'Driscoll at full-back. It did seem strange to pick perhaps the world's best outside centre out of position and it occurred to me that a bad performance might knock his confidence. The obvious interpretation was that Henry was looking ahead to the Test bench; on Six Nations form, you had to assume that Iain Balshaw would be at 15. If Brian could cut the mustard at the back it meant he could fill in if Balsh got injured. As Henry himself admitted: 'We're just looking at options. If there is not a specialist full-back on the bench in the Test squad then Brian might be a possibility to switch to play there. It would be difficult to play him there then if he'd never played there before.' It was not unheard of, of course. England had even once considered playing Jeremy Guscott at the back. And if anyone could do it, surely Brian could?

Rob Howley had first crack at scrum half, ahead of Matt Dawson. Rob, a player I rate very highly, had suffered a drop in form after losing the Welsh captaincy, and had even been replaced in the international side by the nasally-impressive Brummie Rupert Moon, but was now back to his sharp, sniping best.

Keith Wood would lead the side, something he described as a

great honour. His dad, Gordon, had been a Lion in the 50s and Woody has always embodied what is best about playing for the British Isles.

Earlier, we had received some bad news. Those of us not taking part had trained at the nearby Associates Ground, another excellent centre; the quality of club pitches and gyms in Australia really opens your eyes to the poor standard of facilities back home. After a session working on organisation and defence I headed to the gym for a work-out with Blacky and then back to the hotel for lunch. There I was informed that Mike Catt had a pulled calf to add to the back spasm he had been suffering for several weeks. I hoped it would just be a twinge. We did not need any more injuries, especially to someone like Catty. He was a very positive member of the group and a likely Test starter at inside centre.

Our outline plan involved playing Jonny Wilkinson at fly-half with Mike outside him, where his kicking, his change of pace and his big, wide, passing game could do damage. But when I chatted to James Robson he was sceptical, saying Catty might struggle to recover. Feeling a little despondent, and absolutely knackered, I took myself off to my room and tried to kip.

*

IT WAS almost a no-win game. Western Australia were a team of part-timers who we were expected to defeat heavily. The only players of note were the Argentina-born ex-Australia prop Patricio Noriega, flown back from club rugby abroad as a possible Test front rower, and the ex-Saracens fly-half Duncan McRae. Both would be on the bench.

Henry joked beforehand: 'There are 11 Kiwis in the WA side so they must be good.' In fact, they were an assortment of carpenters, brickies and engineers – fair club rugby players but nothing to really worry us. Their English-born captain, Trefor

Thomas, was realistic enough, admitting: 'If we can keep it to 40–50 points, I'll be happy.' My view was that we had to win and win well and we also had to stay injury free. Time would tell.

By 4.30pm, we had rounded up our kit and were *en route* to the WACA, a famous old cricket ground. We did not arrive until 5.15pm, which in my view is too late for a 6.30pm kick-off. I like to arrive with at least 90 minutes to two hours to spare to give me time to get my game head on. The surface looked immaculate, as you would expect at the WACA – more like a bowling green than a rugby field – and a warm-up school game was being played as we arrived. I wandered around the outfield, taking in the great stadium with its day-night cricket floodlights burning very bright.

I did not go into the changing room for the pre-match but hung around by the tunnel with the other guys waiting for our 22 to emerge. The feeling as we clapped them by and out onto the field was immense and as we followed them into the arena to take our seats I felt that adrenalin rush again.

Not forgetting priorities, I got someone to organise a sweep for first scorer and drew Ben Cohen. I thought I had half a chance. Just as the whistle went, I nipped back to the changing rooms and went to the loo and by the time I got back Scott Quinnell had already scored and Jenks was claiming the money. Bang went my tenner!

It rapidly became apparent that the match was not going to be at all competitive and as the total began to mount the only questions were whether we would get to a century, whether they would score at all and whether we would suffer any serious injuries.

Some of our play was excellent, with the guys standing very flat and playing with good pace. Up front, not surprisingly, we outscrummaged them, winning ball against the head which is almost unheard of against serious opposition. Some individuals had a point to prove and did their case no harm at all. Will

Greenwood and Danny Grewcock, both challenging for Test spots but by no means certainties, showed well and Rob Howley, Scott Quinnell and Dan Luger also looked sharp. Best of all, we had not eased up once we had obviously won. Henry said afterwards that he was delighted with how 'ruthless' we had been in still seeking scores long after we had posted 100 points and Western Australia had been well beaten, 10–116.

There were negatives: the Brian O'Driscoll experiment had not really worked, with the Irishman not being as effective as he might otherwise have been, and Ben Cohen had not played his best game. He missed a chance of a try when Duncan McRae barged him into touch and he also blamed for an ineffective tackle to let them in for one of their two scores. A number of us felt this was harsh; it would have been an outstanding tackle. A few passes had gone astray and we had lost our shape in the second half at times. The biggest irritation, however, were those 10 points that they posted. We were very angry with ourselves for letting them through.

As the scoreline suggests, it was not a tense match to watch. We had run in 18 tries and posted a new Lions points record, beating the 97 racked up by the Willie John McBride vintage against SW Districts in 1974.

By half-time, I had just wanted to get out of there with no injuries. My wish seemed to have been granted when the final whistle went, though Iain Balshaw came off holding his shoulder. This looked worrying but it turned out he had merely popped a rib cartilage in his sternum – much less serious than a shoulder injury – and he would not miss any rugby. In the changing room, though, young Simon Taylor suddenly felt his knee go. He had come on for Richard Hill in the second half and had played well with good pace, one lovely behind-the-back pass to put Balsh over and a try of his own. He had taken a knock on the knee 20 minutes before the end of the game but had carried on with the adrenalin masking the pain. Once that had started to wear off he realised he had a problem and the Doc was called. A knee stability test left James very perturbed. He came to me and told me Simon would need a scan urgently but was almost certainly finished on the tour and could be out for months. The scan would reveal all the following day.

Immediately, I sought out the player to console him over the injury. We were all hoping for the best – sometimes the initial diagnosis is wrong – and none more so, obviously, than Simon. At just 21, he had delayed his law degree finals for a year after being selected. Now, after only 40 minutes of rugby, it seemed his dream was over. It also left us with a problem in the back row. With Lawrence Dallaglio, Simon was our only other regular back row line-out jumper. Lawrence was still unable to play so our options in this important area were now severely limited. Martyn Williams had done a bit and Richard Hill was happy to try his hand. Scott Quinnell is a great No8 but at around 20st he is too heavy to jump effectively. Neil Back is probably too small – that will get me chinned. Most disappointingly, Colin Charvis, probably the best option, did not want to try to learn. Colin is a big, athletic bloke with natural ball-handling skills and he ought to make a superb back-of-the line jumper. But when we suggested he try his hand he flatly refused. I was disappointed at his attitude. After the tour was over, he gave an interview to one of the papers. Complaining that he had been overlooked, he said: 'I heard I hadn't been picked for the big games because I wasn't a line-out forward . . . why not tell me to work on this a few months before the tour? I came back feeling like a sub-standard player and the lesson I learned was don't go again.'

Whether or not Graham Henry should have suggested line-out jumping to Charvis months before or not is debatable. What I do know is that when we asked him to try he wouldn't. I do not know why. I believe he could have learned it fairly quickly and he would have given himself a better chance of selection for the Tests if he had.

With Simon likely to be out for the duration, we had to send for our second replacement. Martin Corry, who was on tour with England in Canada and North America, was the choice. I believe he should have been included in the original touring party and it was a mystery to me that he had not been. I could only assume it was to do either with his nationality – Taylor was one of only three Scots to have made the original party, which was heavily loaded with English players – or the fact that he had tended to figure as a replacement for England. Although he had well over 20 caps, only six of them had come from starts. He would walk into most other countries' international sides but has been unfortunate to be around at the same time as an outstanding English back row of Hill, Back and Dallaglio. Possibly the selectors did not take this into account when making up the party. Simon has bags of ability and a great future but only had a couple of caps for his country at that point. Even he himself admitted his selection was a surprise – he had been aiming for the 2005 Tour. Cozza, meanwhile, was a proven international back row with plenty of strength, fitness, pace, nous and skill: just the assets we would need in Australia. He was also an accomplished line-out jumper and an international-standard second row. He got the call in Vancouver and would be with us in Australia a day or two later.

After the match, the guys who had played attended a reception and the rest of us headed back to the hotel. Steve Black had arranged chip butties for us – a great treat – but myself and six or seven others went with Lawrence Dallaglio to a little Italian restaurant he had found around the corner and had pasta and bruschetta. The whole town was rocking after the game, with masses of Lions fans milling around, and we would have loved to go for a beer. However, we had a 7.15am meeting prior to a short morning session and a lunchtime flight to Townsville for the next leg of the tour. Minds on the job, we passed up the opportunity.

*

WITH TWO tries conceded the night before, that morning training run once again concentrated on defence. Phil Larder, frustrated that some players were still not getting his defensive system, gave them a bit of a 'hurry up' and a few of the Irish and Welsh players felt they were being picked on.

It is a common sense system, but it does take practice, confidence and concentration to learn properly. In a nutshell – albeit a pretty big nutshell – Larder's defence system works like this: you stay inside your team-mate as he drifts across the field covering the attack. You make sure you are covering his inside. If he gets stepped, you are there to make the tackle. If he makes the tackle you are there to go in and compete the ball. If the attacker passes inside you are there to smash the guy he passes to. You defend from the inside, where the scrum, ruck, maul or line-out is, out. If it functions effectively, your midfield is covered, forcing your opponents to go wide around your outside if they want to beat you and your cover defence – the back three – can come across and tackle them. A key part of it is communication, with the back row and 9, 10 and 12 particularly important. They should be constantly chattering to each other, identifying problems, making sure everyone is in the right spot, keeping the backs and forwards linked. But everyone needs to get involved – if you are covering a guy's inside shoulder, you must tell him you are there, by shouting or signalling, and he needs to listen and understand what is being said.

If everyone is fully in tune with the system it allows you to compensate for a lack of pace or numbers in your defence. Sometimes, in the modern game, front five forwards can find themselves covering in the back line. If you try and stop attackers individually they will step you and beat you with their pace. If you defend as a team, holding your line, each man covering the inside shoulder of the man outside him, it is a lot easier to keep them out. If you are outnumbered – say three defenders against five attackers – the defenders will cover the inside three attackers, pushing them wider all the time. If the attacking team is poorly organised that can be enough to stop the attack. If the attackers are smart they may exploit the overlap but the cover defence should catch them and bring them down or into touch. It is simple but effective, as Leicester and England's defensive record over recent years shows.

A few of the non-English players were finding the system hard on a number of levels. Some had trouble with the communication – they were not confident that what they were saying was right so they clammed up. Others found their concentration lapsing or were out of position at crucial times. It was frustrating to be working with a team that was of such high quality in most areas but was one which was struggling, albeit only through a lack of time, with a defensive strategy that our club's second XV had mastered (Larder is also Leicester's defence coach). But I understood their problems. While it is not, as I have said, rocket science it does take time for it to become second nature. It was important to avoid sounding negative or patronising and I bit my lip a few times. If it became a 'them and us' situation, with the Celtic guys feeling that the English thought they were superior, the tour could be jeopardised. I tried to remain positive and any criticism was constructive and made as respectfully as possible. Slowly, I felt, we were getting there; the players were talking to each other a lot more and the organisation was improving.

By 10 o'clock we were on the bus to the airport and Simon Taylor had received confirmation that his injury was tour-ending. He had been trying to look on the bright side and had convinced himself he was OK, so it was a bad blow. I really felt for him. Who knows? He may never play for the Lions again. With his obvious ability and at his age, though, I suspect he could well feature in two or three future squads.

More bad news greeted us when we got to Departures. Our

plane was temporarily grounded for technical reasons and concerns over the weight of our luggage. At first the delay was just an hour, which we could live with. It soon turned into a four or five hour problem, however, and, given that the time difference to Townsville meant we would already lose two hours' sleep, we were looking at a very long day indeed.

To kill time, we went back to a Perth casino for food and a chill-out. Austin Healey, wandering past a spinning wheel, put down $10 on a 23-1 shot and won first spin, $230, which kept him happy. Most of the guys won a few quid apart from poor old Rob Howley, who had no luck at all.

After a couple of hours we headed back to the airport for another hour's wait in the charter lounge before finally getting underway. I had been looking forward to seeing the vastness of the Australian interior from the air but by the time we were airborne it was almost dark. I couldn't read – I had lost my paperback, a Tom Clancy novel – so I spent much of the journey chatting to my neighbour, Scott Quinnell. The bigger lads had been allocated business class seats together at the front of the plane and Scotty and I had a good old chat. He is a real gentle giant off the pitch, a very nice bloke and a family man, and we talked about his kids and our clubs back home.

By the time we got to Townsville, after a refuelling stop in Alice Springs, it was nearly 2am. It had been a long, long waste of a day, 14 hours in transit. We were also starving; there had been nothing but peanuts and biscuits on board the plane and we gratefully tucked into a buffet laid on by the Jupiters Hotel, which also boasted a casino, a slight worry given that players are easily distracted. I finally got my head down at about 3.30am and woke just in time for a noon meeting to video-analyse the Western Australia match. Over the course of two hours, we split into groups to assess all the aspects of the game: attack, defence, kick-off, scrummage, line-out and so on. We were also given copies of tapes of the Wallabies' game against the New Zealand Maoris, played as we had been making our painful trip across country. It was their first run-out for several weeks and they had won 41–29, handing the Maoris their first defeat since 1994. But it was not plain sailing. Carlos Spencer had scored twice and two further scores were denied his side by the referee. Given that Australia had also turned a lot of ball over and were defensively stretched at times, the tape made interesting viewing.

Gordon Bulloch and Martin Corry had each arrived by now, Gordon having flown in the day before and Cozza landing that day. Both looked remarkably fresh. I am sure they were both fizzing with the adrenalin of joining the Tour. I took them aside and brought them up to date. They both faced an early entry into the fray; Gordon would be on the bench for the next day's game, against a Queensland President's XV at the quaintly-named Dairy Farmers' Stadium, and Cozza would start at No8.

Graham Henry wandered over and asked him if he wanted to play. 'I'd love to,' was Martin's brief reply. Henry nodded appreciatively; it showed how keen he was to make an impact.

That afternoon we went through lineout spotters, getting Corry and Bulloch involved as jumper and thrower, and I then spent 50 minutes in the gym with Steve Black. Townsville is in the tropics and even with the air conditioning on it was humid and hot but we got through some good work. Back in the cool of the hotel, I watched the Queensland vs New South Wales State of Origin rugby league match before turning in reasonably early. The following day promised to be a long one; those of us not playing in the second match had two full training sessions scheduled.

The tour was becoming crowded now, with two games a week and plenty of travelling to do. We would play on the Tuesday and then fly to Brisbane the following day for the game against Queensland Reds on the Saturday, when I was scheduled to make my first appearance along with Jonny Wilkinson. Somewhere we had to find the time to watch and analyse the games we had played, look at tapes of the opposition and prepare our strategy for the matches ahead.

The only way to fit in the training was to have longer sessions than ideal on the days you had available. Again, some of the boys were unhappy but there was no alternative given Graham's desire to inculcate a defined structure into our play, where the game was mapped out for us several phases ahead.

This was causing some difficulties. Some of the players felt it was too restrictive, too robotic and unrealistic in a fast-moving game. I was in agreement with them but the coach coaches and the players play. We would just have to do the best we could.

On the Monday morning, the players not involved in Tuesday's game drove out to the stadium where we were to train. Townsville is bigger than I had thought, very spread out and home to a few hundred thousand inhabitants. It is a quiet town, right up in northern Queensland, and even though it was the Australian winter it was warm and a good deal more humid than Perth. It is on the coast and locals do a good trade in tourist boats out to the Great Barrier Reef, an hour or so offshore.

The Dairy Farmers' is the home of the North Queensland Cowboys rugby league team and is an impressive place, with typical Aussie grass banks in some parts and multi-coloured seating in others. We found our way to the changing rooms – to be confronted by the biggest cockroach I have ever seen walking across the tiles – before starting on two tough sessions in the draining heat, broken only by lunch. The afternoon one ran on quite late but looking on the bright side that meant most of us missed a planned Mayoral reception in the evening. I hope that does not sound ungracious; these things are important but on a short tour, with few opportunities to rest, I would rather spend the time on the massage table or chilling.

Match day, and for me, once again not playing, that meant training in the morning and then a gym session around lunchtime. I tried to sleep during the afternoon – I still had not got over the jetlag, which had been compounded by the journey to Townsville – before changing and meeting up with the squad downstairs.

I could sense the anticipation, particularly from the guys for whom this was their first game in a Lions shirt. The others – Will Greenwood, Tom Smith, Jerry Davidson, Neil Jenkins and skipper Dai Young – knew what to expect but there is something special about your debut. And guys were obviously already starting to think about Test places.

Martin Corry had a point to prove at No8. In the second row, Davidson and Murray would be looking to play better than O'Kelly and Grewcock had. Matt Perry would be desperate to show that Balshaw was not the only full back on tour. Matt Dawson would be hoping to edge ahead of Rob Howley in what was a very close battle for the No9 shirt. Martyn Williams and Colin Charvis would want to establish that they were the equals of Richard Hill and Neil Back and on the left wing, Jason Robinson was to start. There were those who doubted he could make the conversion from league to union so quickly, including Graham Henry. It would be interesting to see if they were right.

Some 19,000 people were packed into the ground and we spent a lot of time signing autographs for the UK and Ireland contingent. I was even accosted by some guy who had been to my high school in Market Harborough. He sounded like an Aussie, having been out there for 35 years, but had played for Welland Park, my school back home, and we swapped memories for a minute or two.

It was becoming clear that a lot of fans had flown out to support us already, which felt good. The atmosphere was good, too. The hosts had gone to a great deal of trouble, with lots of cheerleaders, fireworks and a band in the middle of the pitch before the game and the general feel was of a party about to kick off.

The Queensland President's XV were a step up from Western Australia, featuring 10 players with Super 12 experience. It was a massive game for them, with possible Super 12 contracts riding on good performances, and they were clearly very determined to give us a run for our money. And in the first half, we let them. We were shocking. Rob McBryde was injured after five minutes or so, and was replaced by Gordon Bulloch. Not surprisingly – Gordon having only had a few hours to learn our calls – the lineout was shaky afterwards. Passes went astray, tackles were half-missed and balls were repeatedly fumbled.

Although we scored two tries to lead 6–10 at half time, we had blown a number of other opportunities and come close to conceding a score ourselves on several occasions. It was frustrating watching in the stands, particularly with a bunch of loudmouth Aussies goading us. It got to the point that guys were having to bite their tongues to avoid getting involved; it sounds silly, but that is what tension can do. One guy in particular was looking for a clip. Jason Robinson was having a quietish first half and this bloke kept yelling at him: 'Go back to rugby league! Go back to rugby league!' Typical Australian humour – not very sophisticated. Later on tour, Jason was stopped by some bloke in the street who asked what the 'ntl' on his clothing stood for. Jase, a very polite bloke, had started to answer him when this guy interrupted him and said 'I thought it was 'No Talent, Lads'?'

In the second half, the team relaxed and stopped trying too hard. And we absolutely smashed them. I had known that if we played well we could take them to pieces but to put 73 points on them in the second half was a surprise even to me. The stand-out man was the little bloke from Hunslett, in Leeds: in a pretty staggering performance, Jason became the first Lion ever to score five tries on his debut. After the fifth, we all turned round to the Aussie pillock who had been yelling earlier – he now had his gob firmly shut – and started shouting 'Go back to rugby league!' at him.

Colin Charvis had a good game in the back row, Martin Corry also played well, particularly for a man with serious jetlag, and

Greenwood and Henderson had looked an excellent centre pairing.

Henry put our dismal first half down to guys failing to play as a team. 'It didn't look too rosy, did it?' he asked a TV interviewer. 'We played too much as individuals but put that right after the break. Guys are a bit too anxious to make their mark but they eventually settled. It was a more satisfying performance all round for us than in Perth. It was good to see people put their hands up for Test spots.'

An even bigger opportunity to do just that was on the horizon. Later that night, the teams for the Queensland Reds and Australia A were decided and the Reds one was announced. I knew everyone would study the names closely, looking for clues as to the make-up of the Test 22. The side for the Reds needed to be a strong selection for what would be our first real test of the tour.

Even without their skipper John Eales, nursing an Achilles injury, they would be tough opposition with Wallabies like Matt Cockbain, Danny Herbert, the front row and the Kefu brothers in their ranks. And ours was a strong-looking XV. The pack was very solid, with Tom Smith and Keith Wood renewing their 1997 partnership and Phil Vickery providing plenty of strength on the tight-head side. Danny Grewcock joined me in the second row and Hill, Quinnell and Back looked a top-class back row (though Scotty would later drop out with a knee injury, to be replaced by Martin Corry).

On form, Rob Howley was probably shading Matt Dawson at 9 and Jonny Wilkinson was always planned as the Test 10. Rob Henderson would wear 12. He had played well in both games to date and, barring a tremendous showing by Mike Catt when he was finally able to play, now looked to be in a straight fight with Will Greenwood for the Test inside centre shirt. Brian O'Driscoll was at outside centre and the full-back and wingers, Balshaw, Luger and Dafydd James, was a possible Test back three.

But we needed a strong midweek team, too. Just three days

after the Reds match, on the Tuesday, we would face an Australia A side which boasted a lot more Wallabies and had been in camp for some time under the eye of the national side's coach-in-waiting, Eddie Jones. Our 22 for Australia A also looked strong on paper, with a number of players certainly well in contention for Test places. Lawrence Dallaglio and Mike Catt were pencilled in to make their tour debuts and had certainly not been written off. Will Greenwood was playing very well at centre and was my first choice No12. Jason Robinson, the party's form winger, would partner Ben Cohen and Matt Perry in the back three. While Luges was probably certain of his place, Jason was nosing ahead of Ben and Daf for the other Test spot. Ben would need a really big game after not performing to his best in his only run-out so far.

Other talented players were still in the reckoning. Colin Charvis made the bench for each game and had the ability to challenge for a spot in the Test team. Austin Healey could never be discounted and his utility skills meant he was sure, at least, to make the Test 22. This 'utility' tag was winding Oz up: he had been named on the bench three times to date (he was a replacement for the Reds game) and he went round telling anyone who would listen that he was planning to dye his hair red and change his name to David Fairclough. Fairclough, for non-soccer followers, was Liverpool's perennial 'Super Sub' in the 1970s.

Jason Leonard was another versatile guy who was suffering, in this case for his ability to play on both sides of the front row. He had also been named among the Lions replacements more often than should be the case for a man with his skill and commitment. He had had a hard tour to date, having to cover for the injured Dai Young both in training and on the bench, but had not moaned once. Jase is a total team man and I felt sorry for him. I asked Donal to let him know that the 'A' game represented his chance to show what he could do for 80 minutes.

After the Reds and Australia A, we would face another Super 12 outfit, the New South Wales Waratahs, completing a set of three tough games in eight days. It all heralded the start of the second phase, after two easy matches.

Now we would see what we were really made of.

Business Begins

TUESDAY NIGHT ended late, with the light out at 1.30am after a steak and chips supper, and Wednesday morning started as most of the rest had, with a long and arduous training session.

We concentrated on defensive technique, tackling and then some full-contact work. Scott Quinnell took the blow to the knee which would force him out of the side for Saturday's encounter with the Reds and we all headed back to the hotel for a very quick lunch and to grab our kit for the move to Brisbane.

Media men were milling around and I had to give one or two interviews. The hotel was also full of fans waiting for autographs, wanting to slap us on the back and chat, which gave us a buzz.

The flight south was frustrating. Instead of chartering our own planes, we were usually on scheduled flights and we often ended up in economy class. Many of us were 6ft 6in or taller, and 18st plus, and cramming our legs into the smaller space you get at the back of the plane not long after two or three hours of strenuous training makes you stiff. We could not stretch out and relax, as we should have and Quinnell, in particular, was in some pain with his knees. Don't get me wrong – I do not need star treatment. When I fly as a private individual, I go economy. But when you are on tour with the British and Irish Lions, playing and training like we were, you need to keep yourself in the best possible shape. If that means chartering plans with plenty of business-class seats, we should have chartered.

The decision not to must have been taken to save money and that was pretty poor, given the money-making nature of Lions tours.

We arrived at the Brisbane Sheraton stiff and tired four hours later. I was pleased to find things a little better there. I had been allocated a really nice double room, with great views over the city, and sank into the bed as soon as possible.

The next day was a rest day for the Saturday team and a few of the guys took the opportunity to put on wetsuits and swim with some big nurse sharks at a nearby aquarium. Jonny Wilkinson and Richard Hill were in the tank with these mean-looking fish circling them.

Outside, Austin Healey was looking through a porthole and banging on the glass.

'What are you doing?' someone asked him. 'Trying to annoy the sharks,' he replied.

I would love to have gone on the trip myself but I was knackered after a long season and I needed the rest so I decided to have a lie-in. After lunch I had my hair cut and at 4pm the forwards met up. We had decided to do some line-out work ahead of the Queensland Reds game. The line-out is key area and guys are not happy if they feel they have not had enough practice going into games.

We wandered out of the hotel and across the road, past a war memorial and over to a patch of grass where we went through our moves surrounded by rush-hour traffic and Brisbane punters walking home from work. We were sharp: you have to be pretty good if people are looking! Later we went out for a team meal at what was supposed to be Brisbane's best Chinese restaurant, the name of which escapes me because the experience was so unmemorable. The boys all love crispy duck – we do not get many chances to eat that sort of food – and a Chinese is always on the agenda. But it was a disappointment. Normally, with a 30 or 40-strong group, we pre-order our food so it is ready for us on arrival but we could not do that and we had to wait. When it finally arrived it was poor. We had had to explain what crispy duck was – duck with the little pancakes and spring onion and celery – and they had clearly never heard of it. When it finally arrived, they had actually made some tiny pancakes – Shrove Tuesday-style – instead of the normal, floury white wraps you should have. Full marks for effort, I guess, but some of the guys snuck a McDonalds into the hotel later.

I got back fairly early, though a few players headed out for a beer, a good thing. It was a rarity for the squad to get out as a group and this was bothering some of them. They felt the training sessions were still too intense, with too much full contact work and too much concentration on Graham's plans for structuring our game.

I agreed with some elements of this. In particular, I was unsure about the over-regimented nature of our gameplans. As to the length of sessions, I discussed this several times with the management. They were not blind and were themselves concerned that the boys were on their feet too long. But on a short tour, in the professional era when you are up against a seriously professional bunch of players, you need to get through a lot of work.

Friday – or the day before a game – is known Captain's Day. We met at 10am, had a quick chat with Henry and jumped on a bus to the Brisbane Grammar School, another great facility on the outskirts of the city. Once again, we found fantastic pitches and a nice club house; I bet only the best private schools back home are as well-equipped. With the sun out, it was a great place to train.

We had a light team run, lasting 60 to 75 minutes, going through our 'menu', a whole group of moves which we could call on during the match. We might use anywhere between a third and two-thirds of them in the game. Although it is called Captain's Day, I kept my involvement to a minimum. I will say something if it needs saying, maybe call a move that needs calling, but most of the time it is good to leave the practice in the hands of the guys who are going to run the team the next day – No9 and No10 linking the back row and the backs, the hooker calling the lineouts, No8 deciding on back row moves – so they can get their communication going.

The idea is to practise those moves that there is a high probability of you using the following day – a midfield scrum that goes right, for instance, or a scrum on the right that goes left and comes back wide – to get everyone into the groove of where they need to be running as the phases develop.

We had analysed the opposition so we practised for them, too. On short line-outs, for instance, their hooker liked to throw and run, taking it off the catcher as he lands and then spinning a flat pass out to someone like Kefu or Herbert in the back line. We needed to be aware of that and plenty of other things they might pull out of the bag.

We also ran gently through play from line-outs and restarts, hitting the first ruck and going through four or five phases of play, all very light and unopposed. The less time we could have players on their feet the better.

Finally, we did a little defence. Phil Larder wanted us to make five or six tackles, just to remind everyone that we would not be the only ones with the ball.

Then we were off. Everyone, including the guys who had been out beering it up the night before, looked very sharp, keen and focused. There had been no mistakes. It was all a lot better for having had the day off and the opposition we were about to face was obviously concentrating minds.

The bus took us back via the Ballymore Stadium, which looked in good nick, with a new surface since I had last played there in 1999 with England. It is always a wake-up call when you visit the ground before a match; it is almost like a confirmation that, yes, the game is really going to happen. A few nerves were starting to show as the big game approached and I was no different: privately, I was hoping that I had not lost any sharpness, not having played for four weeks or so.

After half an hour, I had to leave the players to attend a press conference with Donal and Graham. A Land Rover arrived to pick us up but the driver got hopelessly lost and the team bus actually beat us back. We were late for the media, who had filled a large room at the hotel. Looking at the size of the gathering, it was yet another indicator that the real business was about to start.

The journalists had not been slow to notice that our side looked very close to a Test XV. That it eventually turned out that way, to all intents and purposes, was not pre-determined: injury and loss of form would still have their parts to play. We answered a few questions about injuries and the forthcoming game, but it was all very uncontroversial. That was no thanks to the Australian press. Since our arrival, they had been getting stuck into us in a very one-sided way, far more so than the British rugby journalists would ever do to them. Their attack was two-pronged: they were starting to rake over the ashes of the 1989 Lions tour Down Under, which had been marked by some pretty rough play by the Brits, and they were also accusing us of being dull to watch. A headline in *The Australian* read 'McBain labels Lions boring' and quoted Queensland coach Mark McBain attacking our style of play. In particular, he seemed to think we played too forward-oriented a game.

'The rolling maul . . . it's just not a spectacle, is it?', he had apparently said.

I found that a bit odd, given that we had scored 31 tries in two games at that point, 20 of them by our backs and with a number of the forwards' scores coming not from mauls but from loose play.

We shrugged off the criticism but it was clear who the Aussie media were rooting for. After the press conference I had to pose for photos and TV and by the time that had finished and I had grabbed a bite to eat it was gone 3pm. That was not great. On the day before a big game I like to get everything done and dusted by lunchtime and relax in the afternoon. Still, I planned to jump into the pool and then have a Jacuzzi to work out the aches from the team run. I was on my way when I heard that Paddy Howard, a Brisbane man, was downtown having a coffee with Martin Corry. His father-in-law had recently died and Pat was staying at his wife's family home in the city. I popped over to join them and had an hour catching up with Pat. It was not a great time for him, obviously, but it is always good to see him. Then it was back to the hotel for our team meeting, which I was to take.

I am not a big one for great long speeches. For a start, I do not think I am particularly eloquent when I speak. I also think you can end up patronising players if you are not careful and that, plus tiredness, can make them switch off. So I tried to get across the basics as quickly as I could. The guys needed to play for and support each other and not try to dominate the game as individuals.

With an evening kick-off, I think these meetings have less of an impact anyway; the next day will offer plenty of time to prepare yourself for the game. After we finished, we ate before a few of the squad went off to watch the Brisbane Broncos play in town. I watched the match from the comfort of our massage table – much the better option. I drifted off to my room around 11pm, nerves starting to jangle a little. Tomorrow was a very big day.

*

I LIKE night matches. There is something special about playing under lights: the crowd seems more up for the occasion and that creates a real buzz in me. The downside is the waiting. I normally try to sleep in for as long as possible, to kill time as much as anything. I was up at 11 o'clock, got some food straight into me and then changed the studs in my boots for some slightly shorter ones to cope with hard Ballymore surface.

After lunch I chilled out in my room watching *Dambusters* on the TV. I like all those old war films and the story of the 'bouncing bomb' attacks on dams in Germany's industrial heartlands, attacks in which dozens of guys a lot younger than me had been killed, certainly put my match day nerves into perspective.

Early afternoon, and it was time for a few more line-out spotters down at the picturesque Brisbane Botanical Gardens five minutes away from the hotel. Those last-minute sessions are a little strange: with the game right on the horizon, guys are a little bit anxious and nervous. You do not want to do too much, you never really warm up properly and, occasionally, things can go wrong. This was one such occasion. Danny Grewcock was lifted and lost his balance as he reached for the ball, toppling to the ground onto his shoulder from quite a height. The surface was very hard and we held our breath for a few seconds. But he got up, brushed himself off and said he was fine. Relief all round.

Back at the hotel I headed straight for my room, just really killing a couple of hours on my own. We were due to meet at 5.25pm in the team room. It is always an anxious time for me. You know what is in front of you and in a funny sort of way you do not want 5.25pm to come. You would rather sit there all afternoon, blocking everything out, pretending it is just another ordinary day. Of course, the clock always ticks round to the appointed hour and I found myself downstairs with the rest of the players.

Jonny received his shirt before me and then Donal handed mine over, embarrassing me with a few complimentary remarks as he did so. I had been given No5 but I always wear No4 so I swapped with Grewy. On the journey to the ground my nerves heightened; once again, we were arriving late, with an hour or so before the kick-off instead of the minimum 90 minutes which I like. I had agreed to a BSkyB interview before the match – they have always been pretty good to me – but I was not keen and I turned down another request from an Aussie TV crew. I never like chatting to the media ahead of the game because I am trying to concentrate on what is to come and a friend who watched the interview said it was blatantly obvious that I did not really want to do it. That was fine by me. I did not want to be there, but for the right reason: I wanted to be getting ready to play the game.

Afterwards, I headed back into the changing room for a drink and to get changed into my match kit and then went back out through the incoming spectators to warm up on a practice pitch round the back of the stadium. We were sharp and focused. Again, it helped being watched, with the guys keen not to make any mistakes.

Graham Henry had a last-minute pep talk for us: 'If we don't destroy their composure on the field, we will be second,' he told us. 'That's our challenge. And it is going to require us to think . . . if we are not smarter than them we're buggered.'

As the players huddled, I said a few words myself: 'It's going to be fast and furious. When we've got the ball we're going to take them to pieces . . . let's get the ball and run aggressively. If in doubt, just go forward. Lions v Queensland – it's your only time, ever.'

And out we went. The Reds were clearly also very psyched-up for the match. Their pack was particularly hyped, and especially the front row. Their press had been banging on about the power of our scrummaging and Mark McBain had obviously identified the forward battle as key to his side's hopes of success. They were desperate to stop us driving at line-outs and resorted to pulling mauls down illegally. The game got a little bit niggly with odd punches being thrown here and there. Neither side wanted to back down and everyone was getting stuck in. In one ruck, one of their players was rucking Daf James on the head but, surprisingly, we were penalised after the ensuing scuffle.

It seemed the home team were intent on unsettling us. If so, their plan failed. We got across their line after about 15 minutes when Jonny Wilkinson showed his vision and class, spotting Dan Luger was in space on the left and cross-kicking 30 or 40 yards for Dan to run on to the ball and score. It was great to score early on and it helped us settle down.

Rob Henderson continued his good form, getting over next after a kick by Elton Flatley was charged down by Martin Corry. Ten minutes later Cozza was in action again, smashing back Nathan Sharpe with a shuddering tackle which led to the ball being turned over and Dafydd James going over. Richard Hill had also scored before half-time from a lovely inside pass by Jonny which Hilly sprinted on to, running a tremendous line.

Within minutes of the re-start, Brian O'Driscoll had scored too, shaking off Danny Herbert in the process. It was 3–39 at that point and the game was effectively over. The Reds had failed to threaten us at all, with our defence looking very strong – testament to all those hours on the training ground.

Rob Howley took some punishment, including a nasty whack on the ribs which forced him off after 47 minutes, and they did come back later with a try of their own but the final scoreline of 8–42 said it all. It was the first game of a big week and we had come through well.

Henry was buoyant in the changing room, saying we had made it another step up the ladder that evening. 'There's nine internationals out there tonight who know they've been in a game,' he said. 'But let's keep our feet on the ground.'

At the press conference, I played down the win, pointing out that we had had the bounce of the ball in the first half. That said, we had been the better team, bottling up their two most dangerous runners, the No8 Toutai Kefu and their centre and stand-in captain Daniel Herbert, which had been our plan. After we took a commanding lead, neither of them had looked up for the game. Herbert, particularly, normally takes a lot of switch balls and comes back very hard but that had been missing from his game.

As well as that, some of our guys had had a storming evening. Jonny had slotted in fantastically well for a fly-half who had not played in weeks, missing his first kick at goal but potting the next seven. Rob Howley and Brian O'Driscoll had shown their flair and skill. And Hendo and Cozza were both outstanding. Rob had been known in the past as a bit of a route one merchant – he is bigger and quicker than Scott Gibbs – but he had added guile and a decent kicking game to his armoury and was continuing to press his case for the 12 Test shirt.

As for Corry, just a few days after arriving in the country, he had played himself into the Test squad. Post-match, Graham Henry admitted his mistake in not bringing him on tour from the off, telling the press: 'I think Corry was fabulous. He showed the Lions selectors we made a mistake by leaving him out, which is the ideal attitude. He has put his hand up in a big way.'

Cozza himself, so often a bench player for England, had been desperate to show what he could do. He said in a pre-match interview: 'I'll never get used to the substitute's role and I regarded this game as the biggest of my life. All I want to do is get on the field and do myself and the jersey justice.'

He had been inconsolable when he had not made the final 37.

'How did I feel when they left me out of the initial squad?' he said. 'Shattered, absolutely gutted. Andy Robinson spent ages trying to get hold of me and when he eventually gave me the news I just wanted to bring the phone call to an end as quickly as possible. Suddenly, it's all different. The cards fell for me, what with the call-up and then Scott Quinnell's withdrawal from the match. I want to do the jersey proud because some legendary players have worn that shirt down the years. That is a massive motivation for me, although in this environment motivation is hardly a problem.'

That evening's after-match function, an outdoor barbecue, was sparsely attended by both sets of players and was over quickly.

We were presented with boomerangs by the Queensland Union, and we handed over the usual ties and pins before making our way back to the team hotel.

Later, we announced the team for the Australia A game on the Tuesday and digested the news that Phil Greening was leaving the tour. This surprised me; I had thought we were going to give him two weeks to get fit and this was just a week or so on. We were told it was an insurance issue. I found that a little weak. It is wrong to tell a guy he has two weeks and then ditch him ahead of time.

Phil was clearly very disappointed. He told me he was planning to pay his way to Sydney and try to come back and asked me to speak to the management to make sure that he had that chance if he recovered. A fit Phil would certainly be a valuable impact player and Donal and Graham agreed that he could rejoin the party if he recovered. I had mixed feelings about this. Phil is a great player and a great tourist but bringing him back would be at the expense of another player in the party, probably Gordon Bulloch. You have to be ruthless and select the best team, regardless of feelings, but it would be a hard call to send Gordon home after bringing him out off his holiday.

Around midnight, after a quick meal in the hotel, we headed out for a few beers to a place called City Rowers, a favourite haunt of the Queensland Reds boys. The whole town seemed to be full of Lions fans; I remember wondering what it would be like by the first Test. There was a roped-off area at the back and I chatted to a few of the Reds players, the lock Mark Connors and Danny Herbert, who seemed nice blokes. We watched France beat South Africa, a shock result, and wandered back to the hotel at around 4am. That sounds late but we had been late going out and if I had gone to bed instead adrenalin would have made sleep impossible.

A few of the guys looked a little hungover the next day, with Keith Wood particularly bleary-eyed. That was great; it meant they had enjoyed themselves. Sunday was a rest day for the Reds match squad anyway. All we had to do was recover. Massage, a Jacuzzi, a swim and general relaxation were the order of the day. I spent most of the morning by the pool, reading the papers. The Australian media, and one or two influential figures in their game, were really starting to get stuck into us, building up their whingeing allegations that we were boring and violent.

First the violence: Eddie Jones, ACT Brumbies and Australia A coach, and heir apparent to Rod Macqueen with the senior Wallaby side, accused us of illegal play.

He moaned: 'There were a number of off-the-ball incidents against Queensland that were disappointing. I hope the officials at Gosford (the venue for the Australia A match that would follow on the Tuesday) keep a strict eye on this and take the appropriate action.'

I thought this was a bit unnecessary. It had been hard and niggly but that is what it is all about. There were incidents on both sides although they did seem to have targeted Rob Howley, who had been knee-dropped. As Rob later put it: 'They started it and we stood up to it . . . toe to toe.' It was only when they found they could not beat us up that they started trying to beat us.

Now for the boring play. Here the moaning was led by Mark McBain, the Reds coach.

He said: 'They looked to throw it wide, to use their speed, and if that doesn't work I wonder if they have a Plan B.' This was a laughable statement. It was McBain, after all, who had earlier complained that our only attacking weapon was the driving maul. I treated his remarks with the contempt they deserved. It was nice after a good win to enjoy the feeling and I was not going to let a war of words spoil that.

After lunch we were on the move again, heading to the airport for the two-hour flight to Sydney. The all-seeing ntl cameras were still everywhere, getting on people's nerves. I was actually filmed paying my room bill. I thought this was perhaps the most uninteresting thing of all time to watch, but then I am no expert. By about 6pm, we had checked into the Park Royal Pacific hotel, on the shore at Manly, a relaxed, slightly bohemian suburb of Sydney. It was a nice enough place, not as luxurious as the Brisbane Sheraton but adequate and we would return there for the build-up to the final Test. I was hoping for a magnificent suite, stuffed with Renaissance paintings and antique furniture and boasting a fabulous balcony from which I could watch the ocean swell. Unfortunately, I got a pokey little single with an MFI bed and no sea view. Honestly, the lack of respect was appalling.

I turned in early and awoke the next day feeling more tired and bruised than the day before. This is always the way: the adrenalin keeps you going for 24 hours or so after the match has ended but once it ebbs away you droop a bit.

We analysed the game in the morning. Phil Larder was pleased; our defence had been very good, we had only conceded one try and that was from a charge down.

Afterwards, from 10.30am, we trained. There were a few more moans from guys still disconcerted with the level of training they were being asked to undertake but it was a decent session which included a soccer kick-about to get the boys warmed up. It is always good to introduce something a little different like that and it helped the mood, which was already good after the Queensland win.

I hoped we were not getting too cocky. Before heading for the gym to work on leg weights with Corry, I spent a little time watching the side to play Australia A going through their paces. They did not look great, with a few balls going down and lapses of concentration evident. Catt and Dallaglio both seemed OK, though, and I crossed my fingers for them and their injuries. I do not think either of them would have travelled for any other tour but I understood their desperation to play for the Lions.

We met up around 5.30pm for a talk about forward tactics. It seemed to go on forever and I got a little short-tempered. I felt our meetings tended to drag on when they could have been over in half an hour. People would go off at tangents, not really focusing on the job in hand. It was, as they say, doing my head in and as soon as it was over I headed off to get some food and try to chill out in my room.

Ups and Downs

ON MATCH day, we awoke to yet more nonsense in the Australian press, with Eddie Jones once again having a pop at us for our supposed violence. 'Officials have to be hard on teams that resort to foul play,' he had told a reporter. 'I don't think the officials last Saturday night did that. Don't tell me that some of the blokes who resorted to foul play should not have been put in the sin bin and I mean players from both teams. There has been a constant pattern in how the Lions have played on tour and they are going to try to assert their physical superiority. They do have a master plan in place.'

Donal Lenihan was quick to respond, saying: 'If you watch the video carefully it is beyond me how we can be accused of causing problems.'

In other words, Jones was talking garbage. There was no master plan and we had been victims every bit as much as perpetrators three days previously. And as for this supposed physical superiority, something repeatedly mentioned throughout our time in Australia, that was bullshit too. The Wallabies had not been crowned World Champions by fielding a team of girls.

Did all this media talk unsettle us? I do not know. I tried to ignore it myself and if it had any effect on me it was to irritate me rather than anything more negative.

The non-playing guys met at 9.30am to train at Brookvale, home to the Manly Rugby League Club. Manly used to be one of the top Australian league teams before merging with Northern to become the Northern Eagles – in whose NorthPower Stadium the game was to be played. I followed them slightly during the 1980s and 1990s and it was nice to train at their famous old ground. The morning was hot and close and I was very stiff and tired. My work in the gym the previous day had left me a little drained and it took me a while to get going. We started with a couple of circuits of the pitch and I was struggling even to run properly. But after I loosened up things improved and the session ended well with some sharp drills. I managed to spend some time relaxing on a sun lounger in the afternoon before we got onto our buses for the scenic 100km drive to Gosford along the Pacific Highway. Those of us not playing travelled separately to the team and we stopped at a little hotel for some grub once we got to the town. The food was not at all inspiring – a dodgy pasta dish and a few bread rolls – so we asked them to make us some pancakes.

The mood was still pretty good. After Saturday's result, we were confident the boys would beat the Australian shadow XV and there was plenty of banter as we ate. It continued when we arrived at the stadium, where Henry was giving the 22 a rev-up: 'This will be the toughest game we play outside the Test matches,' he said. 'We've got to play out of our skins. At Tylney Hall we talked about the courage and the heart of the Lions and words like commitment and hunger and ruthlessness. We need to put some meaning into those words tonight.'

Good, stirring stuff which somehow failed to rouse the boys. Roared on by a lot of locals in the 20,000 crowd packed into the intimate stands, Australia A came at the Lions very hard right from the start, looking very organised and very slick on the ball. Their defence was tight, too, and they gave us some problems while not giving much away. It was a different story for the Lions XV. A lot of mistakes were made – dropped balls, wild passes and even guys running into one another occasionally. The side looked very poor, even unmotivated at times, and the home crowd were not slow to spot this. Before half-time, we lost Mike Catt, who pulled up as he chased a kick-through and hobbled off clutching his calf. We went in 15–6 down – not great, but better than it could have been and not impossible to come back from.

Inside, a furious Henry was laying it on the line to the players telling them they needed to show some pride. 'We're flat as bloody pancakes,' he said. 'You guys have got a responsibility here which goes back 100 years.'

Keen to do our bit, we lined up outside the changing rooms and clapped the lads back onto the pitch for the second 40, desperately trying to get their heads up. At first, it seemed to have worked. They looked very determined and I thought we were going to come straight back into the game. Unfortunately, the crucial score came at the other end when the centre Scott Staniforth ran on to a Graeme Bond pass after 20 minutes. With Manny Edmonds outkicking a struggling Neil Jenkins, we were always going to find it hard to come back and so it proved.

Things looked better after Jenks was taken off for Matt Dawson, who took over from Austin Healey at scrum half, allowing Austin to go to 10. We were sharper, scoring three times in the final quarter of the game through Taylor, Perry and Robinson, and Daws, who had taken over the kicking duties, actually missed a penalty almost on full-time which would have given us a draw. We did not deserve it, though. Despite outscoring them three tries to one, we had been well-beaten and were flattered by the 28–25 scoreline.

It was not all bad news. The way we had come back at the end at least showed our fitness was good. There were a few decent individual performances: Robinson, Healey, Cohen and Dawson had looked sharp and Will Greenwood had been outstanding. His defence was great, he was taking the ball up very hard and really creating stuff for us. It had been his third start in the four games so far and he was also due to line up in our next game the following Saturday, against Bob Dwyer's New South Wales Waratahs. He is not normally a workhorse, Will, but his attitude was great and he was taking the extra load all in his stride. He is a top player, performing exceptionally well in most areas in most matches.

But that was about the only gloss we could put on the evening's action. The bald fact was that we had been outplayed by a sharp Aussie second string side who looked better organised, more committed and more skilful than our side had.

The Test team had certainly started to take shape and it did not look as though too many members of that evening's side would be in it. A poor team performance can kill individuals' chances stone dead, which is always the danger on a short tour. The classic example is probably Ben Cohen. Before leaving the UK, Ben had had every chance of being one of our Test wingers. Big, strong and quick, he would be just the bloke to put up against Joe Roff. But a poor first game left him with a lot to do and when his chance came he found himself part of a weak team who were well beaten. Ben himself had played well enough but he had clearly slipped behind Daf James and Jason Robinson in the race for the No14 shirt. Mal O'Kelly and Jerry Davidson were in a similar position. Each are world class players and they both could have been Test starters. But our line-out had been shocking, with Tom Bowman and Justin Harrison outplaying them comprehensively. All over the pitch we had looked very lethargic, particularly in the first half. This really galled me – we should have been really pumped up for this match. They competed for our ball and put us under pressure, which resulted in a lot of silly penalties.

Worst of all was the loss of Mike Catt. It had looked pretty serious when he left the field. He had a nasty calf strain and it was announced almost immediately that he would be going home. Although Scott Gibbs would come out to replace him, this was a major blow: Mike had been a big part of our plans and losing him was little short of disastrous. He was obviously gutted, telling a British newspaper: 'It's a wrench to go off tour but in a way I'm glad it's now all out in the open and over. It has been a bad couple of weeks. My back was always the problem. I almost didn't make it at all but the medics at Bath thought the spasms would work themselves out. It got to the stage where it was embarrassing to be on the tour. I don't think I could have lived with myself if I hadn't given it a go but I'm just relieved now that it's sorted. Scott Gibbs will do a better job than I was able to do in the state that I was in.'

Digesting the news of his loss, I went to the changing rooms to try to lift the players. Jason Leonard was one guy I really felt for. It had been his first start, after sitting on the bench for the three previous games. A storming game and a good win would have put Jase right in the frame for a Test place. He must have felt pretty low but, typically, he did not show it.

The place was dead quiet. Donal was speaking, telling the players: 'Bottom line guys . . . we know we played like a bag of shite. We lost by three points. We scored three tries to one and we know we fucked up. You've got to take the feeling this is what touring's all about – there are ups and downs, good times and bad. We let ourselves down. We know that. This is the last game we lose.'

A few of the players were upset at these remarks. I have to say I think Donal was on the right track. He did not say anything I have not heard at other times when I have been part of a losing team and, while he delivered his words in a way which showed he was upset, he was not abusive or overly aggressive. I was pretty upset myself. Some players out there had not looked good enough or hungry enough to wear a Lions shirt. A few people also blamed tiredness and blamed too much training. This constant moan annoyed me, too. Training had been hard and some days sessions had stretched longer than was ideal. But this was not done for the sake of it. We had been deficient in some areas – this latest result showed we still were – and the only way to put those things right was through practice. We were all tired but that is inevitable on this sort of tour, with all the travelling. We had to pull together and stop whingeing.

Later, Graham Henry did not mince words when talking to the press. 'Our line-out was unacceptable and we lacked basic sharpness,' he said. 'This is a reality check for us to show us where our baseline has to be set. This will tell us what the tour is all about. If we can learn resolve from it, then maybe it will benefit us in the long term.'

Asked how the squad had taken the reverse, he replied: 'The dressing shed was a morgue. This could be a defining moment. Better to strike reality now than in the first Test.'

That was all fair enough. Controversial comments followed, though. 'We might have to concentrate more on the Tests than on the other guys,' he said.

This caused uproar in the press and did nothing to help morale in the camp, which was now in danger of fracturing. A few players clearly felt that they had already been written out of the Test plans – no-one had – and their heads were starting to drop. I was starting to feel a division, not quite a 'them-and-us' situation, but a feeling that some players felt others were being favoured over them. Here, apparently, was evidence right from the horse's mouth.

I had some sympathy with Henry's sentiments. In the modern age, more than ever, touring with the Lions is about winning Test matches. But you do not say that, publicly rubbing the midweek guys' noses in it. You just quietly get on with it. At this point, we needed to be a 37-man squad, not two teams, and we were in danger of losing that.

After a bad day, that long bus trip back to the hotel seemed to take hours. I played cards with Keith Wood and reflected on the match. I found it hard to keep my spirits up. Winning on tour creates momentum and builds team spirit. Losing can have the opposite effect. I thought the main problem had been that we had got too cocky. We had beaten Queensland by what was probably an inflated score and perhaps it had gone to our heads. It was now time to knuckle down.

*

EARLY NEXT morning, I met up with Donal, Andy Robinson and Graham Henry to select the team for the New South Wales Waratahs game. Rob Howley's rib injury from the Queensland match was still causing him some pain and it was decided not to risk him. Instead, Matt Dawson would start at scrum half, with Austin Healey again on the bench, his versatility and fitness meaning he had been involved in every game to that point. Will Greenwood would play at inside centre. The plan was that he would start there in the Tests, too.

Darren Morris would come in at loose-head. Personally, I felt Darren might struggle to play a full 80 minutes given the sort of fast, mobile game we needed from him, but Tom Smith, an outstanding No1, was on the bench if needed. Danny Grewcock would partner me in the second row.

Lawrence Dallaglio would start on the blind side. By his own very high standards, Lol had had a poor game against Australia A – perhaps not surprisingly, since it had been his first outing for several weeks – and, with Corry, Hill and Back all playing very well, he needed a big performance to put himself in the frame for a Test spot.

Scott Quinnell, too, had not been at his best during the 'A' game. His knees were causing him trouble and he, too, needed a good game to dispel fears overt his fitness.

The next day the guys who had played against Australia A trained with the 22 for the Waratahs. It was supposed to be a 60% session: that means guys grab-tackle, rather than putting the shoulder in, and that the man who is tackled should stop. With the midweek guys obviously rankled by what had gone on, they started getting really stuck in to us and it all got a little feisty.

That was something I was pleased to see; it meant they were still bothered.

The needle led to a few mistakes; irritating enough in itself. However, the session ended with an accidental collision between Neil Back and Danny Luger. Their heads clashed hard and both felt it. At first, it seemed not to be too serious and the forwards went off for what turned out to be a good scrummaging practice. Later, though, it was revealed that Dan had fractured his cheekbone. Another key guy gone.

This was a nightmare and very depressing news that we really did not need. Danny was our starting left winger and had the pace and skill to do serious damage, as his England scoring rate of better than a try every two games shows. There were no replacements back home with his ability.

It is hard to think of a more unlucky player. Last season, he spent seven months out with a groin injury, coming back to play well on England's tour to South Africa and to score the try which beat Australia in the autumn. Then he damaged a nerve in his neck in the opening minutes of England's first Six Nations game of 2001, against Wales in Cardiff, and was out for almost the rest of the season. That injury nearly ended his career. In one interview, he admitted: 'My doctor asked me if I did anything else for a living because I wouldn't be playing rugby for a while. No-one seemed to know what was going on. One opinion was that I needed an operation; another not. The best case scenario was that it would take three months.'

Intensive physio saw him through, giving him a clean bill of health just a few days before the tour party was announced. Now it was back to square one for Dan.

It is very hard to cope with the loss of players of the calibre of Phil Greening, Mike Catt and Dan Luger, as talented as Gordon

Bulloch, Scott Gibbs and the Irish winger Tyrone Howe, on his way out for Luges, undoubtedly are. I was starting to wonder whether we were jinxed. I put this thought behind me and spent the evening trying to relax, chatting to Jason Robinson about his days at Wigan. He had been a hell of a boy in his pre-Christian days. Often, he would head out for an evenings boozing. He would stick his training kit in the boot of the car, and spend all night on the lash and turn up at Wigan the next day to join the rest of the team. He is a changed man, now, who rarely touches a drop.

The following day was free, so Martin Corry, Neil Back and I caught the 20-minute ferry into Sydney to have a wander round. You get a great view of the Opera House and the Harbour Bridge as you come into the harbour and later I took the opportunity to climb up to the top of one of the support pillars at the side of the bridge. It is hard work but well worth the effort when you get to the top: the views over Sydney are fantastic.

The three of us popped into the RM Williams shop in town and Cozza and I each bought identical boots in the same size, which was a bit embarrassing. Then we had a bite to eat in the Queen Victoria Mall, a pleasant, turn-of-the-century arcade. The whole city was heaving with Lions fans and we had an enjoyable day before heading back for some line out practice down at the Manly Oval.

The day ended with a squad trip on the jetcat – a fast catamaran – back into Sydney for a team dinner at a restaurant called Doyles. Bit of a problem, here: Doyles only sells fish, and half the boys, including Hilly, Wilko and Darren Morris, do not eat much fish so only 20 or so of us ended up staying. I am not a big fan of seafood myself but I had a prawn cocktail, some lobster and a little smoked salmon, which was very nice.

Gibbsy actually arrived as we were sitting down to eat, having been sent over after getting to the hotel, and it was a lift to see him.

Friday saw us train at the Sydney Football Stadium, where we would face the Waratahs. It was a classy stadium with an excellent pitch. Sadly our session was less impressive. There was a lot of dropped ball and guys looking incredibly casual. It was really very poor and I felt like grabbing hold of people and shaking them. If we played like that against New South Wales we would be slaughtered.

Match day, as usual, saw me trying to sleep in and I made it almost to lunchtime. We were due to meet up for our bus at 4.55pm. Once again, this was worrying to me, particularly since we had been later arriving at grounds than I wanted a number of times. It was a long way into Sydney, through a lot of the traffic. In the event, although it took us almost an hour, we were OK. There was no police escort, which always amazes me. If we were to get caught in serious traffic we would be very late.

It was dark and I was squinting in the bright TV lights which were on us as we walked into the stadium. We warmed up at the nearby Sydney Cricket Ground, which was not ideal. It meant we had to walk for three or four minutes through the crowd surrounding the ground and then go through our paces in an empty stadium with no atmosphere.

The papers that morning had been full of more home jibes at us. The Wallaby coach Rod Macqueen and the Waratahs' Bob Dwyer – my old boss at Leicester Tigers – were the latest Aussies to have a dig, accusing us of illegality in the scrum, line-out and breakdown. So it may have come as a surprise to them when Tom Bowman was binned after just four seconds – probably a record – for elbowing Danny Grewcock in the face at the kick-off. That set the tone for what was to become an infamous game. It started very well, with Brian O'Driscoll scoring early on. The Waratahs replied against the run of play after turning us over but we hit back with two more tries, Jason Robinson playing particularly well and popping up all over the pitch, to finish the first half well in control at 5–24. The second period started less happily. The first 10 minutes we were poor, losing the ball and our shape, and the problems were compounded when Will Greenwood hobbled off with an ankle injury. NSW attacked us in the middle, using dummy runners to open us up and scoring a couple of tries in quick time, bringing the score back to 17–24.

The game had been niggly right from the off and on 55 minutes it exploded. Ronan O'Gara had come on to replace Greenwood and was clearing out a ruck when Duncan McRae launched an amazing assault on him. Pinning Ronan to the floor, he punched him 11 times in the face without reply, leaving the young Irishman with blood streaming down his face from a deep gash under his left eye. It was a disgraceful and bizarre incident; it looked virtually unprovoked, though McRae later claimed O'Gara had struck first, and Ronan did little to defend himself. Referee Scott Young had no alternative but to send a smirking McRae off.

A few minutes later, a brawl broke out between the packs, leading to four players – Lions Phil Vickery and Danny Grewcock and Waratahs front-rowers Brendan Cannon and Cameron Blades – being sin-binned. Ten minutes of completely unstructured rugby ensued, with Young unsure as to whether he could allow opposed scrummaging: eventually, it was allowed with a farcical merry-go-round of substitutions. But we took control eventually and eased ahead, with Wilkinson and James joining Robinson and O'Driscoll on the score sheet. Jason and Brian, incidentally, entered the record books alongside the dozen other Lions who have scored in their first three matches. We leaked a try at the end which was disappointing and I felt that the 24–41 scoreline was closer than it should have been.

We had more injury worries, too: Back had injured a rib and Dallaglio had taken a knock on the knee. Lenihan called everyone together in the changing room. Struggling to contain his anger, he told the boys we had been 'set up' and likened it to a match against Canterbury ahead of the first Test in 1971 when the Lions lost three players to deliberate foul play. Personally, I did not think that the Waratahs had deliberately set out to put Ronan out of action – after all, there were more valuable players they could have targeted – but they had certainly been out to rough us up as a team.

Later, Donal told the assembled journalists: 'What happened to Ronan O'Gara was a disgrace.' Henry said: 'This was a black night for rugby. There appeared to be more to it than just a one-off outbreak.'

Straight after the game, we attended a small function at the stadium. None of us felt at all sociable after what had just gone on and we left after 45 minutes. But it was a long way back to Manly and by the time we got back to the hotel it was nearly midnight. A few of the players went back out into Sydney but it was a long trip so most of us stayed behind. I joined a couple of the guys for a drink in the bar. This was one of the features of the tour and it was brought about by a combination of evening kick-offs and the modern, professional game's requirement for players to be well-drilled. When you have won in those sort of circumstances, that is when the whole party should be out together, having a pint, relaxing, bonding and getting to know one another better. But if you do not get back to the hotel until 11.30pm and you have to be up for training the next day, it is not conducive to having a party so you end up splitting into little groups.

Despite this, I cannot see anything changing in the future. In Australia or South Africa, they have a tradition of night games and the demands of TV back home will also be to keep the scheduling the same. New Zealand has more of a Saturday afternoon rugby culture so things could be different in 2005. However, TV money plays such a major part in sport nowadays and I cannot see the broadcasters back home settling for kick-offs at 5am BST. The Kiwis may have to move to night matches too.

After getting a latest update on the medical situation – Lol's knee looked serious, Backy's rib was causing him a lot of pain and Greenwood was out for at least two matches – I took myself off to my room and ordered a burger while I watched TV until I finally drifted off at about 3.30am.

The next day, predictably, the media concentrated on the violence. The Waratahs, incredibly, were supporting McRae and backed him at a hearing on the Sunday, claiming he had been punched and kicked before he lashed out. There was absolutely no video evidence to support this and the tribunal gave McRae a seven week ban from the game. It was all a bit rich after the press we had had from the local media.

That morning we enjoyed one of the benefits of Manly: its proximity to the sea. Although it was the Aussie winter, the water felt a damn sight warmer than it ever does at Caister so the able-bodied among the boys who had played against the Waratahs all headed down to the beach for a chill-out in the waves during the morning.

Before the Storm

THAT AFTERNOON saw us all hop back onto a plane and fly up to Coffs Harbour, which proudly boasts, on signs as you drive in, that it is the 'Home of the Wallabies Training Camp', which is better than being twinned with Swindon, I suppose. It felt slightly odd being so close to the enemy but we were in town not for them but for an encounter with the New South Wales Country Cockatoos, an exotically-named bunch of semi-pros not much stronger than Western Australia.

The match would be played on a pitch carved out of an Aussie Rules ground, so there was only a stand on the one side, holding around 1,000 people. The whole place had a real country feel to it – very different to places like Ballymore, Gosford and Sydney Football Stadium. It was a game we knew we ought to win quite comfortably but these fixtures are a traditional part of touring with the Lions. It is partly about taking the game to outlying areas in a sort of ambassadorial way and partly about keeping your players match fit. If there are no top sides to play you have to play lower ones: otherwise quite a few guys are not going to get a game.

We arrived in time for the Tuesday forwards to go through a few line-out spotters while the rest of us settled in. The big news of the day came at dinner, when I was chatting to Lawrence Dallaglio. Normally he is quite a gregarious guy but he was very downbeat about his knee and told me that he thought he was finished on the tour. He did not want to say outright 'I can't go on' but it was clear he was not going to play any further part. Watching him in the 'A' game and playing alongside him against NSW, I had seen he was not the player we know he is. The injury was obviously affecting his performance; you cannot run if you have a damaged knee, and much of Lawrence's game is based on his pace, his power and his athleticism. The latest knock, against the Waratahs, had sealed things. He had worked very hard for weeks to get fit but the knee was not right and he was only going to harm the team and himself by trying to carry on. He had spoken to Nigel Melville, his director of rugby at Wasps, who had advised him, correctly, that the best thing to do was pull out and get treatment.

It was kept quiet overnight but announced to the team the following day. I felt sorry for Lawrence but he is only in his late 20s – the tremendous rate of hair loss makes him look older – so he is young enough to make the 2005 tour and I am sure he will.

The Irish openside David Wallace was pulled off Ireland's pre-season trip, to Poland of all places, as a replacement. He was to become the third Wallace brother to play for the Lions, after Richard and Paul. My impressions of him were limited but if he was anything like his brothers – they are a superior physical breed, believe me – he would serve us well.

Another guy going home was Rob McBryde. He had come on late in the NSW game and taken another bang on his thigh. Just as I was going to bed Donal collared me and told me he was calling Dorian West out as his replacement. Keith Wood was battered and bruised – the Doc, when asked what ailments Keith had, looked at a sheet of paper, started to run through them, and then gave up and said 'Everything' – and we needed cover for the midweek team. We did not want Woody having to play weekends and be on the bench, and maybe play, on Tuesdays.

I knew Westie – also known at Leicester as Nobby, The Chieftain (he calls everyone 'Chief') and the Fat Ginger Hamster – was planning to go on holiday. I asked Donal if anyone had been able to contact him and he was unsure so I gave him a quick buzz on his mobile from my hotel room a few minutes later. The conversation went something like this:

'Nobby, where are you?'

'I'm in the baggage reclaim area at Minorca airport, chief.'

'Who have you got with you?'

'Claire (his wife), the kids, my sister-in-law and Toint (his best mate).'

They were all clearly looking forward to some sun, sand and sangria.

'Drop everything and get the next flight to Australia.'

'Oh bugger! What am I going to tell the missus?'

But obviously he was chuffed to bits and, after necking a celebratory pint with Toint, he arranged to fly out his mother-in-law to help Claire look after the children and was gone, on a flight to Frankfurt and then Sydney.

It was bad news for Rob and bad news for Lol but we had good guys coming out. And we needed them quickly – particularly Wallace – so they could play on Tuesday. After the loss of Dallaglio, Martin Corry had been pencilled in for that game. Back's rib injury could yet rule him out of the Test which meant Cozza might end up playing then, too. David was needed to take some of that pressure off.

*

MONDAY SAW a new slant on training. Normally, the sessions would have been split, one for the Saturday side and the other a team run to prepare the Tuesday boys. Today, that went by the wayside.

First thing, we all watched videos of Australia in action.

Then the midweekers were told they would have to play as the Wallabies to try out the Test 22's defence. Already smarting from Henry's remarks about concentrating on the Test team in the wake of the defeat against Australia A, this latest decision really upset the midweek players, and I think understandably so. They wanted time to prepare mentally and tactically for their own game and they were not going to get it. It really was like saying to them: 'You blokes don't count . . . you are just cannon fodder.'

It added to their feeling of being the Stiffs, the Dirt Trackers, and widened their sense of divide. Once again, I could see where the management were coming from: the Cockatoos were a side we should deal with almost in our sleep and the Test matches were what the tour was all about. But again it was not handled particularly sensitively.

To a certain extent, this clash of priorities is inevitable – and will only get worse in future – with the way the game has changed so much so quickly. In 1997, our midweek and weekend sides played basically the same game and we knew pretty well what to expect of the opposition, too. On this tour, the gameplan was changing from week to week. Coaches would spend all hours of the day and night analysing the opposition, looking for chinks in the armour, and preparing tactics to exploit them.

As the game becomes ever more sophisticated I can see Lions coaches approaching mental overload in future years and it may be that the structure of future tours, or the make-up of the parties, are adjusted to take account of these issues. None of which probably mattered to the guys forced to pretend they were wearing gold jumpers.

But however down they were, things were put into some perspective by tragic events later that day. After lunch, I had gone with Steve Black to the gym. It was a nice spot, with an outdoor pool, and a great place to train hard. A lot of the guys had gone out whale-watching on a boat trip. I was doing some weights in front of a window that looked out, through some trees, onto the beach. We noticed a couple of players running down there, a little more urgently than if they were training, but though nothing much of it. Then the physio, Mark Davies, walked in. I just knew from the look on his face that something, not just bad, but tragic had happened. Blackie and I immediately had the same thought: 'Who has died?'

Steve went up to him and said: 'What's wrong?'

Mark just said: 'It's Anton . . . he's gone . . . he's had a heart attack . . . he's gone.'

Anton Toia was our ARU-supplied liaison officer, a Maori whose main job was helping to move our huge amount of baggage between hotels. In the old days it would have been a few balls and some kit; in 2001 our luggage filled most hotel receptions stacked two deep. Anton was a jovial, friendly guy, very quiet, not one to push himself on you but a good bloke to have a laugh and a beer with. He would have been in his mid 50s, and married, I think.

He had been on the boat with the guys, watching the whales, and as it had returned he had jumped into the water to swim the last 100 yards or so back to the shore. The players had watched him go thinking he was OK but as the boat turned away he had a massive heart attack in the water and died. Neil Back and Jonny Wilkinson had been on the scene quite quickly and someone tried to revive him with mouth-to-mouth. James Robson also sprinted down there but there was nothing he could do. He spoke later of the poignancy of seeing this poor guy lying there, covered in sand, beyond help.

It was the latest – and, of course, the worst – in a series of misfortunes that were befalling the trip. As one of the Aussie guys at the hotel said to me later: 'Jeez . . . how many black cats have you guys seen?'

Once the news got around the squad, the mood in the camp was naturally pretty bleak. Anton had been a popular member of our party, quite well known to some of the party from national tours to Australia, and it was a horrible thing to have happened. I remember thinking that, however the tour finished, whatever pressure we were under, at least we would all be going home. Not Anton.

The guys to play the Cockatoos were due to meet in the evening for a team talk ahead of the match. Dai Young, the skipper, scrapped it and sent his players off to get away from it all. Somehow it would not have felt right talking gameplans. I had some friends who had just arrived from the UK and who had driven down to meet up. There were plenty of spare tickets floating around the squad for the game so I got some for them and took a cab down to the harbour to join them in a bar. They were on holiday and clearly having the time of their lives. They were shocked by how I looked, saying I seemed very low and as if the weight of the world was on my shoulders.

The unhappiness of some of the players, the tension of the approaching Test and now Anton dying were taking their toll on me. People – even good mates – sometimes do not realise that a Lions tour is not necessarily great fun for the players. It is not a holiday, it is work and work under high pressure and the media spotlight. Now they knew!

The flat mood continued all Tuesday and right up to the match, when things were not helped by the sight of Neil Jenkins hobbling in pain after he had warmed up. Jenks was in dreadful trouble with his knee and, although he played the 80 minutes, it would be his last run-out on tour, apart from a brief appearance as a sub in the second Test.

During the match, the guys played as though it was just a question of waiting for the final whistle. It did not look an enjoyable experience for them. We played some nice rugby at times, and scored a few tries. Scott Gibbs got one and was named man of the match. He also had stitches for the first time in his rugby career, a lovely gash about his right eye opening up after a clash of heads. Scotty has a phobia of needles but very bravely underwent the procedure and returned to the fray with a big white bandage right across his forehead.

Despite our tries, most of the game was scrappy and pretty passionless, which was a shame for the two or three thousand Lions fans who had made the trip. The opposition were tougher than expected, better organised, and they could play. The combination of that, a pernickety referee and our mistakes prevented a cricket score, though we eventually won 3–46, defending well and preventing them crossing our line.

It had been no fun to watch, and by the end of the game we were sitting there saying 'Come on, blow your whistle, let's get off here without any injuries.' One moment of humour came as we left the stands: An Australian woman came up and said 'I'm really sorry that you are injured and you are going home, dear'. She thought I was Lawrence Dallaglio.

No laughs in the changing room, though. I was shocked when I walked through the door. Gibbsy, one of the South Africa tour's most enthusiastic members, was back and Tyrone Howe and Gordon Bulloch had made their first Lions starts. David Wallace had come on from the bench to make his first appearance in a Lions shirt. Nobby had been on the bench, also a Lion for the first time.

The room ought to have been jumping with the excitement and adrenalin but it was just dead. No-one had enjoyed themselves and they seemed happy just to have got the match out of the way so we could move on.

It was the second week on the trot, after Australia A, when the midweek players had failed to get any buzz out of their game. I guess the combination of the previous day's events and the general feeling among the midweek guys that they were second class citizens was to blame.

It was not ideal; for the tour to roll along, those guys needed to go and get things buzzing. A big victory for the Dirt Trackers gets the whole party going. In 1997, the midweekers developed their own tremendous team spirit and took a real pride in their games. And they played a crucial part in the Test team's success with their victory against South Africa A before the first Test, where they played very well, denting the senior Springbok side's confidence in the process, and the thrashing of Freestate between the first and second Tests, where they were brilliant and put on probably the best performance of the tour.

In 2001, I felt too many players were getting no sense of satisfaction simply out of being on the tour. Playing midweek was not enough for them. Who was to blame for that? Partly Graham Henry, who had not helped matters with his bluntness and his attitude to their fixtures, and partly some of the players, who had, frankly, gone out with unrealistic expectations of playing in the Test side.

I am sure that, towards the end of the tour, some of them were sitting there thinking 'What the hell am I doing here?'

*

WE LEFT the players at their after match function and headed back to the hotel, where we had to pick the team for the first Test. A certain number of guys selected themselves, as is always the case. Much of modern team selection is about getting the bench right. You are looking for guys who will make an impact if they come on and also ensuring you have cover for the vital positions. For instance, with Austin Healey available we had a choice between having a spare scrum-half or a spare fly-half on the bench, because Oz can cover both of those positions. In the end, Austin covered 10 and Daws was included in the 22 as well.

The front row was reasonably easy: Tom Smith was chosen at loose-head where, to my mind, the only challenger was Jason Leonard. Jase had been a victim of his own versatility, having been involved in nearly every game but often coming on at tight-head. Again, he would be on the bench. Keith Wood was always going to start at hooker, with Gordon Bulloch his replacement. Phil Vickery was at tight-head, with Dai Young not quite mobile enough for the game we wanted to play.

Danny Grewcock would partner me in the second row, the other locks generally not playing up to their undoubted ability. There was a little indecision about the back row, where playing Scott Quinnell, Richard Hill and Neil Back did not give us great line-out options. We were talking this over in the selection meeting when I asked 'How are Backy's ribs'. He had injured them against the Waratahs. No-one seemed to know, which surprised me a little.

I said: 'Jeez, we need to find out . . . let's get the doctor.'

James Robson came up to see us. His view was that Neil could play on the Saturday but there was a serious risk that he could exacerbate the injury and put himself out for the remaining three games. That solved our conundrum. Corry would come in on the blind-side and Hill would switch to 7. That gave us the extra line-out jumper and balanced the back row, though we would lose Back's tremendous linking abilities.

Rob Howley had just nosed ahead of Matt Dawson at 9, a very close decision, and Jonny Wilkinson would go at 10. Rob Henderson, who had come from nowhere to play really well, but had not been involved since the Queensland Reds match, claimed the inside centre spot ahead of Scott Gibbs, with Catty gone and Will Greenwood injured. 'God' – as Brian O'Driscoll is known in Ireland – would play outside him. Poor old Brian took some stick on tour for his back-home nickname. He only had to pour a glass of water and guys would enquire whether he was turning it into wine. Same with bread: 'Got any fishes to go with your loaf, God?' someone would enquire.

There was more debate over the back three. We had a few options on the wings. Had Luger been around he would have started, but he was gone. That left a choice of Ben Cohen, Tyrone

Howe, Austin Healey, Iain Balshaw, Dafydd James and Jason Robinson. Ben had been unfortunate and I felt sorry for him. He had made a couple of mistakes in the Western Australia game and had then played well against Australia A in a poor team performance which had tarred him with the collective brush. Since then he had not really had a chance to show what he could do, given that the New South Wales Country Cockatoos game was almost a non-event in selection terms. I rate him highly: he is a big, powerful winger, 15st and quick, and he makes a big impact. He punches holes in defences and is a difficult guy to tackle, believe me. It can take two or three blokes to bring him down. Added to which he is a quality finisher, having scored a lot of tries for England. If he had been in the right place at the right time he would probably have made the Test team but he had been in the wrong places at the wrong times. He had been first choice for England in the autumn so going from being in the middle of everything to playing in the Lions midweek side was tough for him. His attitude was always good and his head never dropped but I could see he was down about it and I tried to cheer him along, telling him to keep going and that he could still get his chance. Tyrone Howe had probably arrived on tour too late to force his way straight into the Test XV and Austin was condemned to the bench by his versatility. Balsh would either play full-back or be named among the replacements. Daf James was a top bloke, who kept himself very fit. He was solid in defence, which we needed against the likes of Roff, and, while not an out-and-out speed merchant, had enough pace to cause damage himself. In the absence of Luger, we decided he would start on the right wing. That left Jason Robinson. Early on, Graham Henry had confided in me that he did not think Jase was ready for a start in a Lions Test. He did not say this in a negative way: he just said: 'I've yet to be convinced by him.' His eyebrows had definitely been raised by Jason's five tries on his debut – the only Lions player to have achieved this – even though the game was against the low quality

Queensland President's XV. A try against Australia A and two more, and a great performance to boot, against the Waratahs, had removed those doubts. We decided Jase would start on the left wing.

That just left full-back, where the question was simple: Matt Perry or Iain Balshaw. When the party was named, the management's intention had been to play Balsh at 15 and if Iain had been our Test full-back I would have been perfectly happy. He has played well there for England and would not have let us down. However, I think he was suffering, in a perverse way, because of his meteoric rise during the season. He had gone from being almost an unknown to being heralded as one of the greatest backs England had ever produced and that is a lot of pressure to put on such young shoulders. He felt everyone was expecting him to do something startling, and maybe felt himself that he should be doing that, but it was not happening. As a consequence, he was trying to get hold of the ball and force things – which you cannot do against good teams – and had fallen into a bit of a rut. It was a shame for him but we had another top quality full-back in our party in Matt Perry and Henry was adamant that Perry had now moved ahead of Balshaw.

Pezza is a very solid player, England's most-capped full-back at just 24, and a man you can rely on. It had been hard on him to be dropped from the national side for the previous Six Nations so I was pleased for him that he was back at the highest level.

It was a strong-looking line-up, given all our injury problems, with a good bench, too. Guys like Balshaw, Charvis, Leonard, Healey and Dawson were excellent impact replacements.

The hardest thing was going to see Backy to tell him that he was not being considered because of his injury. I refused to go on my own, taking Andy Robinson and the Doc with me in case he started knocking bodies about; he was so desperate to play, after only starting once in South Africa, that there could have been a chinning. It is a difficult job, when you captain a side, to go and tell your long-time teammate, colleague and friend something like that. But he took it well. He knew he was not fit and understood it was the right decision. He had tried to play through a knee injury for England some months before and his performances had dropped off as a result. He did not want that to happen again. Neil is a very organised bloke who likes things mapped out for him: we told him to get himself ready to play in Melbourne and he was happy enough with that.

One other issue was raised: Neil Jenkins. It had been abundantly apparent, since before we left the UK, that Jenks' knee was dodgy. By the Cockatoos game, he was, to all intents and purposes, unable to continue on tour. Adrenalin and pain killers will take you so far but it was obvious to everyone that he was nowhere near fit. It was a real shame for Neil. He is a Lions legend and people's lasting memory of him in that jersey should have been his fantastic performances in South Africa, not those pain-wracked showings in Australia. It was not fair on the other players to keep him out there and it was not fair on Jenks. I think in his heart of hearts he knew this himself but it is a big call to expect a guy to pull himself out of a Lions tour, especially when he knows it will be his last.

Graham Henry, almost in passing, said: 'Shall we send for Gregor Townsend?' I felt this was the right option – Gregor has great class and would have added a lot – but I never heard the issue raised again, unfortunately. Henry should have taken the difficult decision and Gregor Townsend should have been on a plane on the evening of that Cockatoos game, June 26. But it did not happen.

On Wednesday, we trained in the morning and I had to attend a long press conference for the team announcement after lunch. It was a busy old day – trying to fit in videos, training, team meetings, press conferences and, finally, packing your bags to travel back to Brisbane.

We flew from Coffs Harbour in two very small planes instead

of the usual 80-seater. It was a short flight but a few of the guys who are nervous of flying hated it, being batted about in these little aircraft, and they were glad when we landed and got into the bus to our destination, the city's Sheraton. Thursday was to be a day off for everyone, either getting ready for Saturday or recovering from Tuesday, and we really needed it, with the Test match looming and having had a horrible week so far. All the guys were looking forward to getting their feet up and doing their own thing: no 'You must be here to do so-and-so at such-and-such a time'.

Then, as the coach headed into Brisbane, the announcement came over the PA: 'Guys, day off for everyone tomorrow, meeting at 3.30pm.' And you could feel the morale just drain away from everyone. I felt for them. A day off is not a day off if you know, at the back of your mind, you have to be back at the hotel in the afternoon to think, talk and plan rugby. I could see all the players' shoulders drop and them saying to each other, 'Well, what's the point of having a day off?'

A few of them suggested meeting up in the morning to get it over with – they did not want to be out trying to relax with that at the backs of their minds. Other guys said no, they preferred a lie-in.

There was no easy solution and when I spoke to Andy Robinson about it I could see the stress in his face. Robbo and the rest of the management team were under massive pressure to succeed in Brisbane and they had called the meeting just to tweak those areas they felt needed it. It was for the best of motives. But they had just gone about it the wrong way, forgetting the psychology of players.

Robbo should have called me and Jonny Wilkinson, who was *de facto* leader of the backs, on one side and said 'Fellahs, we need to get the boys together this afternoon for a run-through.'

Jonny and I would have suggested it as though it was our idea and they would have been fine about it. It would have felt informal and casual and would just have continued what we had already been doing. On the Thursdays before the Queensland Reds and Waratahs games, for instance, the forwards arranged among themselves to meet up and spend some time working on a few line-out spotters. We met about 5pm in the local parks, all very relaxed, and everyone was fine about it. Sometimes unofficial sessions are best in the immediate run-up to a game. If they go well they give you confidence and make you relax. What players do not like as the match approaches is too much talk or too many meetings. It makes them tense and nervous and they start getting into 'game mode' in their minds.

The session went ahead, though – there was never any question of guys not turning up – and, once we were into it, it was fine. Danny Grewcock, who is known as 'Danny One-More' for his love of just one more throw, and the rest of the guys were happy to stay out there for 50 minutes until, in the end, I had to call a halt.

The funny thing was that we went to a park down near the water in Brisbane which was overlooked by the Wallaby team hotel. When we had been based in the city earlier in the tour, we had run through our line-outs in the middle of the same park. If the Aussies had wanted to watch us training, instead of having to sneak into our practice they could have booked rooms in the hotel, strolled out onto their balconies, cigar, brandy and pair of binoculars in hand, and watched us. This time, cunningly, we hid behind some trees.

Earlier there had been an interesting insight into the life of Johnson. I had been planning to spend the day dozing until I was asked by our press liaison people if I would take a trip to the Gabba for a photoshoot with John Eales and the Tom Richards Trophy, for which we would be playing the Test series.

My initial response was: 'How about, 'Bollocks, it's my day off'?' I had done a 90 minute press conference on the Wednesday while Ealesy, as far as I knew, had done nothing public. The Aussie media supplied questions to the press officer who then put them to the players and had their answers filmed by an in-house cameraman and returned on videotape. We could not expect that luxury with 40 or 50 press guys following us around but there has to be a limit.

'No, no, no,' they said. 'We've told them you'll do it!'

'How about, 'Bollocks, it's my day off'?' I replied.

Unfortunately, you cannot really take that attitude although I could not see the point of the exercise. The game was sold out – it was not as though we needed to drum up interest. So around lunchtime I headed for reception for my transport to the ground. Except, er, there wasn't any, our press officer having forgotten to arrange it, so we had to find a taxi. You can imagine my mood. Which worsened when the cabbie did not know where the Gabba was. Eventually, after turning down a few blind alleys, we arrived and I strolled out onto the turf and over to shake hands with Ealesy. At that point, some Aussie said: 'Right, gentlemen, let's have the first question.'

I had seen that there were quite a bunch of blokes there but had not noticed that a lot of them did not have cameras.

Johnson's grumpy mood now turns grumpier.

I said: 'Hang on, I'm here for a photoshoot, not a press conference.' After all, I had done one of those yesterday and was to do another the following day. And I walked off to inspect the Gabba's wicket, forming the impression that it would definitely be taking spin on the fifth day. Unfortunately, I could not jam my keys into the surface to be sure because the hotel used those plastic swipe cards.

For all my reputation as a fairly brusque person, I am normally fine with the media and would usually have stood there and answered the questions because it is almost easier to do that. But I was so wound up about the game and the week in general that I snapped. I actually surprised myself. Ealesy, good as gold of course, gave them a few lines and I wandered back for the photo. It did not stop there.

We were holding the trophy, a big cut glass affair created in honour of a World War One hero who actually played for both the Lions and the Wallabies, and pictures were being taken. Then one of the snappers said: 'Can I have a photo of the two of you walking towards me from about 25 yards away, carrying the trophy down low?' I looked at John and John looked at me and we both turned to this guy and said: 'Er, no.' It would have looked distinctly odd, almost as though we were hand-in-hand, though John Eales is a very nice guy and if I were to walk off into the sunset with any bloke it might well be him.

That is the problem with the media: they are always looking for something different and if it makes you look like a fool . . . well, hard lines.

With that, a halt was called to proceedings and I left, though I had to walk all the way from the Gabba to the main road to hail another cab.

All in all, Johnson peeved.

*

BY THURSDAY evening, the pressure was really on everyone. The support we had had in the early days of the tour was excellent but the amount of British and Irish people in Brisbane was literally incredible. The Welsh public, in particular, had responded brilliantly and every other fan seemed to be from the Valleys. Some of the Welsh players who had been out around town came back and said 'Bloody hell, it's like being back home . . . my whole village is here.'

We were out of it a bit, our team room being stuck up in the penthouse of the Sheraton, which was sometimes a bit of a relief. You were taking your life in your hands trying to get out of reception. That was an amazing feeling too – it was like being a pop star or something.

On Friday, we went to the Gabba so the rest of the guys could have a look round. Obviously, it is one of the world's great cricket grounds and, out of season, it is primarily used for Aussie Rules. That night, they had a Rules game on so there was pitch marked out and no posts in place. We had to try to imagine what it was going to look like as a rugby field, which was not easy, and Jason Leonard tried to imagine his pub XI playing there, which was harder still.

Another factor which was unusual concerned our warm-up, which we had been told we had to do inside so we did not affect the pre-match entertainment. That is often the way in the Southern Hemisphere, where they go to town with fireworks, bands, cheerleaders and, sometimes, curtain-raiser games before big matches. With this in mind we were keen to see where we would change, rather than turning up and being a bit surprised. We found it was a big gym area with a few chairs dotted around. Unusual, but fine. Then we went off to the Reds' ground, Ballymore, for a final training session. The strain was now massive on everyone, including the management. We huddled on the pitch before we trained and Graham Henry spotted Austin Healey was talking to someone.

I could see the pressure on Graham's face. He snapped: 'Oz are you with us?'

Healey said: 'Yes, of course I am.'

'It's about bloody time,' replied Graham.

I winced – it was exactly the wrong note for Henry to be taking and another example of his blunt way with words. It was an exchange which did him no credit and not something I think he would have wanted to say. In the tension of the day it came out and it underlined how big this game was for him too.

I could see Oz thinking 'What have you said that for . . . there was no need for that' so I grabbed hold of him and said 'Look mate, just ignore that . . . just get on with it.' And we trained well.

That evening's team meeting continued the theme of nerves and pressure. I have never been in a team that was so anxious before a game – and I include the second Test of the 1997 series, England's World Cup semi- and quarter-finals in 1995 and 1999 and Leicester's European Cup finals. You could see it in people's faces and their body language. Even experienced guys. Jonny Wilkinson, the backs' moves and our gameplan whizzing around and around in his head, looked like he had the weight of the world on his shoulders. Everyone, to a greater or lesser degree, was the same. I think it was due to a combination of factors. Australia were World Champions and formidable opponents, probably a better side, relatively, than the one we beat in 1997. Thousands upon thousands of people had spent a lot of money travelling halfway around the world to watch us. The media presence and interest was huge. The whole thing felt enormous.

Phil Vickery put it well in an interview when he said: 'It's a great thing to play for the Lions, one of the best things in your life, but if you play poorly and get badly beaten it could be one of the worst.'

A final factor was the general air of unhappiness in the camp. It now did not feel like we were a team together. There was a definite split in the squad at this point between the Test 22 and some of the others, one or two of whom did not feel part of the tour any more. Their heads were down, they were not getting any joy out of being there and I could tell that, given the choice, they would have gone home. They were counting the days.

A good win just might reintroduce a bit of feelgood. But if we kicked off the series with a loss those final two weeks were going to feel very long indeed.

The 'Captain's Meeting' gathering was set for 6.30pm. I tried to relax the boys as much as I could. You want to stop the players thinking about the game too much because that will increase the tension.

My final words were something like: 'We're going into this together, we're going to stand shoulder to shoulder, we're going to come through it and we're going to win.' It is very easy to feel alone at times like that and you want everyone to know they are not.

I was nervous, too. Tomorrow was a big day. We were going into the unknown.

The Real Thing

EVENING KICK-OFFS have great atmosphere and drama but they do present the difficulty of what to do with yourself during the day. I tend to try and stay up until about midnight the night before, reading or watching TV, to give myself the best chance of sleeping in for as long as possible the next day.

I got up about 10am and had a breakfast of yoghurt, muesli, fruit and scrambled eggs with brown toast, no butter. I killed a bit of time chatting to the guys, fielding calls from family and friends and checking my kit. After lunch – steamed chicken, vegetables, pasta and a baked potato – we had another brief team meeting, just chatting through objectives and making sure everyone was OK. Then the forwards wandered down to the same grassy area in the middle of Brisbane, a few hundred yards from the hotel, where we had gone through our line-outs ahead of the Reds game.

There were hundreds of supporters in the reception and I was dreading them grabbing the guys for autographs as we left; by now they had their game faces on and were not very approachable. But the fans held back, just cheering us out and following us down to watch. I suppose for them it was quite interesting; I would be exactly the same if the San Francisco 49ers were leaping

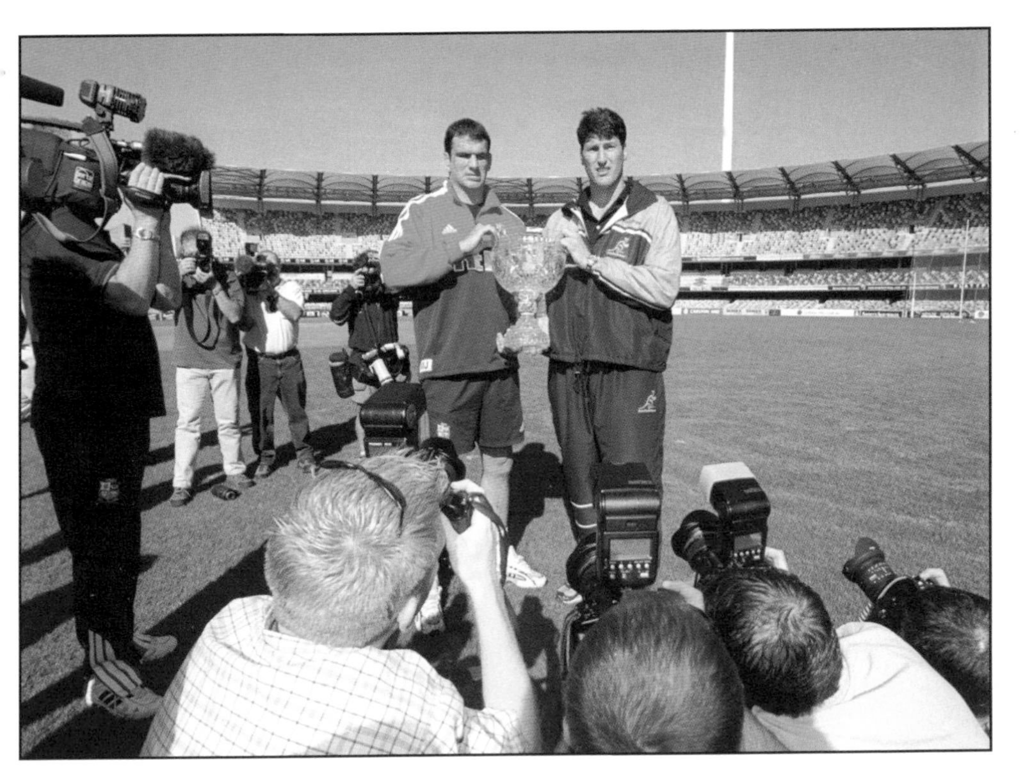

'How about, "Bollocks, it's my day off?"'

Dan Luger massages his cheekbone. It was fractured in training: one of many injuries we suffered on tour

Lawrence Dallaglio was another injury victim and a great loss

Everybody needs good neighbours. Austin would not be one

Tom Smith, a 1997 stalwart, a quiet guy and a top bloke

A finely-sculpted Johnson shows his ball skills. Gibbs shows why Wales don't play much soccer

First Test: Jason Robinson scores one of the best Lions tries ever...

...Brian O'Driscoll scores perhaps *the* best

Daf James, a solid citizen, was another scorer...

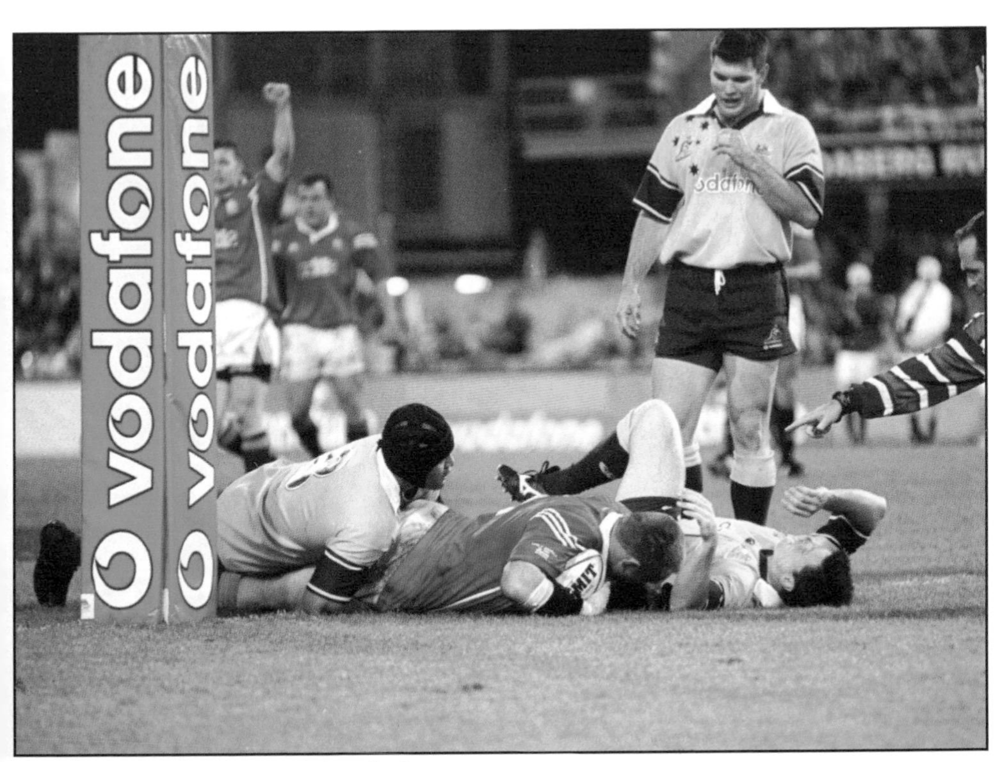

...and Scott Quinnell makes it four

The First Test won, and we are off to a flier

Scotty Gibbs, a talisman on the South Africa tour, walks me off the pitch

Richard Hill was a key factor in our First Test win...

...as was Keith Wood. Nice stitches

Our magnificent travelling support await a Jonny Wilkinson kick

Graham Henry faced a lot of press questions about the supposed 'bad boys' of the tour, Austin Healey and Matt Dawson. Here, Austin (l) celebrates scoring his second try against ACT Brumbies - with his nemesis, Justin Harrison, stalking off in the back-ground - and Matt (r) kicks the con-version which sealed the win

Martin Corry lays down the law to his fellow forwards

Second Test: Neil Back gets us underway

Richard Hill - with Rob Howley - was a major loss

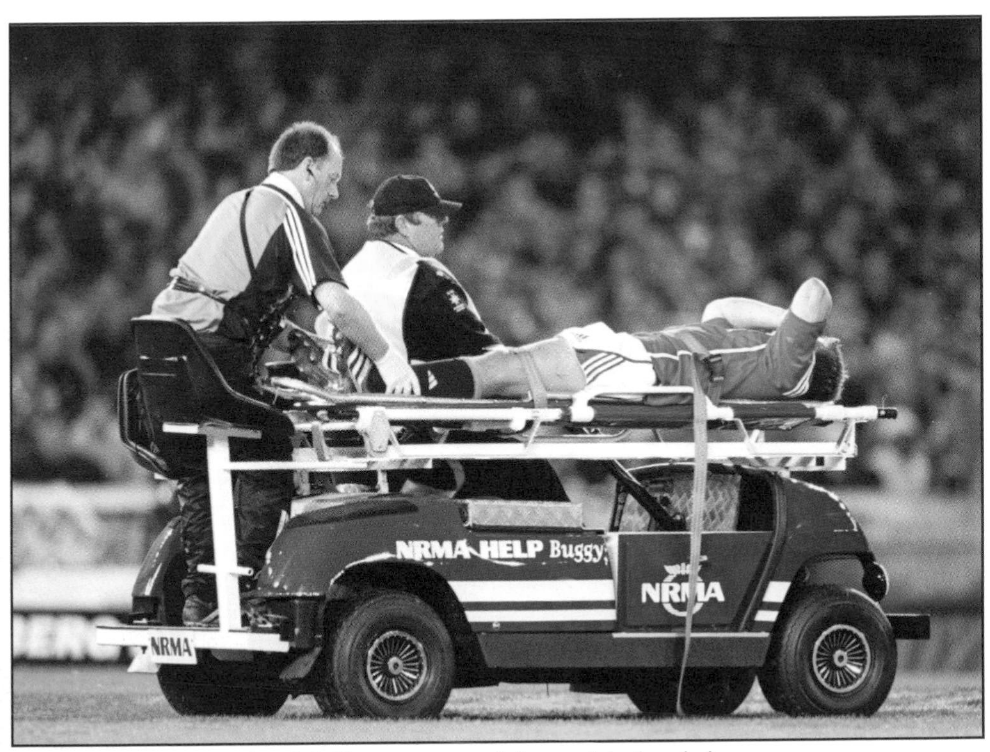

Jonny Wilkinson, thankfully, recovered from this leg injury

Jonny's kicking, while slightly below his England level,was still excellent

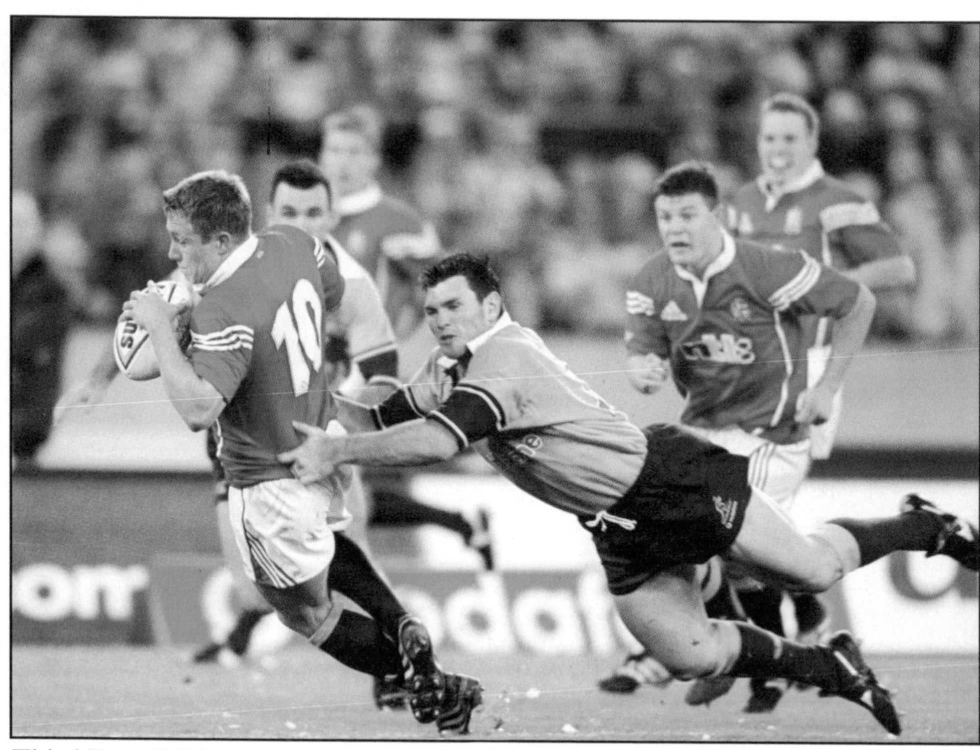

Third Test: Wilkinson breaks through for a great try

The agony...

...and the ecstasy. Rod Macqueen and John Eales, worthy winners

Neil Back scored his 50th try for the club during the season

Deano celebrates

Leon Lloyd, two-try hero of Paris

Champions of England: the boys celebrate our Zurich victory

Champions of Europe: the Schnozz and I with the trophy that proves it

The Leicester faithful: a great day out in Europe

about in the street. A lot of people were taking pictures, which was fine. It would have provided good photo album fodder, 11 blokes throwing balls to each other and leaping up and down like performing seals. And we had a good session, though we nearly had a mishap on the slippy grass. Tom Smith lifted me up but must have lost his footing slightly and we both fell, he on his back and me almost on top of him. As I dropped I had this flash through my brain: 'Bloody hell, I'm going to put Smithy out of the game right in front of all these people.' It must have been in his mind, too, because he almost bounced straight back upright as though it had not happened. Then we were finished and heading back to the hotel.

As we left, one fan came over and collared Leonard, who was on the bench. 'Oi, Jase,' he said. 'I know your dad!' How do you follow that? Jason just said: 'Oh, right, that's great,' and carried on walking. I hope the guy did not feel too miffed: it is just that, at times like that, players cannot deal with mundane things that would otherwise be perfectly OK.

Around 3pm we had another meal, trying to get enough protein and carbohydrates into our bodies for the game. You want to have eaten enough early enough so that you have the energy for the match and are not hungry. And we were free then until we met up for the coach at around 4.45pm, so I retired to my room. Just sitting there, having packed, everything going round in your mind, it can be an awfully long wait. So I opened a book my dad had lent me, *Glory In The Centre Spot*, which is the autobiography of the former Wigan and Great Britain rugby league player Eric Ashton. It is an interesting read, particularly the passages about his league tours to Australia forty years ago, but I found myself going over the same paragraphs time and again. I could not concentrate.

And then it was time to go. In our penthouse team room, high above the streets of Brisbane, the Lions legend Willie John McBride was waiting for us. The lads filed in and sat down and then Willie John started speaking. He could have stood there and made some 'fire-and-brimstone, let's kick their backsides' kind of speech. But that is not his way. Instead, he spoke about how he had felt pain and nerves and anxiety before his matches . . . everything that we were all feeling now. He was playing 30 years ago, in the amateur era, but his words really struck a chord with us. He had been there and done it and it gave us a good feeling. He handed out our shirts and we were on our way.

*

THE GABBA was not far from the hotel but much of the city was fairly quiet as we drove through it. When we reached the ground, however, it was a different story. There were Lions fans everywhere, thousands and thousands of them. There was a pub not far from the stadium called the Gabba Hotel – a Colonial-style building with old, covered verandas all the way round. It was 15-deep with red shirts. Everyone seemed to have the colours on. Most of us had played Test matches in Australia before with our home countries and we had never seen anything like it. On short tours, you do not take 20,000 people with you – you might take 250 to 500 and pick up a few expats.

It was an incredible and moving sight and the only thing that came close to it was South Africa in 1997. The difference there was that the stadia were much bigger and the home support much more fervent so the impact of the British and Irish fans was reduced.

We found our way into the changing room with 90 minutes to go before the game and most of the boys took a wander out onto the grass to acclimatise themselves and check they had the right studs. The pitch was firm apart from a hard, bare area where the cricket square normally was. The ground was still fairly empty, with the supporters sucking down the Toohey's and Castlemaine XXXX outside, but when I went out 45 minutes before kick-off for the toss it was a different story. Wall-to-wall red. Winning the toss – it is pretty irrelevant in rugby, unless there is a strong wind, a slope or maybe a low sun – I told Ealesy we would bat. I am not sure he got the joke. Then I went back inside.

'Boys,' I said. 'This is going to be like a home game.'

Sometimes, before club games, the time can drag but when you are playing a Test match it seems to shoot by in a blur. I do not have much of a memory of those minutes, more an impression. I remember the tension, the anticipation. I remember, too, the ntl cameras being in there, but I tried to avoid the distraction. I like to focus. If you want to create a distraction of your own, a joke with one of the lads, that is fine. But in a team situation, if outsiders come in and crack the same joke they would be told to get stuffed. It is quite strange, quite territorial. With England and Leicester, if I am in our changing room and someone walks in who should not be there before a game I just tell them to get out and would physically remove them if they refused . . . no-one walks through there. It is a confrontational feeling brought about, I suppose, by the natural adrenalin and aggression building up in you.

We channelled those feelings into a good warm-up in our team area deep in the bowels of the Gabba stands. With guys running around, hitting tackle pads and shouting, the noise was bouncing off the walls and it gave us all a lift and a feeling of togetherness.

Graham and Robbo had a few last-minute words, and I gave the lads a final pep-talk: 'This is what separates the men from the wannabes,' I said. 'We stand together and we put our bodies on the line if we have to. These guys don't rate us. We're going to show them.'

Then the ref popped his head round the door and gave me the nod and we were on our way. Normally the away team goes out first and you see the other side's changing room door open a minute or so later. But we were in different ends of the stadium and we came out together, our 22 heading up some steps through a forest of red-clad arms and flags, everyone going berserk. I had the cuddly lion in one hand but I hate carrying that thing around so I threw him out of the way as quickly as possible and ran out onto the pitch.

Looking around the guys, they were all really wired, really hyped, all right on the brink of something huge in their lives. We stood for the Australian anthem – it is a shame the Lions do not have one – and then the game was underway.

Right from the off, the pace was high, with things happening so quickly and balls pinging everywhere, Smithy and Woody getting their hands on it and making yards, the backs getting involved. I remember thinking to myself 'We've done all this work on structure and the game is just all over the place.' We just had to play rugby, which I think was good for us because we had some good, instinctive players in our XV. I could see immediately that the Australians were rattled by our intensity but I did not expect us to score so soon . . . all tour we had been reminding ourselves that these guys had the best defence in the world.

Try telling Jason Robinson that. We won a line-out on the half-way line in the third minute. Danny Grewcock caught it and gave quick ball off the top to Rob Howley. Rob passed to Jonny, who missed out Hendo to find O'Driscoll. He was brought down by Grey 35 metres out but managed to throw the ball back out of the tackle. Howley made a brilliant pick up, right off his feet, and formed the ruck as he was tackled by George Smith. Scott Quinnell picked up and popped a short pass to Jonny who handed it on to Matt Perry. Pezza, with soft and very quick hands in the face of an onrushing defender, passed the ball to Jase. He still had three or four yards before he hit their 22 and Chris Latham, the full-back, seemed to have him covered, even showing him the outside.

Two seconds later he would have been regretting that: Robinson's awesome step and high pace took him straight past to the line. It felt like 10 minutes into the game because so much had been going on but the score was timed at 2 min 44 sec . . . the whole move had taken just 18 seconds and we were five points up.

The crowd were going wild as Jase ran round behind the posts, punching the air and whooping before disappearing in a swarm of Lions. It was a dream start, just what we had wanted. Seeing one of their key players skinned like that so early in the game gave everyone a belief that we could win. Latham or Burke must have been a difficult call for the Australians. Matt Burke is very solid in defence and a tremendous goal-kicker. Latham, though, was a more attacking full back and Australia's player of the season the year before. We had spent a lot of time looking at videos of him in action. He is the master of the chip-and-chase, has a lot of pace and looked very dangerous running with the ball. Robinson had just proved his defence was suspect.

Jonny missed the conversion and a couple of subsequent penalties but the 100mph action continued. Hendo broke through and almost released Brian, only for Roff to intercept just outside his own 22 and race downfield after a chip kick. He was defeated by the bounce just outside our 22 and Jonny picked it up. Wood, Quinnell, Vickery and Corry combined to bring the ball right back down to their end where this time O'Driscoll put in the chip for Robinson to chase, forcing Walker to touch down behind his own line. The ball had gone end-to-end-to-end in about 60 seconds. It was horribly fast and furious.

As the half wore on, they started trying to play wide on us. It worked to a degree, dragging our defence across the field a lot, which is not ideal for a tight five forward. We do not have the pace to compensate for being out of position so I was constantly checking that I was in the right place.

Although their pack was slightly heavier we had the edge on them and our second try came off a scrum in the 34th minute. We went right and Rob fed O'Driscoll, whose pace and balance beat the Wallaby blindside defence. Jason Robinson had come across to make the extra man and he passed to Daf James who dived over in the corner, Latham again missing his man and Jonny converting. It was especially pleasing because this was a set move. We had felt we could exploit Owen Finegan's lack of pace and it had worked beautifully.

Half-time rushed up on us and the score was still close: 3–12. In the changing room, the nerves had gone and we felt good. The amazing thing was the ease with which we had been able to break open their much-vaunted midfield defence. Hendo and Brian had both made good breaks and the back row had been charging through too. Everyone had been playing well. But they are a team that does not panic and we knew we had to keep the heat on.

We did this better than we could have hoped. Danny took the restart kick and a maul formed, driving up 10 metres. The ball was fed out down the backline to O'Driscoll, who lost it. Richard Hill dived on the loose ball and flicked it to Balshaw – on for the injured Matt Perry – who made five metres and set up a second maul. The ball found its way back out to Brian, five metres inside our own half, and he set off on an amazing run. He stepped Nathan Grey and shrugged off a tackle by Jeremy Paul, who tripped George Smith as he fell. Still 30 metres out, Brian had Matt Burke – on for Latham – ahead of him. He feinted right and stepped round the diving full-back to the left, racing on to score under the posts as Roff dived to tackle him.

Forty seconds of the half gone.

It was one of the best tries ever scored in a Lions shirt. I watched the Sky Sports coverage weeks later and Stuart Barnes came out with a memorable line: 'They call him God . . . well I reckon he's a better player than that!' A pretty fair comment.

Jonny knocked over the conversion to the unfamiliar strains of *Bread of Heaven* and the score was 3–19. But the Wallabies had come back from further behind than that in the past so we could not relax. Still, O'Driscoll, Robinson and Henderson were cutting the Australian midfield apart and they were forced to give away a penalty, which Jonny kicked to give us three more points.

In the 50th minute, we won another penalty and I told Jonny to kick for touch. Our line-out, which Cozza won at the back. The ball was fed out quickly to Hendo, who beat tackles from Larkham, Burke and Roff before finally being dropped five metres out by Eales. The ruck formed, Howley gave it short to Balshaw but he, too, was brought down agonisingly close. A second ruck, and Scotty Quinnell picked up and drove, taking Burke and Toutai Kefu over with him. Four tries to nil, Jonny converts to make in 3–29, scarcely more than half the game gone, and we are in dreamland.

It was a weird feeling: we had built ourselves up that this was going to nail-bitingly, agonisingly close and suddenly we had all-but won the game. We should have carried on playing in the same way, keeping them under pressure without taking unnecessary risks. But I think, subconsciously, that we became defensive in our mindset, trying to protect what we had. At the same time, they had been stung and were finally coming back at us hard. It is always tough playing rugby on the back foot and the Wallabies grew in confidence as the game wore on.

I do not think they were ever going to overhaul us – it might have been a different story had they scored straight after Scott – but they did score two tries in the last 15 minutes, the Lions having played most of the last 25 minutes with only 14 men, with first Corry and then Vickery sent to the sin bin.

One irritating factor was the number of penalties we gave away as we defended. We felt that in the first half they had got away with work on the floor which we later found ourselves being pinged for. I think the referee got a little bit down on us, thinking we were trying to kill the game off, and we should have been a little smarter in the way we played. We should have let them have the ball and relied on our tackling, which was good, instead of committing ourselves to trying to nick the ball on the floor.

A Burke ‘try’ was denied by the video judge because he

touched the flag before he grounded the ball but, after 65 minutes, their pressure told and Andrew Walker did score. Their second try, five minutes later, was one of those things: we had centres committed in a ruck so I was out wide defending. My positioning was good when Roff switched the ball back in to Nathan Grey and Rob Henderson or Brian O'Driscoll would have caught him had they been where I was. Unfortunately, I do not have their pace and he went over with me lumbering in the background.

We held out from then, the match ending 13–29, and the relief when the final whistle went was tremendous. I actually felt the pressure lift off me: it had been the worst and hardest week I have ever had in rugby, with all that had been going on behind the scenes, and to get that victory was priceless.

I hoped, above all, that the win would bring us all back together. Sitting there in the changing room, basking in the warmth of a win, everyone together, relaxing and joking, is the best time you get as a player. I said to the guys 'This is what it's all about, winning these games . . . everyone's a part of this.' I was trying to get the whole squad feeling good about it. Whether things had gone too far I do not know. I think everyone was in good spirits – obviously the guys who played the match were euphoric – but it is difficult to judge how people really feel.

As usual, it was not all good news. Perry was hurt – as was the Wallaby hooker, Jeremy Paul, with a shattered knee – and Charvis, on for Scott towards the end, had been cited for knee-dropping someone. He could be looking at a ban, which was something we really did not need with Quinnell suffering with his knees.

Pretty soon, I had to leave to go to the press conference and the TV interviews, which takes you away from the players. I would much rather stay with the boys but it is a part of the job so you just have to get on with it. We were greeted by a British press corps who only wanted to talk about one thing: a fairly sensational newspaper column, written by Matt Dawson, which had appeared back home on the morning of the Test and was starting to filter through to the media Down Under.

Donal dead-batted the questions, saying he had not seen the article. I had not done so myself so I could not really add anything to that. The first I had know about it – in fact, the first any of the players had known about it as far as I am aware – was when Daws came up to me after the game in the changing rooms.

He said: 'Johnno, I've got a bit of a problem' and went on to explain what had been printed.

The British press, he said, were all over him – something which was now being confirmed by the journalists in front of us. One recurrent theme was the question of whether Matt would be sent home. My attitude was simple. Whatever he had written, I was not personally bothered about it. Words did not matter. What mattered was his attitude within the squad. I saw him in training every day, I saw his commitment and his desire for the tour to be a success. I knew he was a valuable and talented member of the party and I would rather have him on the tour than not. I hoped this would smooth the affair over and kill it off as quickly as possible, not let it run and run because, ultimately, the constant attention could start to affect team preparations. I understand the press's need to find stories and, in the modern age, when players are kept on a tight rein, this must have felt like manna from Heaven to them. They were determined to hype it up for all they were worth. I had a feeling we had not heard the last of it.

It was the usual empty changing room on my return so I hopped in a people carrier back to the hotel, still in my game tracksuit. We got a fantastic reception there. The fans were absolutely loving it, and rightly so – we do not put one over on the Australians that often. As a single Test match, leaving aside games which have clinched a series, it was one of the Lions' best ever performances. Set against the fact that it was the last day of June in a very long season, and with all that had gone on in the last week or so, it was a hell of an achievement for the guys to play at the level they had.

A lot of my mates were at the hotel, and my mum and dad and my wife were too, so I stayed and had a chat, a sit down and a few beers. I did not go out on the town – it was late and I was knackered – but a few of the boys did though they were not going berserk. We had serious business still in hand.

Later that night, I spent a lot of time with Daws and his agent, Dave Williams, in his room, mocking him while I had the chance. He was pretty upset with himself and, I think more than anything, embarrassed about what had happened. He was obviously thinking 'Oh my God, what have I done?'

He was also thinking of what the consequences might be and was asking me what Donal and Graham would do to him. At worst, of course, they could send him home.

I said: 'Mate, if they send you home we are all going home.'

I absolutely meant that. I am a friend of Matt's as well as a colleague so, naturally, I felt a loyalty to him. If he had been playing badly, moping around the place, not bothering to train, then I would have been the first to say to him myself 'If you want to go home, go home'. But that is not Matt. He is not like that. He wanted things to go well. If the management had put him on a plane I would have been on the seat next to him and I like to think that the rest of the squad would have been too.

I left him, troubled, miserable but, I hope, reassured to turn in myself at about 2am. I was shattered but sleep was elusive. I kept thinking about the match and the games to come.

We had shocked the Australians, who had been over-confident. Before the match, they had been grinning at the cameras and waving to friends in the crowd. They would not fall into the same trap again. Next weekend, they would be a different side. Of that I was sure.

Midweek Guts

THERE WAS precious little time to celebrate the win. The next day, we had two problems to deal with. The first, as I had feared, was the continued fall-out from Daws's article. The second was the back row set-up for our final midweek game, against the ACT Brumbies on the Tuesday. Colin Charvis had been banned for two games for violence during the previous night's game. It was nothing serious – other people on both sides did worse things which were not picked up – but that was of no help to us. The ban stood and it created difficulties for the ACT match.

Matt first. I had now had chance to read his article – a full page diary of the tour to date – and it was rather more revealing of his inner feelings than these things normally are. He accused the management of treating the players like children and of forcing 'mindless' training upon us. We were 'spending too much time on set-piece and not enough to reacting to what's in front of us . . . everyone too bogged down by calls.' He also claimed some of the younger players had decided to 'leave the tour'.

What can I say? It was a stupid, silly thing to write – as he himself had immediately recognised – and I was amazed that a player of Matt's experience allowed it to be published, under his name, when he did. It is one thing to make criticisms – however valid they may be, and some of them were – in a book or interview after the tour has ended. It is quite another to publish them just before you are about to play the first Test of a British and Irish Lions series against the World Champions.

All that said, I meant what I had said to the press. Matt's diary did not matter a toss to me nor, I think, to any of the other players, many of whom probably felt the same way as he and whose main reaction would be one of glee that Daws had done something they could take the mickey out of him over. Ironically, it is other things, thing that look minor to outsiders, which are more likely to cause a genuine rift within a team but these tend to pass the media by.

Later, I met up with Donal and Graham to discuss what action would be taken. They had each copped some personal criticism in the pieces, and they were hurt, upset and angry. I could understand their feelings. But they were taking a mature attitude. Thankfully, it rapidly became apparent that they were not considering ditching him, a decision made a lot easier, I think, by the fact that we had won. I think he may well have been on his way if we had lost, because to treat him more leniently would have created a lot more pressure for the management and the players to handle. As it was, the victory made his remarks less damning. Additionally, Donal and Graham knew that, whatever he had done, we needed him as a player and they knew, too, that sending him home would only have increased the furore surrounding the affair. Instead, we decided on a hefty fine and an apology to the team. He was made to sit in front of everyone and say sorry, like a naughty schoolboy, with the players all giggling and pulling faces at him, and he desperately trying not to catch anyone's eye. Personally, I felt the punishment should have gone further: in my opinion, a public flogging, with his naked buttocks being whacked through the streets of Brisbane, was probably the way forward.

So why did he write it? I am sure he was pretty down: we have all had days when we felt like saying things like that. He was losing out to Rob Howley in the battle for the No9 shirt, which cannot have helped, and I think he felt Graham and Donal did not respect his abilities. A big part of the problem was in the interpretation of the words he used. For instance, he described our training as 'mindless'. People read that and think it means the coaches do not know what they are doing. In fact, it is just a word we use to describe very strenuous work. If I do a really hard training session, I'll say 'Bloody hell, that was mindless'. That was how Matt meant it. It was still a criticism – he felt we were working too hard – but it was not as aggressive a remark as some people felt. Overall, the column was his way of showing he was unhappy with the way the tour was going. He was trying to say we are at a certain level but we should be much higher.

And I agreed with some of his points. I certainly felt that Graham Henry's desire to play a structured game meant we *were* spending too much time worrying where we were supposed to be at a given moment and not enough to reacting to the game as it developed.

The bottom line, though, was that the forum for raising this sort of issue was in private, with the management, and not in the press.

A second problem we faced on the Sunday morning was the composition of our side for the final midweek game, against ACT. It was a massive game against the Super 12 champions. We desperately needed to win, especially after all the Dawson controversy, to give everyone a good buzz to take us into Melbourne. The plan had been for Charvis to start in the back row but that was no longer an option. Backy still was not right to play so that only left Martyn Williams and David Wallace, plus the three guys who had started on the Saturday in the Test – Hill, Quinnell and Corry. Scotty suffers badly with his knees and was also playing superbly so we did not want to risk him. Hilly was vital to the Test XV with his ability to play 6, 7 and 8. That left

Cozza, playing for the third time in seven days, to join Williams and Wallace. It was short straw time for Martin. He had been on for an hour in the previous midweek game, against the NSW Cockatoos, then played for all of the first Test, and now he was being told he had to turn out again three days later. He must also have known that, effectively, it meant he would not start in the second Test, despite a good display in the first. But his attitude was outstanding: when we broke the news to him he just said 'Right . . . fair enough' and remained very positive. We were still in a bind with back row replacements, however. In the end, myself and Mal O'Kelly sat on the bench. The thinking was that the starting second row, Jerry Davidson and Scott Murray, were both very athletic, mobile locks. Jerry had actually played international rugby at 6 and Scott could probably play 8 in a crisis. They would cover the back row with myself and Mal to cover them.

Austin Healey immediately started calling me 'Token' as in it being a token gesture that I was in the midweek squad, but it actually made for a busy couple of days for me. On Monday, when most of Saturday's Test team were taking it easy, I had to go and train with the Tuesday team and on the Tuesday morning, when that evening's team were chilling out, I had to train with the Test squad for the following weekend. I also had double the team meetings to attend.

Remember: we are now in July, the season having started for me 11 months previously. I was pretty bloody knackered. If I could have caught Austin I would have chinned him but then that's the story of my life.

We flew to Canberra on the Sunday evening and found a characterless new city which reminded many of us of Milton Keynes. We were in another open plan hotel, with all the bedrooms opening out onto an indoor balcony overlooking reception. The sprinklers had gone off and flooded the place and all the carpets were soaked downstairs . . . the only noise you could hear, 24 hours a day, were these heaters blowing warm air over the floor to dry it out. Canberra is a chilly, soulless place, which did not add to the enthusiasm of the midweekers. I remember reading one article talking about how amazing the city's War Memorial was and suggesting, in a fairly pointed way, that it was a shame the Lions could not find time to go there. I wish I had been able to. We spent so much time training, watching match videos or resting our battered bodies that we literally did not have enough time to see it – we were only there from Sunday evening until Wednesday lunchtime, after all.

The game was to take place at the Bruce Stadium, home to the Canberra Raiders rugby league side as well as ACT, in front of a buzzing 20,000-strong crowd made up of a lot of locals and plenty of British and Irish fans who had made the detour. The Brumbies were missing some key players – Roff, Walker, Larkham, Finegan, Smith, Paul, Gregan, Giffin – but they had been to New Zealand for a couple of warm-up games and, with guys like Jim Williams, Graeme Bond and the newly-returned Pat Howard in their side, they still had a strong line-up. Dai Young, the skipper, made the point to the boys beforehand that the ACT players still had a chance to wear a Wallaby shirt in that series: they would give us a real game.

As I made my way to the bench, I had a nagging feeling of doubt about our side: for the third week running, the midweekers had been very flat in the changing room, very quiet, with no excitement or anticipation. I was concerned about how they would play, and that was reflected in the pattern of the game.

In almost no time we were 19–3 down, having conceded three tries, and struggling with their pace and organisation. We defended poorly, our line-out failed to function and whenever we did get into a position to put pressure on them we made silly mistakes and turned over ball. Our only first-half try was Austin Healey's interception of a Pat Howard pass. He anticipated where Paddy was going to throw it – maybe it helped having played alongside him so much – and jogged home under the posts. At one point, he turned back and seemed to be wagging his finger at Pat and the other ACT players – he now says he was checking with the ref that he had been onside when he nicked the ball – and this seemed to enrage the lock Justin Harrison. Harrison ran back after Oz, barging into him and saying: 'You've only scored one try, tosser!'

At half-time Graham delivered a bollocking: 'What's this shirt mean? What you talked about before the game, is that all bullshit? Where's the fucking honesty? 22–10 out there. We can do these bastards if everybody gets right up there and on their toes and does the business. And you can look at yourself in the mirror after the game and say I gave 100 per cent . . . I'll tell you what, a lot of you couldn't do that right now. It's a huge honour to wear that shirt but a hell of a big responsibility and we're not taking on the responsibility.'

And to be fair, the guys turned it around in the second half. Ronan made a break for David Wallace to score early on and penalties were exchanged. Daws, who was not having the best of games with the boot, missed a couple of fairly easy chances but potted some others to edge us nearer to their total. As the game wore on, we seemed to get more and more into it. We started knocking them back in the tackle, we were pinning them back and tempers started to fray. Balsh was sin-binned for a high tackle and their flanker Peter Ryan was binned for punching. But despite the pressure we were exerting they were holding us out, with a five-point lead. Eighty minutes came and went, and injury time stretched on. Then the hooter went, signalling the end. The guys knew if the ball died the game was lost so they were desperately fighting their way closer to the ACT line while retaining possession. We looked dangerous and I could not sit down. It had gone from a horrible game to one of the tour's most thrilling and I just had that feeling that we were going to do something, that we were going to score.

Eventually, in the 89th minute, Darren Morris took the ball forward, attracted a couple of defenders and managed to flick a pass out the back. The ball went wide to Austin and he stepped inside two players to score. As he touched down one of the Aussie players – it looked like Peter Ryan on the video – dropped the knee on him and he had more words with Justin Harrison who had run over again. That little confrontation ended with Oz saying 'That's two tries . . . and you've lost!' and Harrison hurling his scrum cap at him. Don't laugh: I've seen it cause some horrible injuries. Ryan's knee led to another comedy moment, typical Healey: Martyn Williams and Mark Taylor were jumping all over him as he got to his feet. He stood there for a moment and then just dramatically fell to the floor. He is never one to under-exaggerate but he paid for it later, when everyone spent the evening mocking him and falling over theatrically. It was just desserts. England fans will remember Will Greenwood's excited, rather girlish, little skip just before he grounded the ball when scoring his first try against Wales in our Six Nations encounter in 2000-2001. Austin had given Shaggy plenty of jip for that and even went so far as to execute an effeminate little hop of his own when he scored in one of the later games. Now he would get it back in spades. Meanwhile, we still had a chance to win the game. In one of sport's poetic moments, it fell to Matt Dawson, villain of the recent past, to become our hero by converting Oz's try. He had not been kicking well and the bench had earlier sent on an instruction to switch to Ronan O'Gara. But Ronan apparently said to Matt 'No Daws, you keep going at it and keep your head up', which was a top thing to do.

It was not a particularly hard kick but it was not particularly easy either. It could have gone either way and, with Matt under tremendous pressure, no-one would have been surprised it he had fluffed it. But I just remember thinking 'He's going to redeem himself here, he's going to redeem himself here', and, sure enough, he smacked it straight through the posts. It was a great sight and it was great, too, to see Matt being hugged and back-slapped by the other players as they came off. It really had been an unbelievable comeback after the way we looked in the first half and it gave those players – some of whom might never wear a Lions shirt again – a great buzz. In the changing room, Matt was very emotional, close to tears and very choked up. Healey broke the ice by saying: 'Hey, Daws . . . good job you kicked that . . . otherwise we would have had to stone you publicly!'

Henry came in, buzzing. 'Absolutely superb performance guys,' he said. 'Magnificent guts and character. You can look at yourselves in the mirror and feel bloody proud.'

Later Dawson said: 'The win was a big moment for everyone. I personally got very emotional but I think there were many others who felt likewise. The conversion was like a pressure valve being released. It blew out all the emotions of the previous few days. I did break down in the dressing room, reflecting on all the negatives of the preceding 72 hours. Dai Young and Scott Gibbs had given a very important and passionate talk at half-time, reminding us all what it meant to wear a Lions jersey. There was 40 minutes left for me to make amends. I was so glad to be actually playing. If I'd not been involved my head would have been all over the place. It was a pressure game and a pressure kick. But knowing myself as I do, I do like to accept challenges although I certainly wouldn't want to recreate the circumstances. When Austin Healey scored in the last second I dropped to my knees. I was completely gone. The doctor rushed on to see if I was alright. I just needed time. I realised this was a great opportunity to put some things to rights. I cleared my head and went through all the routines I had spent hours and hours doing on the training field with Dave Alred. I blocked it all out and let rip. It was a good contact and a good feeling.'

The Leveller

ONCE AGAIN, there was not much time to sit around soaking up good feelings. The 22 for the second Test needed to get back to the hotel and get their heads down as soon as possible – every moment of lost sleep is bad news on tour, and the following day we had a tough schedule of training in the morning and travelling in the afternoon.

We changed as quickly as possible and headed outside to where the bus should have been waiting. It wasn't. Forty minutes later, we were still hanging around outside the stadium. The Aussie liaison officer who was supposed to have sorted it out did not seem too bothered – 'It'll be here when it's here' was all he would say – so we wondered idly whether we could get away with strangling him and burying his body in the bush. We could always blame the wildlife . . . 'Dingos ate our liaison officer' struck me as a possible headline. It was irksome, having to stand there on a cold Canberra night when we should have been back at the hotel.

Wednesday morning's training session was light. At this late stage in the season, with tired players nursing battered and bruised bodies, you look to do the minimum. A number of guys were carrying injuries and the latest bad news to filter through from the doctor was that the knock Austin had taken in scoring his second try meant he would be doubtful for the Test match. Matt Perry had gone off at half time in the first game so he was touch and go. Quinnell's knees were sore and Brian O'Driscoll and Rob Henderson were a bit banged up too. In fact, almost everyone was carrying some sort of knock or another. After training, a press conference, a little lunch and then bags packed and off to the airport for the flight to Melbourne to prepare for the second Test.

It was going to be a massive game and one we felt we really had to win if we were to take the series. The Lions support, once again, would be huge in a city which was not a hotbed of rugby union. In Sydney, the sheer size of the stadium meant there would be more home fans and if the Australians went there with the rubber drawn one-all they would have the upper hand. Thursday was a day off so I met up with a few friends and had a wander round Melbourne. It struck me as more British in climate than Perth, Sydney or Brisbane, with the spring weather very much like an English autumn, a bit grey and dank. It lacked the quaint feel of parts of Brisbane and it did not have Sydney's water but it was a pleasant place, nonetheless; the trams and the look of the place reminded me of a flatter San Francisco or a European city.

The game was to be played at the magnificent Colonial Stadium, which we could see, lit up at night, from some of the bedrooms at our Holiday Inn base. We visited the ground on the Friday. As usual, we wanted to acquaint ourselves with the venue and to sample the atmosphere of a stadium with a closed roof. It was almost unnaturally still and quiet but was obviously going to be jumping when 60,000 people were packed inside. We poked our noses into the changing room – again, we were going to have to warm up inside and we wanted to have a look at how much space we would have – and then headed off to Olympic Park, where they had the warm up track for the Melbourne Olympics, to train. The two stadia are 10 minutes apart and within a stone's throw you also have the huge Melbourne Cricket Ground, the Vodafone Sports Centre and the Rod Laver Centre. That is not to mention all the big Aussie rules grounds they have. The facilities are just amazing, compared to ours.

As the game approached, we were more relaxed and felt that some of the pressure had shifted to the Wallabies. And we were sure of great support again – Melbourne was absolutely heaving with Lions fans.

Our hotel was next door to a big casino, which kept one or two of the boys happy. Rob Henderson, in particular, was often to be found on the blackjack tables. Again, it was not a particularly private base. The team room was in the basement and the main lifts stopped at the first floor so you had to take an escalator down into reception and then another down to get to the team room. That made life interesting when there were two or three hundred fans milling around. At one point we found another, smaller lift outside the business centre, which was on the first floor, which did go to the bottom floor. There was a button to stop at reception but we were obviously whizzing all the way down. However, the supporters soon cottoned on and would hang around outside this lift's doors in reception, randomly pressing the call button so they got to us that way! It showed good British initiative, if nothing else. I did not have a problem with the fans being there at all. The difficulty, though, was when guys were in a hurry to get out of the hotel. Not surprisingly, the supporters – who, let's face it, are on holiday and having a great time – sometimes forget that the players are there to do a job of work and that sometimes involves having to be at a certain place at a certain time. Sometimes guys would have no alternative but to turn down requests for autographs and whatever you say to people I think they always get a little upset if you refuse. Most of us signed 99 per cent of the time quite happily but there was always going to be the odd disappointment, just because of the nature of it all. It is all about give and take. The fans need to know when to back off and the players need to respect the supporters' interest.

On the Friday afternoon I went to get my hair cut in Melbourne. I had spotted this Italian barber shop, way out of town, and decided to go there to avoid the city centre. The guy was a big Juventus fan, so I sat in the chair chatting to him about Juventus losing Zinedine Zidane to Real Madrid, and in the mirror I could see loads of Lions supporters walking by, doing a double take and walking by again to see me getting my hair cut. It goes with the territory.

In the evening, we had a team meeting at which Graham and Andy Robinson laid out our objectives.

Henry identified the difference between the next day's game and the first Test: 'It's a different psyche. For Brisbane, it was a fear-factor psyche, an underdog psyche. The psyche now is 'Are we good enough to be No1?' It is totally different. None of us have done it before. They have had plenty of experience of doing it and they want to maintain it. If we want to be No1 we have got to be magnificent, huge, psychologically.'

Robbo put it simply: 'Tomorrow, we need winners.'

Later, I tried to chill out. My wife Kay and my parents were in town and they came over for an hour or two. I doubt I was very good company, though. My mind was on the following day's game.

The nerves and anxiety which had been there the week before had subsided slightly. We now had a real belief that we could beat these guys. They had taken us a little lightly – probably subconsciously – the week before but we knew they would not make the same mistake twice. We knew it was going to be a big game and anticipated a major Australian backlash, expecting them to come out and really try to put us under pressure early on. They had made a few changes: Chris Latham, beaten by Robbo seven days earlier, had gone and was replaced by Matt Burke. In the front row, Paul was out with his nasty leg injury and Panoho had been dropped; in their places came the experienced hooker Michael Foley and the prop Rod Moore. We felt this gave them a bigger, stronger pack: Foley and Moore were better scrummagers.

The only change to our line-up was Back, in for Corry after being passed fit. Pezza was OK to play too, as were all of the first Test side. Austin Healey had not recovered from haematoma in his leg, caused by the knee-drop in the ACT match. We had planned to play Oz on the right wing instead of Daf James. It was not that Daf had let anyone down, just that Healey probably has a little more pace and flair to his game and we felt he might spring a few surprises on the Wallabies.

Will Greenwood, too, was taking a while to recover from his ankle injury. It had always been touch and go as to whether he would be fit for this match, though, and we concentrated on getting him right for the third Test.

The Aussie press had been full of tales of how Brisbane had been almost a home game for the Lions. I read a few interviews with Wallaby players and they were moaning about it, too. Apparently, it is the same when the All Blacks visit – there are more Kiwis in the ground than Aussies. The ARU was determined to counter the effect of all those red shirts and had hung gold bunting everywhere and was giving away free yellow t-shirts and caps to the locals on the afternoon of the game.

We had a last team meeting before leaving the hotel. Graham Henry was very pumped up as he told us: 'They are apprehensive, they are concerned, they are brittle, they are starting to fall apart, we have got to continue that process.'

Donal Lenihan laid out the size of the job in hand: 'The Lions are 125 years old and in all that time, once ever have they achieved back-to-back Test series wins, in 1971 and 1974.' It was in our hands to be the second Lions side to do so.

Then we were off.

There was little sign of gold as we came out of our team room and walked up the stairs and through the hotel reception to the coach. Four hundred or more Lions supporters were there and the noise as we appeared was like that as you run out for a match. The hairs on the back of my neck stood up and I remember Dorian West, who was on the bench after playing his first game on the Tuesday, saying to me: 'Jesus, I've got a lump in my throat already after coming through all that.' And he was right, it was tremendously emotional.

You could multiply it by ten when we ran out for the game: the sensation was awesome. Huge noise, very bright lights, an immaculate, bright green pitch and gold glitter raining from the top of the stands to give the home side a bit of a boost. Tickets had been changing hands for £500 a pair and plenty of them looked to have been bought by people wearing red. The welcome we got was fantastic.

The surface was very dry and firm and it made for a tremendously fast game. At first, we seemed to be playing most of the rugby, keeping them out of our 22 and creating plenty of opportunities ourselves. We had been shocked in Brisbane at how easy it had been to break through their midfield, given that their defence was supposed to be the best in the world, and early on we were at it again, Daf James bursting clean through within five or six minutes. He was tackled but he failed to spot Jason Robinson outside him – to be fair to Daf, I was running across at the time and I did not see Jason either – when a pass to Jase would undoubtedly have led to a score. Another very quick try and it would have begun to feel like Groundhog Day for the Wallabies. Who knows what would have happened if that score had come? As Daf was caught he went down and knocked the ball on, which seemed to sum up the whole match for us. In terms of breaking them open, we probably played better than we had in the first half of the first Test. Brian O'Driscoll got away, Danny Grewcock got away, Keith Wood got away, I even had a dart myself . . . we had plenty of attacking breaks from around halfway, but we were never able to finish them off. Whenever we got to within 15 metres of their line we seemed to make an error. At first, it seemed as though we would get away with this carelessness. Wilko put in a nice cross-field kick, Hilly smashed Andrew Walker and the ball into touch and, from the resulting line-out, we drove them over for a well-taken try by Neil Back.

Jonny had slotted a couple of penalties and they had posted just one in return, so as the halfway stage approached the score stood at 3–11. Then, on 37 minutes, Nathan Grey put in a disgraceful tackle on Richard Hill, hitting him with a flying elbow as he went by. If you watch the video of the game you will see Grey's eyes are on Hilly even before he hits the ground. He knew he could be looking at a yellow card at the very least. Richard was obviously in a bad way and Corry replaced him while he went off for treatment. After a couple of minutes he tried to come back on but he was clearly concussed and was not all there. When you are in that state you feel distinctly weird. You only appreciate what has happened when you come round from it and you realise you have lost the last 20 minutes – you get a sort of *déjà vu* feeling, with all your short-term memory gone. I was concussed in my first game for England in 1993, against France. I carried on but had this strange sense that I was watching the game on TV. I remember coming round during the match and thinking, 'Bloody hell, I'm actually *playing*!' In the old days guys could play on with concussion, and often did, because there was far less to remember in terms of moves, calls and so on. I was also concussed in the third Test in New Zealand in 1993. For the life of me, I could not understand any of the line-out calls. In those days, the response was simple: they just didn't play the ball to me and I got on with the rest of the game as best I could, on autopilot. Now, I would be straight off and that was the decision on Hilly, too. It is not just about the game; playing with a concussion can lead to serious brain injury.

Amazingly, Grey was not sin-binned for his actions. Even more incredibly, the match referee later refused to hold a hearing into the incident. I thought that was disgusting, especially when set against the far less serious incident which had seen Charvis banned for two games. It was pretty amazing after all the crap we had taken before and throughout the tour about our supposed dirty play and intimidatory tactics. It was the height of hypocrisy but there was nothing we could do. We could not dwell on it.

Right at the death of the half, Burke kicked another penalty to bring them up to 6–11 and we went off, wondering why, with all our possession, we were not much further ahead. We had clearly been the more threatening side. The first thing we said in the changing room was 'If that's their backlash, let's not be too worried about what they've got . . . let's just go out there and play the same way but finish off the chances'. There was plenty of room for improvement on that front. We had made a lot of mistakes when we had been close to scoring positions: we had dropped balls, thrown wayward passes and been turned over a number of times by George Smith, who was having a great game. But it was not all down to our errors. The Wallaby defence was certainly better than it had been in the first Test, although we had still been able to break through them a number of times. They had worked hard to nullify the threat of Henderson and O'Driscoll. Hendo, in particular, was not having as good a game as he had in the first Test, when he had been tremendous, and he and Brian were being closed down a lot.

They had obviously spent time on our line-out, too. In the first Test, we had thrown a lot of ball to me at the front, where they had not been defending, but they had tightened up there and we were finding it harder to take that ball off the top and attack with it as we had done previously. So we decided to change the lineouts. We would throw more to Danny and, now he was on for Hill, to Martin Corry at the back of the line.

In terms of threats from them – well, there had hardly been any. The final thought before we ran back out was that we needed to play for territory as well as possession. It is crucial against sides like Australia to play the game in their third of the field and not let them play in yours.

What can I say about the second half? Well, the first 30 seconds were great. We won the kick off and drove the ball back at them, making a lot of yards. Then Jonny Wilkinson took the ball up the blind side and tried to throw a pass over the top of their defender towards Hendo and Daf James. Joe Roff made a good interception to nick the ball, Rob Henderson grabbed his jersey but did not have the purchase to hold him and he got away to score in the corner.

As captain in this sort of situation, you gather the players round you while the conversion is being attempted and say all the obvious things: 'Look, let's calm down, it's one of those things, let's start again.'

But that score had rattled us. We had felt we were getting on top of them and that had been confirmed by the nature of the restart. Now – bang! – they were right back in it.

Jonny has said since that he would throw the same pass again, so it must have looked on to him. It was just a great piece of anticipation by Roff. These things happen.

It was a turning point in the match, because it lifted them and knocked us back, but it was not *the* turning point. If we had replied quickly it would not have mattered. And once again, we started well: we kicked off, won the ball and drove it up. Unfortunately, I turned over possession, losing the ball in contact and knocking it on, and from that play we gave away a penalty which Burke kicked. The half was only four or five minutes old and it had started badly.

The real turning point, though, and the killer blow, came when they scored again pretty quickly. They got into our half, there was a scrum and it was our put in. We had had the upper hand in the first half and we hit this one well, taking two small paces forward which meant we had the ascendancy. But they used our forward momentum against us, letting one side advance while trying hard to hold the other. That wheeled us slightly, throwing us off balance, and they were able to push us back on an angle. It was a good technical move by them, relying on their eight working very solidly as a team and with good cohesion and timing, and was a move we had used ourselves earlier on the tour to similar effect. Sometimes sides get penalised for it – you cannot pull in a scrum, only push – but sometimes you get away with it.

The ball squirted out into their side. Losing it against the head is so rare in international rugby that our guys were not ready. Eales picked up and ran, Roff got his hands on the ball, evaded a half-tackle and was in again in the corner. The conversion was kicked and the score was suddenly 21–11. We had gone from being on top of the game to conceding two tries and a penalty in 10 minutes and we never really recovered from that.

They played with growing confidence and we just seemed to make a lot of mistakes. Matt Burke, who banged over three more penalties, also scored in the 65th minute to rub salt into our wounds after Owen Finegan got the ball away to him out of the tackle. All we could manage for the entire half was one penalty amid a litany of further errors – late or high tackles in their 22, running the ball into touch from promising positions – and the game ended 35–14, a record defeat for the Lions against the Wallabies.

That was not the worst of it. Our first-choice half-backs, Jonny Wilkinson and Rob Howley had both left the field in trouble. Jonny had gone on a motorised stretcher with what looked like a broken leg. Lying on the turf, he had feared the worst: he had taken a big knock on his leg and could not feel it. He did not want to look down, fearing some catastrophic injury . . . a foot pointing the wrong way from a shattered ankle. Luckily, it turned out to be less serious. Rob had walked off clutching his ribs and looking in a lot of pain. Both went straight to hospital. Against this, the Australians had seen Stephen Larkham go off late in the game after the last in a series of big hits. The Aussie press later suggested we had targeted Larkham for special, and illegal, treatment. That was rubbish. We certainly wanted to hit him hard but there was nothing dirty about it.

In the changing room, the overwhelming feeling was one of disappointment. I think a lot of us had felt, deep down, that it was our night, and the first half had seemed to confirm that, when we had been on top of them physically and mentally. Then, in the second half, we had hardly got into their 22.

I sat there feeling really down about how ineffective we had been. We had let them back, not just into the match but into the series. And to lose in the way we had was very galling. Roff had done well for his first try but his opportunity had been created by our mistake. The second try was almost the same story. Competent play by the Wallabies and a blunder by us. If you score like that you think 'Great, we did well, turning their scrum over'. If you concede like that you think 'That should not have happened'.

In that last 40 minutes we had allowed ourselves to be rattled and I feared for our mental composure as we headed for Sydney. We would be facing a Wallaby side who had played themselves into form – their third try had been a typical Aussie effort, building momentum and phases before striking – so we would probably face them at their best the following week. Somehow we had to raise ourselves from the disappointment of losing and also from the physical toll 11 months of rugby had taken on us. Woody had a go, standing up in front of the boys and making a really emotive speech about what it meant to be a Lion and how we could turn things around.

Then I headed off to the press conference as the other guys showered and changed. By the time that was over and I had returned, the changing room was empty – a particularly depressing feeling on this occasion – so I grabbed my stuff and went back to the hotel to shower and dress.

Later that evening, I checked on the injuries. Most people seemed to have something wrong with them. Scott Quinnell's knees were sore, Hendo had the same problem, Brian had a dead leg and a sore shoulder – he was getting everything taped up before going out for the game – and James Robson was being kept very busy. The Doc had been called from his bed on 22 nights to date to deal with the walking wounded and the pace was not slackening. Richard Hill's concussion meant a mandatory three-week lay-off. It was bad news, but we had good cover in the back row. The half-back situation was more worrying. Rob Howley was definitely out with his rib injury, poor bloke. He is a superb professional and a great guy who has not had a lot of luck with the Lions, missing all three Tests against the Springboks in 1997 with a dislocated shoulder. Jonny Wilkinson's x-ray showed his left leg was not broken after all but merely very badly bruised close to the bone. It was still way too early to say whether he would be fit for the next match but you had to work on the basis that he would not be.

Our back-up for them looked thin. We had Neil Jenkins and Ronan O'Gara covering at fly-half and Matt Dawson and the injured Austin Healey at 9.

As far as 10 went, since we had not sent for Townsend, Ronan would have to start if Jonny did not recover. This was not ideal. It may sound a harsh judgment but I did not feel that he was quite up to it – I would have started a fit Healey ahead of him. As world record points scorer, Jenks is one of the greatest rugby players these islands have ever produced but he was once again in all sorts of trouble and was, effectively, out of contention. We just had to hope Jonny would recover.

On the face of it, we were OK at No9, as long as Austin recovered from his leg injury, as the medics assured us he would. If he did not, we were in trouble. What if Dawson also suffered an injury in training, or even tripped getting out of the shower? Imagine if *both* of them were unfit to play.

With this thought in my mind, I went to see Graham and Donal to talk about getting a replacement – perhaps England's Kyran Bracken – flown out immediately. Kyran was in prime form and was match fit, having just captained England on their tour of North America. He was also well up to speed on our defensive patterns.

Donal and Graham listened to my argument, ummed and ahhed and asked me to leave it with them. And that was the last I heard about it. The subject was never raised again with me and, as history records, Bracken, like Townsend, was not sent for.

*

I JOINED a few friends for a beer on the hotel's mezzanine floor and we chatted for half an hour, all feeling very down. I could not help reflecting on how different the atmosphere would have been if we had won. Ifs and buts. No good to anyone.

I turned in about 1am and found the game was on TV, so I watched the second half. It did not actually look as bad as it had felt while we were out there. We got into their half on plenty of occasions but just turned the ball over or made silly mistakes – and I was just as guilty as anyone. They had kicked poorly out of their 22 on a couple of occasions, only for us to be penalised and lose good field position. They had played well but not brilliantly so I felt a little better as I turned the light out. If we could tighten up our basics there was every chance we could do the business in Sydney.

I was looking forward to getting down there for a couple of days of relaxation before starting to focus for what was now a huge final game.

The Decider

ON THE Sunday morning we decided to leave Rob, Jonny and Hilly in Melbourne for an extra day, to delay their flying. The Doc was becoming more confident that Wilkinson would be fit for the weekend and Hill's hospital scans were a cause for some amusement: they revealed that his skull was twice the thickness of the average. Clearly, he is Salisbury Man – the missing link. When they dig his bones out of some hillside grave in 200 years' time the newspaper headlines will be 'Neanderthals roamed the earth in 21st century'.

Sunday afternoon saw the majority of the party back at the Park Royal Pacific hotel on the seafront at Manly. For a lot of guys, it was going to be a very long week. Many of them had no chance of being involved in the game, they were just there to help us train, and that cannot be easy. Again, training was being kept to a minimum. By that stage of the tour everyone had the gameplan after we had been playing together for so long. And after almost a full year of rugby, we were ready to drop. It was a question of trying to keep ourselves fresh and sharp for the final Test.

On the Monday morning I went to the gym, enjoying the feeling of lifting a few weights. It is important to do your strength work but it is sometimes hard for guys to motivate themselves for this on a long tour. A shop next to the hotel rented out surf kit so in the afternoon we tried our luck in the Manly swell. Some of the squad went for the proper surfboards but my inbuilt aversion to making a complete idiot of myself stopped me joining them; instead, I chose a cut-down body board, which I was told was easier to handle. You are not supposed to do it without a top on, because the contact between your skin and the board in the salt water gives you a rash. The only one in the shop which fitted me was a tight, purple lycra affair.

Fortunately, there were only two or three hundred people gawping at us from the Manley front, and probably three or four sets of TV cameras, so no-one really saw me and my woeful attempts to conquer Sydney's big breakers. One or two of the boys were constantly looking over their shoulders for sharks but I was more worried about the current. I did not fancy going out of my depth because it was very strong, and you could feel it dragging you along the beach. I had visions of being sucked away to my untimely death. That is never going to be a good thing, but a few days before the deciding Test it would have been a real downer.

After 45 minutes of looking very English, we gave it in as a bad lot and I plodded back up the beach in my purple lycra. In the evening, to round off a pleasant day, we went out to a place called Ribs & Rump where we tried to eat our body weight in fat and red meat. The management presented me with a set of steak knives which I immediately gave to Cozza as his wedding present. It is the thought that counts.

Throughout the rest of the week, we concentrated on a lot of line-out work. The Australians are very cute, very astute, with their line-outs, both in defence and attack, and there was an added factor. Giffin was unlikely to play – he had been a doubt even before the second Test – and Austin's friend Justin Harrison looked certain to take his place. We knew from the Australia A and ACT games that he was a very good line-out forward in the Ian Jones, Scott Murray sort of mould, light, quick on his feet, able to steal ball. We felt he and Eales together would be a serious combination. Equally, we felt that if we could hit the back of the line-out and win ball there we could attack off it.

We named our side on the Wednesday. Austin Healey, now back to full fitness, was in on the right wing ahead of James. Matt Dawson replaced Rob Howley at 9. Corry came back into the starting line-up in place of Hill.

Rob Henderson was only just about holding himself together so we had hoped Will Greenwood would be fit to win his first Lions Test cap. The medics had thought he would be touch and go for the Melbourne Test, and we had seen him jogging around in Canberra, so it was a surprise when he was ruled out. How unlucky is he on Lions tours? Hendo would have to give it one last go.

Wilkinson was in, though we were still not 100 per cent sure he would be fit. Austin would cover for him if he withdrew or had to come off during the game.

The Wallabies waited until the following day. As we had expected, Harrison was in. But he was not the only change to their XV. Steven Larkham was also gone, having failed to recover from the knock he had taken at Melbourne. In his place was Elton Flatley, a capable replacement who maybe did not quite have Larkham's flair – he certainly did not have his reputation – but who could damage us and who would want to put in a big game.

Earlier that day, we had travelled out to Stadium Australia, the magnificent venue where the Olympic Games had finished nine months before. That trip highlighted a problem – it had taken about an hour in the coach. Manly is a great place to stay if you are on holiday in Sydney it was a long way from our hotel to the ground. A matchday journey like that is not ideal and we discussed ways around it. One suggestion was to hire a boat to dock near the stadium. That was bombed out because of the fear of players turning up with seasickness a couple of hours before the big game. We also considered changing hotels on the Friday afternoon and moving to Paramata where the Australians were staying. That was rejected because of the hassle factor and in the end, in the absence of an ideal solution, we decided to leave things as they were. I felt this showed bad planning, though. The venue was no secret and we had had a recce party out months beforehand.

Walking out onto the pitch, I knew something was different from the last time I had played there, in the 1999 Centenary Test. It took me 10 minutes to realise the track had vanished, along with a lot of the seating, which was in the process of being refurbished and was replaced with bare concrete . . . draped in yellow plastic. The ARU was up to its old motivational tricks again.

There was a confidence among the 22 that we were all in good enough shape to play, that if we got the line-out and scrum right and cut out the mistakes we could win. We also wanted to get that last game played and get home. It seemed like we had been together for six months, not six weeks.

On Friday, we trained lightly in the morning and had the afternoon off – it was down on our team sheet as 'compulsory rest'. I nipped into Manly to buy some shaving foam and found the streets absolutely packed. There were supposedly 20,000 Lions supporters in the city and most of them seemed to have come over on the ferry from Sydney harbour to take a wander down the seafront. It took me ages to get to the shop and on the way back I cut through the hotel's underground car park and took the lift straight up to my room, rather than face the front entrance again. I just wanted a moment of peace and quiet. The afternoon before a game, even a club fixture, players like to switch off and relax, have a doze, watch a video, maybe get a massage . . . just do anything to get away from rugby, because once you start thinking about the match the adrenalin starts pumping and you start to feel anxiety and nerves. It was nigh-on impossible to forget about things in Manly that day!

One way was to face the fearsome inswinger of Rob Henderson. Our team room was large enough for us to set up an indoor cricket pitch and Hendo, a very useful cricketer, was moving this spongelike tennis ball through the air like a boomerang, making me look an utter fool as I groped for the ball several inches from where it actually was. Before long he bowled me so we swapped over and I charged in off the long run, getting some pace going which is not hard on a 15 yard wicket, and ripped out his off stump 4th ball, with a stupendous yorker. Naturally, I celebrated like a man who has just taken a hat-trick at Lord's. That irritated him somewhat so he decided to take me on with a stump instead of a bat and started to smash me around the hotel room at will. At which point I realised that he was the better man and retreated to my bedroom, beaten and demoralised.

We played a few times on tour. There were some pretty good players. Jonny Wilkinson, being the product of an English public school, was immaculately coached and extremely correct. O'Driscoll was strictly a thrash-and-hope man. Corry was pacey and a mad keen Yorkshire fan, as you would expect of a bloke brought up in Kent. Backy, who played for Warwickshire schools, was humiliated by Hendo, which was amusing. Those little games kept the eye in, which came in handy when we got back to the UK. In August, the Tigers had one of our regular charity cricket matches, against Ibstock, a decent Leicestershire league side, and I performed pretty well, yorking one of their key batsmen and helping us to keep our unbeaten record going. At one point, the umpire turned round and said 'Some of you boys can play, then?' I was not sure whether he meant me.

Meanwhile, as our cricketing drew to a close, Austin Healey had been in town, and disaster had struck. He had felt sore for a couple of days; it actually heralded something serious. His back had gone into muscular spasm and had almost seized up. He had to stumble back to the hotel, walking like a geriatric, which is very amusing if it is not the day before the third Test. On the way, he had been collared for autographs, which he had refused to sign in his pain and urgency. He had been abused for this by some fans in a café.

It is unlike Oz not to have a smile on his face and a wisecrack ready but when I saw him he was pretty down on all counts. He went off to the doctor and physio and it rapidly became clear that he might well have to withdraw from the side. It was no exaggeration to describe this as a catastrophe. We were now down to one fit scrum-half in Matt Dawson and Austin could not cover 10, either. The nightmare scenario I had worried about in the aftermath of the second Test defeat had become a reality.

The management scrambled to deal with the situation, finding themselves in the horrible position of having to hunt around Australia for a British scrum-half to sit on the bench.

That night, I actually approached Neil Back. I knew Backy had been a schoolboy scrum-half.

'Could you fill in if it came to it in an emergency?' I asked him.

'Er, yes,' was his slightly hesitant reply.

It was obviously far from ideal and not the sort of thing any of us needed to be worrying about a few hours before a game like the third Test.

Word got out that Andy Nicol, the Scottish No9, was over leading a tour group and he was contacted late on the Friday to see if he could stand in. Poor bloke, of course he said yes but how would he have been feeling? It is always a massive honour to wear a Lions shirt, and that would have been in his mind. But imagine the pressure on him if Dawson had twisted his ankle on Friday in training. Andy Nicol, who has not played a game for weeks, is suddenly our starting scrum-half.

Don't get me wrong: Andy would not have let us down. He is an international player, with plenty of bottle and ability, and he would have done the best he could in the circumstances. But he would have effectively been walking out of a bar and onto the pitch for the biggest rugby game of his life, never having played – Tom Smith apart – with any of the guys in his side, having had a few hours to learn our tactics and moves and obviously not at peak fitness. Farcical. And totally unfair to Andy.

First thing Saturday morning, a hospital scan revealed Austin had disc damage and confirmed his unavailability for the match. I felt gutted for him. Like Will Greenwood, he had now been on two Lions tours without starting in a Test. Like Will, he could well have featured in all three on this tour if bad luck had not intervened. He kept his chin up but he was clearly pretty down.

Andy Nicol, who had reported to the team hotel on the Saturday morning as requested, was immediately handed some kit and a set of notes detailing our moves. He looked extremely nervous about the possibility of playing.

I said: 'Look mate, at the end of the day it is a game of rugby . . . you know you can play, we know you can play. You're good. You're experienced, you've been around for a long time. If it happens you will be fine.'

He said: 'Yes, that's how I'm trying to think myself.'

Andy actually has a unique place in Lions history. He came out on the 1993 tour to cover for injury and again sat on the bench, getting three minutes against Taranaki before leaving the tour party once the guy he had replaced recovered, as the rules then dictated. So, technically, he has been on two Lions tours and played 180 seconds of rugby. He was certainly good enough in his prime to have started for the Lions but was unlucky in that his best years, when he was injury-free, did not coincide with tours. Still, he is a Lion and no-one can take that away from him.

It was a mad situation, though, and we should have had Kyran sitting there.

*

AUSTIN HAD also, inadvertently, handed us another issue to deal with that morning in the shape of another controversial UK diary piece. This one had been published in the *Guardian* back home under the headline 'And For Our Finale . . . Stuffing The Arrogant Aussies.' In a column ghostwritten by Eddie Butler, Austin was quoted as describing Justin Harrison as 'a plod', 'a plank' and 'an ape' and attacking the 'Aussie male'.

A fuming Graham Henry described it as 'a ready-made team-talk for Rod MacQueen'. Unlike Dawson's piece, we knew a little about this before the match and the management had to contend with a few media questions but I was all but oblivious to it until I logged on to planetrugby.com to have a browse through their pages. There it was. 'Oz,' I said. 'What have you written now?'

He replied: 'Not a lot, really.'

And that was the general attitude throughout the squad, I would say. We certainly were not worrying about whether it might motivate the Wallabies – teams like that do not need motivating. The outside world, or course, did not see it that way and two or three months later, bizarrely, I would find myself on a disciplinary panel in Dublin sitting in judgment on Healey . . . a friend and a team-mate who I had gone on holiday with immediately after the tour. I could have withdrawn but felt that would have been to dodge my responsibilities, although it felt a little bit like a waste of time to be doing it in September.

We dished out a fine for bringing the game into disrepute – even though it later transpired that Butler had used a large amount of journalistic licence in composing the article – and that was that. But I could not help spinning back to the second Test and Nathan Grey's illegal challenge on Richard Hill. Did that not bring the game into disrepute? It is a strange world, when words mean more than flying elbows.

Back in Sydney, we were building up to the third Test. Jerseys were handed out and Rob Henderson gave one of his to Will

Greenwood in a nice gesture to the guy whose place he had taken.

Inside the changing room it was important to put all the nonsense behind us as much as possible. One way was to crank up the team stereo as loud as possible. Westie is a big fan of The Jam, as am I, and we stuck on a 'Best Of' CD. A lot of the other guys were in nappies when Paul Weller, Rick Buckler and Bruce Foxton started out – I was only seven or eight myself – but they all seemed to get into it. The sound of That's Entertainment, Town Called Malice, Down In The Tube Station At Midnight and Going Underground bouncing off the walls at high volume helped the adrenalin to flow nicely and we warmed up inside again.

The night before, Graham had emphasised the historic nature of the match we were about to play, saying: 'When you guys are my age this will be one of the things you'll talk to your grandchildren about. It is a defining moment in a career, in a lifetime. We are good enough. There is no doubt in my mind we can smash these buggers. We get one opportunity to do it right.'

It was a theme I followed in the changing room, laying out to the players that it was there for us: we could be the side which won a Lions Test series or the side which lost it . . . that was how we would be remembered. 'Big hearts, cool heads,' I finished. 'Thinking all the time. Put your bodies on the line, put your minds on the line. There is nothing else after this.'

I was careful not to rant on for too long. The guys were well aware of the enormity of the match and I felt that the more I kept saying it the less impact it would have. We also needed to treat it like any other 80 minutes of rugby. Thinking about the result too much was a waste of energy; thinking about the performance would bring the right result.

Looking around at them, I saw a lot of blokes who would have been declared unfit for any other game. Painkillers, anti-inflammatories, cortisone jabs, sticking plaster, adrenalin and willpower were about all that was holding them together. They could just about go out and play but they would pay for it later.

Out on the pitch, the stands looked very yellow. The proportion of Lions fans in the 80,000 crowd was significantly lower than it had been in the smaller Gabba and Colonial Stadium, and there was no sense that this was a home game. But we had not expected one.

It was another quick, frantic game without much pattern to it. Early on, there was a bit of ping-pong between Perry and Burke and a few penalties were given away on both sides. At 9–3, we were behind but I felt good and thought that we were well in the game. Twenty minutes into the half, Jason Robinson showed once again that he is one of the world's great finishers. Henderson made a good break, the ball went through the hands of Wood and Smith and out to Jase, who raced over. Jonny converted, to give us a 9–10 lead.

Irritatingly, we then missed tackles on Finegan and Kefu who were able to put Danny Herbert away for a response which Burke, kicking very well on his 50th cap, converted.

We restarted well and got down into their 22, putting a lot of pressure on through a series of phases. You felt as though a score would come at any moment but they held us out and we had to be content with another penalty, banged over by Jonny.

Still, going in at half-time with the score at 16–13, the feeling in the changing room was that this was a very finely balanced game and that we stood every chance of winning. The penalty count against us was still way too high but we felt confident. Scotty Quinnell had been struggling to make his usual impact, with his knees clearly giving him a lot of trouble, so he was whipped off and replaced by Colin Charvis.

Henry stood in front of us as we drank our fluids and were re-taped up, saying we needed to show discipline and character to come through.

And the second half started very well, with Jonny beating Kefu to dive over after Martin Corry won ball at the back of a line-out and some good driving work by Keith Wood and Danny

Grewcock. The conversion meant the score now stood at 16–20 and we should have accelerated from there to kill the game off.

Instead, we suffered from a moment of madness from Charvis. In his own third, with no support, Colin took a quick lineout to himself and suddenly realised he had nowhere to go. With Australian attackers bearing down on him he tried to hoof it clear but his kick was horrible. From there, the Wallabies pinned us back in our own 22, building pressure until Herbert scored his second, which Burke converted to make the score 23–20. It was a bizarre and almost suicidal passage of play but at the time you don't think, 'Oh no, why's he done that?' You just have to react to what has happened and try and keep them out. Sadly, we couldn't.

Shortly after that, Herbert was sin-binned for a high tackle on Brian O'Driscoll and we had an opportunity, against 14 men, to make that count. But we failed, in the face of some excellent defence, to add anything to our score. Jonny Wilkinson drew us level with around 20 minutes to go but two more penalties gave the Aussies a 29–23 lead.

We now had to convert a try to win the game. And we kept pressing and pressing, creating two golden opportunities right at the death. Two minutes to go, and we won an attacking line-out around five metres out. If we held our own ball we felt we could drive them over. Experience suggested that if they could not stop us they would try to pull us down, as they had done throughout the series, and we might win a penalty try. Sometimes in the earlier games they had been penalised and sometimes they had not but we felt the referee would be looking out for that at this crucial stage. I called the ball to me because we had been struggling elsewhere. I got up OK but Justin Harrison came up in front of me and got both hands on the ball to nick it. Looking at the video later, the throw may have been slightly low but Justin, who was going very well, may have beaten me even if the ball had been perfectly positioned.

The ball was cleared but we brought it right back at them. I knew time was ebbing away. I didn't notice the crowd. I was totally focused on doing something, anything, to help us score the try we needed. It is a desperate, desperate feeling, a sense of straining and struggling to make that tackle, get that pass away, gain those few yards, and all the while, in the back of your mind, you know the clock is tick, tick, ticking away.

As the seconds passed, I sensed that time was virtually up. Then the hooter went and I knew for sure we were on borrowed time and that the referee was waiting for the ball to go out of play. The whole tour and a big part of your life has come down to this: can we get over their line before the ball goes dead?

Everyone was frantically trying to retain the ball and keep it alive. We were in their 22, they were under pressure, they could not afford to infringe, because the referee cannot end the game on a defensive penalty. They looked as desperate as I felt. We were still in the game. The ball was recycled and recycled and suddenly it moved out towards their left corner, reaching Matt Perry. And a charging Iain Balshaw was coming up on his right shoulder at full pace. If the ball went to his hands he was in . . . but Pezza's pass went slightly behind Balsh, he lost momentum and the ball was turned over. Walker ran it into touch.

And the whistle went.

Different games leave you with different feelings. There are those matches, thankfully rare, where you have been stuffed and you know, with half an hour to go, that there is no way back. I am thinking, for instance, of the 1995 World Cup semi-final against New Zealand, where Lomu went on the rampage. We came back in the second half but there was too much for us to do and, deep down, we knew it. You do not give up but you know you have lost long before the whistle goes.

This time was not like that: right up until the last moment, we could have won the match and with it the series.

And horribly suddenly, it hit me. Everything we had worked

for in the last six weeks, the dreams we had all had . . . all ruined. It was a defining moment: out there, on the pitch at Stadium Australia, in front of 80,000 people, we had lost and everything was ruined.

I just stood there feeling very emotional and close to tears. I looked at the players, dejected, hanging their heads, some on their knees on the grass. A few of the boys were looking at me and I could see the disappointment in their faces. They were just totally gone. Desolate. The cruelty of sport.

A few of them had walked off into the changing room so we fetched them out to acknowledge the fans. I felt awful for them, too. A lot of my mates were in the crowd and a lot of them had scrimped and saved to be there. I am sure that was a pattern repeated hundreds of times over. A bunch of supporters had spotted me on the Wednesday as I sat in the hotel, quietly minding my own business and trying not to think about the match. They were already madly hyped-up and they came over chanting: 'Go on, Johnno! Lions! Lions!' I had thought: 'Bloody hell, they should be playing . . . we could do with a bit of that!' It had made me feel humble and proud at the same time and I felt bad for them now. All our supporters had been brilliant.

Justin Harrison came over to me and asked if I wanted to swap shirts. I couldn't because I had already arranged to do so with John Eales.

'Danny will swap with you, mate,' I said. This was my last Lions Test match . . . if I did not want to give someone my shirt, surely that was up to me? It was no big deal – or so I thought. But later his mum wrote a letter to the Australian papers calling me rude and a bad sport because I would not give her Justin my shirt and Donal was collared about it by the Aussie media as he headed home. This was a bit bizarre and unnecessary.

The Australians were jubilant, fifteen players and 60,000 fans going wild. I did not blame them but I did not want to watch them.

We stood there as they collected the trophy. A fine line, between us and them. But it might as well have been a mile.

I did a couple of brief TV interviews and made my way to the changing room. It was a bad place to be. A lot of the guys – myself, Backy, Keith Wood, maybe Scotty Quinnell and Hendo – were never going to wear that Lions jersey again. Winning the series would have meant the world to us. I looked around at the players and started to get choked up once more.

There were no recriminations, no harsh words from Donal or Graham. There was no need.

Lenihan's voice broke with the emotion he was feeling as he told us: 'It's hard to take but we've no choice. You couldn't have done any more, boys, and I want to thank you from the bottom of my heart.'

Beaten, bruised and weary, we made our way into Sydney. I met up with my family and friends and we shared a few beers. I didn't hang around long. I was catching a plane to Hawaii with Austin Healey and our wives early the next day. We were scheduled to attend Martin Corry's wedding two weeks later and had booked the flights months before to give ourselves a decent break on the beach.

More importantly I had to get Oz out; there was a danger of a good old-fashioned lynching.

Aftermath

SO WHY did we lose?

We lost the third Test because we were beaten in two key aspects of the game: at the ruck and maul, where we turned over too much ball – George Smith played brilliantly – and at the line-out, which was worse than it had been all tour. We lost five of our 18 throws, including the very first and that crucial last, and won just one of their 10. Who was to blame? Woody, myself, Danny or Martin? I guess all of us. Tactically, we tried to throw too much ball to the back when the front is always a safer option. But you have to say that the Wallaby line-out, particularly Justin Harrison, played a blinder.

Deeper than that, we lost the tour for a number of reasons.

Credit, first, to the Wallabies. You do not win a World Championship and a Tri-Nation championship without being a very good side. They have some excellent players and they combine well. They rarely panic, they are intelligent footballers and they are well-coached.

That said, we were the better side for more than half of those 240 minutes of rugby, though we tended to tail off towards the end of games and never scored any points after 60 minutes in any of the Tests.

Our training regimen was one factor in our loss. This upset many players. I had misgivings, too, though they concerned Graham's determination to structure our play, rather than the amount of training that we did. You have to accept that, in modern rugby, you need to spend time on the training field. With a scratch side playing the World Champions, obviously you need to train that much more than normally.

It has all changed so quickly. Here is a telling fact: we did more defence work in the first week of the 2001 tour than on the whole of the 1997 trip and on the 1997 trip we did more defence work than I had ever done before; indeed our defence was one key to our success in that series.

Then there is the organisation of attack, the scrummage, the line-out, kicking, fitness . . . the list is almost endless, with each area coached by specialists all screaming out for more time. That is not a criticism: it is a fact of modern rugby life.

Where Graham Henry went wrong, in my opinion, was in loading massively complicated pre-set gameplans onto players on top of all that.

He wanted to orchestrate multiple phases of play and gave individual players detailed instructions as to which rucks they would go into and which rucks they would not.

Imagine a line-out. If I win the ball jumping at number two and we run it, I am unlikely to be the first guy to the resulting ruck because I have been up, caught the ball, hit the deck and passed it to the scrum half. The back row will be way ahead of me. That is fairly simple.

But from then on our gameplan might dictate that I get involved with the next – second – ruck (third phase), avoid the third (fourth phase) but make the fourth (fifth phase). And so it goes on. On top of that there would be multiple options to deal with depending on where the ball went. For instance, I might be tasked to get into rucks 3, 5 and 7 if we took the ball up but to be elsewhere if the ball went wide.

This might shock people – some readers may want to sit down – but I regard myself as quite an intelligent player. I generally know instinctively where I should be at any given moment but I must admit I found sticking to Graham's plans difficult at times.

I would catch myself running round the field thinking 'Should I be there or should I stay where I am?' instead of just seeing what was happening and playing it accordingly.

I was not alone. Other guys had the same problem. Many were worried about making a mistake and going into the wrong phase. This overloaded us and at times caused a kind of mental paralysis, as we tried to avoid doing the wrong thing. This, in turn, led to delay, as we tried to remember the plan. The delay might be fractions of a second but that may be enough for a top team to rip you apart and while the Wallabies never gave us a hammering they were able to capitalise on our hesitancy.

Ultimately, the plans demanded a level of foresight that verged on crystal ball-gazing. Rugby is not like that. The opposition will not always play as you expect them to and you cannot even predict how your own players will perform from minute to minute.

Sometimes you will hit a ruck and find three bodies on top of you. It might be late in the game and you are trying to push knackered blokes away . . . you may not make either of the next two rucks if there have been two quick plays. Equally, you might get to a ruck but find the ball has already been won. You do not need to hit the ruck so you are free to go to the next phase very quickly. What do you do? You are not supposed to be in that next phase – you are still supposed to be piled up in the ruck you have just arrived at and you need to be sure you will make the next-but-one. Or you might be running a decoy line to keep the defence from drifting – that might work really well but then you find yourself out of the game because you have made that run. It is very difficult to be able to say for sure that you can make rucks 3, 5 and 7 – you might make 2, 4 and 6. It is in the nature of the game.

The potential for problems is clear. While I understood what Graham was trying to do we tried to be too regimented, too structured. We had some very talented 'heads up' rugby players in our party and we should have been a lot simpler in our strategy.

Look at the tries we scored in the Test matches: they were not down to any plan, they were down to good play by skilful guys reading what they saw and doing it. The best rugby is played like that: instinctively, naturally.

Graham wanted to use us like chess pieces, to control everyone's moves all the time. Sometimes you can do that but more often you cannot and a coach, certainly a British and Irish Lions coach, has to be able to trust that his players can play, that they can read the game.

The Australians have it about right, as I have learned from Pat Howard and Rod Kafer. They, too, are very organised and pre-planned in the way they attack. But it is a more generalised approach: rather than saying to the openside flanker 'You must be here at this point, there at that point and over there at that point' they lay down a general policy for the way they will work and players fit into that policy. It is much less specific but every man, from 1 to 15, knows what the team is trying to do.

Graham's attitude to some players was also a little counter-productive. He could be blunt and he was not one for suffering fools gladly. Look at the remarks about concentrating on the Test team, at the decision to make the midweekers play as Australia, at his sharpness with Austin ahead of the first Test. These were not out of character. That is not to say I did not like and respect Graham. I did. We will never be bosom buddies – Donal Lenihan, a real players' manager, is much more my type of bloke – but probably only because we don't know each other very well. I suspect he is the kind of guy who I would really get on with given time to find out.

One or two players let us down, too. I am not thinking of Dawson and Healey, who have been unfairly vilified. I am thinking of the player who, while still at Tylney Hall, was already complaining about the training, and guys whose heads dropped when things did not go their way. To be successful on tour everyone needs to be together through thick and thin; it is a massive honour to go on a Lions tour even if you only play midweek games and some people lost sight of that.

I spoke about selection errors right at the start of the book and I stand by those comments. But a bigger problem than the personnel we took were the injuries we suffered. Look at the names: Taylor, Greening, McBryde, Dallaglio, Catt, Luger, Howley, Healey, Back, Hill, Greenwood – all out of action for all or part of the Test series. Never mind that half the 'fit' personnel – Scott Quinnell, Rob Henderson, Brian O'Driscoll – went into the final Test having been unable to train all week and that Neil Jenkins could hardly walk by the end of the tour.

Which brings me to a key question: how can we give ourselves the best chance of winning in 2005?

Firstly, we need to play less rugby. I read somewhere that Jim Williams left ACT for Munster having played 40 games for the Brumbies in four years. He will obviously have played lower-level club games too but these will have been of a far lower intensity. Meanwhile, the English international player can expect 19 Premiership games, up to five in the cup, up to nine in Europe, plus eight internationals. That is 41 games in one year.

It was no wonder that half of our squad were being held together with sticking plaster by the end of the tour. An agreement is now in place to limit the number of games played in England; maybe this will leave players fresher in future. The other Home Nations need to look at their calendars too.

Secondly, we need to make sure all our players are singing from the same songsheet right from the off. Rather than pulling the guys together in May for a week before sending them abroad, I would suggest naming a group of 60 players around Christmas; they could then get together in January for two days to be run through basic Lions training. That pattern could be continued every month, with the numbers being pared down as and when deemed necessary. That way a lot more groundwork – look at our problems early on with defence and the general workload – will have been covered by the time the party leaves.

Thirdly, we need to guard against splits in the camp. That may mean taking two complete sides – one designated as the Test 22, the other as the midweek. There were raised eyebrows at the size of the 2001 squad: 37 players for just 10 games. I risk sounding wise after the event but I was relaxed about this. If everyone stayed fit then two or three guys might end up just playing in a couple of games. However, if we sustained a lot of injuries – as we did – everything would change. The theory behind taking 37 was that, at 22 plus 15, you should be able to keep your first XV from having to sit on the bench midweek and, possibly, play more rugby. The old days of sitting on the bench and being an injury reserve are gone. You are there to come on and make an impact when needed.

There are always key players on a Lions tour – this time they would be people like Keith Wood, Richard Hill, Jonny Wilkinson, Brian O'Driscoll – and it is important not to have them playing Saturday games and then sitting on the midweek bench too.

Quite apart from the extra risks involved if they have to come on, they will have to train with the midweek guys and will not get enough rest.

To avoid that, effectively you have to take players just to cover for others. That may sound harsh and it may lead to some guys feeling left out. One way around that in future might be to take two separately defined and entire squads, a total of 44 players. Before they even leave, one group would be told 'You are the Test 22' and a second group told 'Unless you are clearly playing better than your opposite number in the Test group, you are the Midweek 22.' At least then they know where they stand and they are not going to get out there and be disappointed. Instead, they may even be more motivated, to show the management they have made wrong decisions.

Even with all this, though, a Lions tour is never easy. It presents massive challenges to the players and management and brings the best out in the opposition.

New Zealand in 2005 will be a big test.

I'll be there . . . this time as a fan.

Leicester's Great Treble

THE LOW of Sydney had been preceded by one of the most amazing domestic rugby seasons I have ever known.

I have won championships with Leicester before. I have won a Grand Slam with England before – in 1995. But I have never been part of two sides, club and country, which were this exciting to play in.

Leicester had finished top of the English Premiership the season before, hardly losing and producing some of the most thrilling play around. We had had a bad season in Europe, though, and we faced a twin challenge: the first was to maintain our standards as an exhilarating side to watch, to nail our defence even more tightly shut and to win an historic third domestic championship on the trot; the second was to prove we could beat the best in our half of the world.

If the Tigers' rugby was exciting, how would you describe England's?

We had won in South Africa over the summer after a Six Nations in which we had swept all before us until coming a cropper in the rain against Scotland. Fabulous new talents, like Iain Balshaw and Jason Robinson, were waiting in the wings to take the national side to new heights. Again, we had a twin challenge: two autumn Tests against Southern Hemisphere superpowers and then the pursuit of that elusive Grand Slam.

I could not wait.

*

PRE-SEASON FRIENDLIES serve a useful purpose in blowing away some of the team's cobwebs: I would not want to go into the first league game of the year without having played in a competitive game. However, players do not take them as seriously as proper fixtures and at Leicester we have actually made a habit of losing them in recent years.

Our curtain-raiser was against Cardiff; on paper, it looked a more interesting proposition than most, since it was a match-up between the English champions and our Welsh counterparts to be played for something called the Jewson Challenge Trophy. It was the same old story, though, as Cardiff rolled us over 29–17. They played a quick, physical game through guys like Dan Baugh and Pieter Muller, the big Springbok centre, who did a lot of damage and took the ball up well. We missed a few tackles and deserved to lose in the end. The Welsh fans were jubilant but we did not feel too despondent; we would rather have won but the important thing was to shake off a bit of ring rust and get home without any serious injuries.

My brother Will – known at Leicester as 'The Schnozz', because his nose has been broken so many times – was getting married in Bristol the following day, so several of us drove back across the Severn Bridge after the game and spent that Saturday night having a few anticipatory beers. We had been looking forward to a really good night – we do not get that many chances once the season proper has started – and the club had originally said we could have the Monday morning off. Unfortunately, they changed their minds and organised a three kilometre fitness test, so it was a more sober weekend than might otherwise have been the case. A few of the guests at the wedding were a bit surprised at how restrained we were but the image of players getting seriously hammered on a regular basis is a myth. It is simply not practical when you have to play or train 36 hours later. A few of the guys were a bit upset but they were all there bright and early on the Monday morning putting in a hard session.

Later that week, the squad sat down together at our training ground in Oadby, on the outskirts of Leicester, for what the coaches call a goal-setting meeting. It was led by the players, with myself and Paddy Howard as chairmen. There were two main topics of conversation: winning the championship again and succeeding in Europe.

Domestically, we were absolutely determined to top the Premiership. It meant a great deal to us, particularly after we had read in the newspapers that we did not have the 'hunger' to triumph again. We wanted to prove those doubters wrong and really used this as motivation.

On the bigger stage, we also wanted to go well in Europe. There had been a lot of media rubbish written about the Tigers and the Heineken Cup. One particularly laughable piece I read explained that we would never succeed in Europe because we were a very 'insular' team who did not have the 'vision' to 'take in' the whole European scene. Whatever that means. A lot of the journalists covering rugby are good guys and decent writers but they do occasionally over-complicate things in order to fill their column inches.

It is actually very simple: we had not done particularly well in Europe over the years because in crucial matches we had played badly and been beaten. 'Vision' had nothing to do with it.

It is not as though our European record is exactly bad: we got to the final in 1997, though we lost – again, because the other side, Brive, played better than we did. We were probably a little over confident and they punished us for that. The following year we lost to Pau in the quarter final where, once again, they were simply the better side. The next season a run of bad results meant we did not progress beyond the group stages. Along the way, though, we had beaten Pau and Toulouse away and I felt confident that, given a fair run with injury and the bounce of the ball, we would be tough to beat this time around.

As the goal-setting session got underway, we divided the season up into chunks. The first two groups of games were a five-match series of Premiership fixtures followed by three more league games. Then Europe kicked in.

Our initial priority was that first set of five games: Wasps, Newcastle and Saracens away and two home encounters, with Rotherham and Northampton. We set ourselves a points target. A key part of this was the new bonus system, which would be in operation for the first time that season. Sides would receive an extra point for scoring four tries or more or for losing by seven points or fewer. The idea was to reward sides who attacked more and those losing teams who strove to get back to as near level terms as possible. We looked at how things might have differed if that system had been in operation in 1999/2000 and discovered that the answer was not at all – we would still have won the championship. However, it was obviously a factor from now on in. We resolved to really try to kill sides off where possible, denying the others as many 'within seven' bonus points as we could and also looking for the 'four try' bonus point ourselves.

We decided our target for that quintet of matches should be 19 points. We allowed one loss – we did not identify the team we might lose to, since that would be negative – and made up the 19 as follows: four victories (4pts each), two four-try bonus points for the home games and – assuming we did lose one of the five – a 'within seven' bonus point too. It was a tough ask. There were no easy games in the group, though we did not expect to lose to newly-promoted Rotherham at Welford Road.

The first game was Wasps away. Loftus Road is always a tough place to go – the season before we had won our first-ever victory there in an evening midweek match when Geordan Murphy had dotted down after chasing up a miscued drop goal – but they would be without Lawrence Dallaglio, who was sitting out the first few games recovering from injury. Lol is always a key player, both in terms of his play and his leadership, and we knew they would miss him badly. They had a good, strong pack, with Joe Worsley and Phil Greening among the key names, but Dallaglio gave them extra options in what was not a great line-out. In the backs they had guys like Rob Henderson, Josh Lewsey and Kenny Logan – quick players who can make you pay for missed tackles or wrong decisions.

Saturday, August 19 marked a very early start to the season – remember that, for some of us, it would stretch through to July 14, 2001 – and an unusual day to find yourself at Loftus Road. It is primarily the home ground of Queen's Park Rangers and soccer tends to take precedence, with rugby often shunted to Sunday. I hate that. Sunday is not a day to play rugby, it is a day to chill out, a day to recover from a few drinks the night before. Somehow it does not feel quite right. Saturday afternoon comes around and, without a game, I find myself mooching around the house, feeling listless, not quite knowing what to do. I do not think the spectators enjoy Sundays as much, either. Like us, they cannot go out and have a few beers after the match because they have work the following day and I think that mutes the atmosphere. It also gives you less time to recover if you have a game the following Saturday, of course.

It was a warm summer's day, with very little wind, and temperatures at pitch level must have been in the high 70s. Heat can sap players' strength surprisingly quickly and I do not enjoy playing in those conditions so we made sure there was plenty of water ready in bottles along the touchline.

The Wasps game gave us a successful but somewhat shaky start to our campaign. We started off with a couple of early tries, including a debut gem by our new Canadian signing Winston

Stanley. Winston, a slight, blond lad who had come in to replace his countryman Dave Lougheed, showed his great pace in gassing Rob Henderson on the outside to go over. Another try was added and the signs looked encouraging. Shortly afterwards, however, Andy Goode damaged his ankle ligaments and had to go off. Austin moved from scrum-half to fly-half, was himself replaced at No9 by the young James Grindal, and somehow we lost our shape. As the game wore on, Wasps fought their way back into contention and finally took the lead with a chip kick over our defence to score. Things seemed to have gone from bad to worse when they won a penalty in injury time at the end of the match. It was the result of a silly error by Ricky Nebbitt – the sort any player can commit – and when the three points were added it could and maybe should have been curtains for us. But, bizarrely, it helped us to win the game. Without that penalty kick we would probably have spent the next minute or so until the whistle trying to find a way out of our half, or might have punted deep for territory and then had to try to get the ball back. Instead, we had a restart from the halfway line, from which we recovered the ball and started to put Wasps under pressure. We won a lineout in the corner, failed to drive them over but attacked in midfield and recycled the ball quickly from where Austin Healey managed to score. Tim Stimpson converted and the game was ours, 22–24.

That match illustrated two things. Firstly, it showed how important it is never to give up. Secondly, it proved once again that Leicester has that never-say-die attitude. Under pressure, seemingly out of nothing, we had conjured up a win.

The Championship was underway.

*

THE FOLLOWING week saw us head north to Newcastle. I was glad to be going up there so early. I am not keen on playing rugby in the heat but I don't like the Arctic either. Northumbria can be a freezing, sleeting, icy hell on earth if you happen to visit at the wrong time.

In the 1999/2000 season we had played the Falcons on a Friday night two weeks after England had been knocked out of the World Cup. I remember walking out onto the pitch and standing chatting to Jonny Wilkinson about 90 minutes before kick-off. It was very still, almost balmy, a lovely November evening. 'Jeez, Wilko,' I said. 'This is the best weather I've ever seen up here. This is going to be almost enjoyable.' Jonny just grinned at me and we walked back inside.

I did not poke my nose out again until 30 minutes before the start, when I wandered out in my t-shirt for the warm-up to be confronted by a stream of red-nosed guys in waterproofs coming the other way. The wind had got up, it was now raining horizontally and it was about minus 10°C. Unbelievably, we played the game in what were the worst conditions I have ever encountered. During the match, the forwards were setting up maul after maul just to keep together and keep warm. Meanwhile, both sets of backs were fighting the cold by running up and down the pitch, utterly oblivious to the game. When the referee finally blew his whistle we just ran straight into the changing rooms without the traditional handshakes where Paddy Howard promptly went into the foetal position and had to have blankets piled all over him.

Luckily, this season's game was played in more clement conditions. Newcastle had the better of things early on and were leading but we managed to claw our way back into the match after a classic piece of Austin Healey genius. The Falcons had given away a kickable penalty and I was calling for the three points when Austin, ignoring me, suddenly spotted an opportunity and put in a low cross-kick to Geordan Murphy. It bobbled up, Geordie caught it and scored. It is one of those things: if it comes off you are a hero and if it doesn't you aren't. Matt Dawson is another who likes to take these options: some of England's best quick penalties have been taken with me shouting 'No! No! No!' I am not one to blame a player for being adventurous if the play fails to come off, as long as it was feasible in the first place. If a guy showboats, maybe trying a million dollar pass, I might have something to say about it. This was not one of those situations. Oz knew when he kicked the ball that if he got it wrong an easy three points had gone begging but he had the guts to back himself and that move got us on the road to winning the game.

Afterwards, we had a laugh about it. I said: 'I was screaming at you not to take the quick penalty . . . if you'd messed up I would have had to chinned you.' His reply was typical Oz: 'Yeah, but I've got the magic . . . just leave the skills to me.'

It was a comprehensive win, though the 22–25 scoreline might have suggested otherwise. We had battered them up front all afternoon and put too much pace on the ball out wide for the Falcons to cope with, notching up four tries to their one and establishing a club record of eight successive away league wins. Only a rare nightmare afternoon for Tim Stimpson – who missed five attempts at goal in the first half alone – kept them in the hunt.

After seeing his team comprehensively outplayed, you would have thought Rob Andrew would have kept his head down or at least had the grace to accept his side had been beaten by the better team on the day. Instead, he went berserk in the press. 'If we all played like that we might as well all go home,' he raged. 'They kill the ball. It's cynical. They do it year after year. Why won't referees be brave enough to do something about it? I didn't realise they had done away with the sin bin.'

He picked out me and a few other players for particular attention.

'The referees are not prepared to put Martin Johnson or the front row in the sin bin and I am fed up with it. It's their reputation. Why do you think Johnno spends half the time talking to the referee? It's clever but it's not right. We go to referees' conferences every year saying we want the game to flow but nothing is ever done. All this will ever do is encourage everyone else to do the same.'

It was self-evidently nonsense: I get my share of time in the bin and so do our other England players. Look at Backy, an international with a fairly big reputation of his own. He was binned the year before during our Championship-winning game at Bristol, live on TV, for instance. That does not sound like a referee without bottle. And Rob needed to take a closer look at his own guys. He was accusing us of cheating but he was ignoring Newcastle's own tactics: their flanker Richard Arnold, one of the Premiership's most 'uncompromising' players, whacked Tim Stimpson in the face, leaving him bloodied and unable to continue, but we did not whinge about it. Rugby is a physical game and occasionally these things happen. You just get on with it. As for me talking to the referees, how else are you supposed to find out why you are being penalised? Even when there is a genuine infringement it might have happened 20 or 30 yards away from the captain; how else is he supposed to know where his side are going wrong?

Rob was just using the same old tired argument – Leicester are boring, they play forward-dominated rugby, they kill the ball to keep other sides out, they intimidate the referee – to excuse his own side's poor performance and deflect attention away from himself. That view of Leicester is just not true. A side with footballers like Pat Howard, Geordan Murphy, Austin Healey and Leon Lloyd in it is hardly going to be a boring outfit and we proved that by playing some of the Premiership's most exciting and imaginative rugby throughout the season. Yes, sometimes we deserve to be penalised but in this particular game most of the instances where we had been pinged had either been down to silly – not premeditated – actions by our players or, I felt, the referee being a little harsh on us. That is not to say we are perfect. All sports have laws but no team ever takes to the field and adheres scrupulously to every one of those rules, and that includes Newcastle Falcons.

However, there is not, and has never been, any team policy at Leicester which instructs us to 'kill the ball'. We compete vigorously at the breakdown – guys like Neil Back are among the best in the world at this – but sometimes a referee will construe what a player does as illegal. In those circumstances, the rest of the players will be furious with the guilty party because we believe we do not need to infringe to keep other teams out. Our defence will do that job for us.

Rob and I were England team-mates, I think he is a good bloke and I understood why he made his outburst. But I did fear that a few officials might take notice and might 'ref' us more strictly and that did happen over the next five or six weeks. To that extent I think Rob himself was using a little gamesmanship to influence results.

Meanwhile, we were sitting in second place in the Premiership after two wins. Northampton Saints were our next opponents, for our first home game of the season. There is a lot of East Midlands rivalry between the two sides and I always enjoy our encounters. They have some really good players, internationals like Matt Dawson, Ben Cohen and Budge Pountney, and were the reigning Heineken Cup champions. Our players were very fired up for the game. We felt that Northampton were likely title rivals both domestically and in Europe and that we could not afford to lose to them. Saints matches are usually fiery and played in front of big crowds and this one was no exception: 14,278 fans saw Alistair Newmarch and Ben Cohen binned in a niggly game and Martin Corry was off for 20 minutes having 19 stitches put in a nasty head wound. The wound was inflicted by the boot of the French second row Olivier Brouzet in a slightly dubious encounter; Cozza returned to the fray with typical bottle and again we chose not to complain about the injury, instead looking to do our talking on the pitch. And we were successful, winning 33–19. I was pleased that, under the new points system, we had denied our rivals even the available bonus point. I knew that could be vital at the run-in. There were tries for Corry, Healey and Lloyd and 18 kicked points for Geordan Murphy, standing in for the injured Tim Stimpson. It was a typical Geordie performance: cool, calm and collected. He is perhaps the most talented footballer in the Premiership, with pace and ball skills most guys can only dream of having, and it is an utter mystery to me, and a crying shame for him, that he has not played more times for Ireland. He was included in their squad for the Six Nations games delayed by foot-and-mouth but was forced to withdraw through injury; all I can say is that he would have been in my England squad for the last couple of years if he had been born on this side of the water and I had any say in the matter.

The Saints game took us to the top of the table but there was no time to sit back and relax. A hard week lay ahead, with a midweek game at home to Rotherham and then a Sunday visit to Saracens. I was pleased that the Wednesday night fixture was at Welford Road. Playing away from home midweek is tough; you sit for two or three hours each way on a coach, you arrive home at around midnight and then you can't get to sleep until about three or four in the morning. My body is still so full of adrenalin and the buzz of the match that going to bed is a waste of time. I stick on the telly and watch whatever late-night rubbish is on – anything to kill the hours until I start to get sleepy! The next day you have to be up for training because you have a game three or four days later and it is hard for players to be at their best under those circumstances. Playing at home cuts a lot of that out. We were very keen not to underestimate Rotherham, who we felt would present a physically hard challenge, though we took the opportunity to rest some senior players and give younger guys like Ricky Nebbett and Adam Balding an opportunity and to give 19-year-old lock Louis Deacon and a trialist scrum-half, John O'Reilly, their debuts. With a big squad you must give everyone a crack because it keeps them interested. It also gives the first choice side a rest, while at the same time keeping them honest – you need players coming through behind you, challenging you, pushing you. And the visitors played well, scoring first through a penalty, never letting us settle and refusing to be intimidated by coming to Welford Road. As the game wore on they seemed to grow in confidence and were the better side for long periods of the match. They would rue a fluffed opportunity by the centre Jim Naylor, who missed a glaring overlap to come inside where he was tackled, and five missed kicks by Mike Umaga. In the end, two typical Neil Back tries, one from a forward drive and the other from a dart round a maul, gave us the victory. The 26–18 scoreline shows it was not easy. It had not been the best of Tigers' performances – we had created chances but failed to finish them – and it left me feeling irritated and tetchy.

So did the refereeing. We were repeatedly penalised; the whistle seemed to go almost every time we competed for the ball. As I have said, sometimes the referee gets it right and sometimes he gets it wrong: he is only human. And some of the penalties must have been justified. But I lost count of the times the whistle went when I felt we were doing nothing wrong. I was sin-binned near the end. The official blew and I just walked off, without even waiting for the card I knew was coming. I was fuming: on another day, against another side, we might have lost because of the whistle.

Afterwards, Dean Richards spoke for us all when he said at his press conference: 'I have no doubt that the referees are looking more closely at us than they are at other sides.'

Let me give one example: the Rotherham No8 made a break and Neil Back tackled him to the floor. Because of my blistering pace and uncanny ability to read the game – or possibly because of luck – I was the first man there. I was standing over this chap trying to lift the ball off the floor. The laws of the game are clear: at this point, he has to let go. You might give him a second, maybe two, to do so but once an opposing player has his hands on the ball it must be released. It was as clear a penalty as you could get and, sure enough, the whistle went. But the referee was penalising *us*! Incredulous, I asked him why. 'Back was stopping the ball coming out with his knee,' he said. I could hardly believe my ears. Even supposing you actually *could* stop a ball coming out with your knee in those circumstances, why on earth would Backy have been doing so? I had it in my hands! It was a bizarre explanation. This sort of thing had happened throughout the game. I am not suggesting for a moment that the official was deliberately against us. I am sure he felt he was being impartial. I just felt, like Dean, that Rob's words might have affected him. I also felt that it was important for us not to become paranoid. Just as other teams thought Leicester had some sort of hold over referees, so it was possible we might begin to feel victimised. We were bound to get the odd performance we would rather forget; we must not let it affect our play.

Saracens, away, completed that initial group of five games, and, with 18 points, we had almost hit our target. It had been a good start to the season. But we had felt all along that this could be the toughest game of the five. Vicarage Road has been a hard place at which to win since the advent of league rugby and Sarries had a very strong side at that time. They were certainly, I believed, likely to challenge us for one or more of the trophies. We felt the biggest job would be to subdue them up front: in recent years, their scrum has been world class, certainly as good as most international representative packs. Over the last few seasons they have been able to choose their front row from the likes of Paul Wallace, Julian White and David Flatman, Roberto Grau and George Chuter. The second row in the 2000/1 season was Danny Grewcock and Scott Murray and they had guys like Richard Hill and Tony Diprose in the back row which meant they had an excellent line-out. In the back line they had skilful, quick players like Thomas Castaignede and Danny Luger. They also fielded some guy called Duncan McRae, an Australian about whom I did not know too much at that point. Added to all their obvious talent and flair, they have traditionally been well-drilled, aggressive and tough and that meant this was a slightly niggly game, as our visits to Watford often are. People find it strange that you can be playing together for England one week and then knocking lumps out of each other the next in club rugby. To the players, it is just a part of the game. Danny Grewcock, for instance, is a very physical, aggressive competitor and sometimes his opponents bear the brunt of that. But if I am on the receiving end I don't hold it against Danny – it is a part of why I respect him and why I want him on my side at international level. There is a line that people do not generally cross – kicking, biting, gouging and so on – and as long as they don't you just get on with it. Our league encounters with Sarries had also usually been tight and this one was no different. Unlike other recent matches, though, it was a dour, uninspiring affair which cannot have excited the spectators. At half-time, we were 8–9 up, with the home team having scored the only try when McRae intercepted a Martin Corry pass. We had played poorly, failing to cross their line and making a lot of handling errors. On the positive side, our defence was holding well: an intercept try is rarely due to a defensive mistake. In the changing room, we were all frustrated with the way the match was going. Our routine is always the same: the players sit down, attending to any injuries – Vaseline on cuts, strapping on joints – and taking on fluids. I speak first, the coaches next. I told the boys we needed to tighten up our game, cut out the mistakes and play in their half of the field. That way we could put pressure on them. I did not climb into specific players. When I get wound up by a performance – be it with Leicester, England or the Lions – I tend not be a ranter and raver. I take the view that, 99 times out of a hundred, the boys are doing the best they can – though if I sense they are not, I will give them a rev-up. Most times the players themselves can see what is going wrong. The question is whether we can do what is needed to put things right. On this occasion we could not. They 'nil-ed' us in the second half, while managing to add three penalties themselves to win 17–9, and we trudged off feeling down and dispirited for the first time in the season. The mistakes had continued, handing the ball and the momentum to Saracens and leaving us unable to mount much of an attack on their territory. We had not even managed to get a penalty to earn the bonus point and had missed our 19 point target.

Afterwards, we warmed down on the pitch. Martin Corry, agonising over the pass intercepted by McRae, said: 'Sorry, guys, that was my fault.' In a good-natured way, we told him to shut up. You could hardly find a more dedicated, committed team-player than Cozza and no-one held it against him. It was just one of those things. Later, as we sat in the Vicarage Road changing rooms, heads bowed, in near-total silence, I felt really down. It is not a nice feeling, losing, and it is worse when the victors are a team that you know will be challenging for the title. We had felt great after beating Wasps away – we would be favourites to win at home in the return fixture, so we were halfway to a likely double over Dallaglio's side. Conversely, we now had to beat Sarries at Welford Road just to stay evens with them. The journey back was a little flat, as it always is after a defeat. We all sank into our seats, going over our individual mistakes in our minds.

It usually takes me a few days to get over the disappointment of being beaten. You work hard all week, and you don't work hard all week just to go out there, play poorly and lose. But as we neared home I began to chill out a little: you cannot win every game and sometimes, whether through bad luck, poor refereeing or, more likely, bad play by yourselves and good play by the opposition, you lose. We lost – now move on.

Heading into Europe

DESPITE ONLY posting 18 points, we had won four out of five and we now looked forward to a trio of Premiership games which led into the opening European Cup fixtures. At first sight, London Irish at home and Bristol and Sale Sharks away did not look like a minefield. Irish and Sale we would hope to beat and we had a good record against Bristol in recent seasons, having retained our title at the Memorial Ground in 1999/2000 in a game the West Country side needed to win to get in to Europe. And things got off to a good start, with a win over Irish. They had beaten us heavily in the Tetley's Bitter Cup the previous season but we had later beaten them well in the league so honours were fairly even.

We always have a group session on the Friday before a match when we will sit down and talk about the strengths and weaknesses of the opposition, watch a few videos of them and try to work out our strategy for the game. With Irish, it is not always easy to pin them down. They seem to have a lot of player turnover, and a lot of Southern Hemisphere guys, so each season sees them bring in a few new Irishmen, South Africans and Kiwis who no-one has seen before. Additionally, they are not perceived by the TV people as a 'glamour' side so there may not be too much video of them to watch. So we tend to concentrate on their style of play: they are generally a good but perhaps inconsistent side, playing quick, exciting rugby. They recycle the ball very well and have a lot of runners available, with plenty of pace on the wings through guys like Paul Sackey and the former Leicester player Nnamdi Ezulike – a top man known to all at Welford Road as 'The Bread' . . . well, his name does sound a bit like 'naan'. We planned to work on cutting the service to those guys and defending out wide.

And although they scored first, our tactics were generally right, enabling us to run out 33–20 winners with a bonus point for scoring four tries. Among them was one by Neil Back – his 50th league try for the club. That is a fantastic record for a forward and underlines just how important Backy has been to us over the last decade. His attitude and commitment serve as a fantastic example to all young players and he thoroughly deserved the massive Welford Road cheer he received.

It had not been all plain sailing though; there had been some missed tackles and wayward passes and we had not fired for the length of the game. This had been the pattern of a number of matches thus far and it was a worry. As Dean Richards put it to the press: 'In phases we played some outstanding rugby. However, we lapsed into moments of indecision. We have got to play well for a full 80 minutes. Going into Europe, we would like to be a lot more cohesive.'

Still, we headed to Bristol three points clear at the top of the table. Or at least some of us did. I had left the field after 60 minutes during the London Irish encounter, having not been quite right all week. That feeling persisted over the weekend and I missed Wednesday training. I went in on the Friday to do the pre-Bristol team run and I just knew I was not 100 per cent. I was not ill exactly – if I had been back at my old job with the HSBC I would probably have gone in to work. What counts as 'illness' for an athlete may be almost imperceptible for most people: for me the only sign will often be in my training, when I do not hit my usual targets. But today, I definitely did feel off colour and I was sweating up too quickly after the exercise. I had something to eat at lunchtime but a queasiness had developed and I told Dean to get Louis Deacon prepared in case I woke up feeling worse the following morning.

With two hours before we were due to board the coach for Bristol, I nipped home to get my kit. Almost as soon as I walked in the door I threw my lunch up. That was that. I phoned Dean and said I was going to go to bed. The option was still there to drive down myself the following morning if I was better but I did not hold out much hope. It is very unusual for me to actually feel bad but when I awoke the following day I was in awful shape and clearly I was not going to play. I called in to tell them and when I did I got the news that Neil Back and Austin Healey were also suffering with the same bug. Backy stayed in bed in the team hotel and Austin managed to come on for the second half but he could not affect the result much and we lost 24–20. From talking to the guys I actually do not think losing myself and Neil was the main problem, though obviously it was bound to disrupt the team a little. Bristol just played well and made better use of a strong, gusty wind than we did. Whatever the reason, it was a disappointing loss. As a club we take the view that we should not lose if we score three tries but somehow that had happened. Moreover, games like Bristol away can be key to a season; if you win those they can make all the difference to the table come May because they are no mugs and other teams will definitely lose to them.

Again, Dean summed things up in his post-match press conference: 'Too many passes didn't come to hand and even established players didn't play as well as they can. I expect the players to react positively to the defeat in training next week.' Two losses in seven games did not look much like championship form, particularly given the patchy way we had played.

Dean added: 'During the autumn internationals we are going to lose a lot of our guys and it is going to be hard for us to win the league.'

This was a feeling the players shared. Things were not quite right and in our training meetings the following week there was a lot of recognition that we needed to improve.

Sale was our next destination. The night before the game, Gareth Roberts at the brewer Tetley's had arranged for the squad to attend the Tetley's Super League Grand Final play-off between Wigan and St Helens. Most of the boys had never seen a live rugby league game – I had seen the London Broncos play, but never a really top side – and it made a change from the normal Friday night routine before an away fixture. Usually, a few guys will slump in front of the TV in their rooms and the rest will kill time by playing cards or a word game. A favourite is 'The Name Game'. Random pairs of letters are drawn up and players have to come up with famous names with one of the pairs as the initials. As long as at least one other person in the group recognises the name, you are OK. One or two of the boys have demonstrated a shocking grasp of names over the years.

Neil Back once had a B and a K. It came to his turn. 'Barry Kello,' he says. Puzzled looks all round.

'Who's Barry Kello, Neil?' someone eventually asks.

'He's that racing driver,' replies Backy.

'Er, do you mean Rubens Barrichello?' someone asks.

'Ah,' says Backy. 'That's him.'

There are points for using your imagination. Someone once pulled out C and X and came up with Chris Cross. You might have tried to get away with Charles the 10th (Charles X) but you would probably be challenged because while we all know Spanish kings were called Charles no-one knows how many there were. There is a lot of bullshitting and a lot of stupid names called out, but it is surprisingly good fun.

Another classic is 'Who's In The Bag?', which involves pulling the name of a person from a sack and describing him or her to the rest of the guys. The Irishman Eric Miller coined a new nickname for himself when trying to describe one TV 'personality'.

'The laughing squirrel,' he said. 'You know, big ears and all that.'

It turned out he meant Basil Brush. For younger readers, Basil was very clearly a fox. Forever more Miller will be known to Tigers players as 'The Laughing Squirrel'.

Those two games are a lot safer than some other things we have played. 'To My Left', for instance. To My Left is a game we tended to play on the coach back from away games in the old days. Broadly speaking, it involved punching the person to your left in the face from a two-inch distance. The power of the blows would increase as it travelled round the circle. Imagine that with the likes of Deano or Darren Garforth or Peter Short . . . boys with big, heavy fists. To My Left would often mutate into another favourite of the Reg's – 'the Reg' being Deano, don't ask me why he's called that because I don't know – called 'Do You Mind If I Butt In?' This involved sticking the nut on the guy instead of punching him. For variety, Deano sometimes changed the name to 'Do You Like Biscuits?' His catchphrase for this was: 'Here's a ginger nut' . . . bosh! That was seriously mindless and we had to stop in the end because someone was going to get badly hurt.

The whole culture of rugby is different now. Ten years ago, a trip back from a game you had won would see the coach descending into something approaching a booze-fuelled riot. Nowadays, we are more likely to break out a box of Magnum ice lollies than a crate of beers, which is quite sad in a way. It shows how times have changed. Occasionally, we'll have fish and chips all round on a long trip. That is a particular favourite of mine but it has to be a really special occasion.

As a certified sports bore and son of a man from Wigan, I am a bit of a rugby league fan. I was brought up on tales of the great sides of the 50s and I found that Wigan vs St Helens game fascinating. It was particularly interesting watching the positioning of the players off the ball, which is something TV does not always show. For instance, when there's a long kick in rugby league, most of the defending forwards walk or, at best, trot back and let their backs play the ball up through them before they get involved again.

The speed of the game was impressive, and the finishing at times awesome. There were clearly some very talented guys on show – Kieron Cunningham, Paul Sculthorpe, Sean Long – who all played well for St Helens and they thrashed the home side by 50-odd points. Half way through, a Samoan monster called Fereti Tuilagi came off the bench to a rousing cheer, and some increased interest from our ranks. 'Freddy' was due to switch clubs and codes and move to Leicester at the end of the Super League season. He had already down been to Welford Road to watch games a few times on his days off and had even turned up one Sunday with his whole family – wife, kids, brother – to see us play in a pre-season cricket game against a local club side for Stuart Potter's testimonial. This had impressed us all. It was a fair way for him to travel and it showed he was keen to join us and was basically a good bloke. We were glad to return the favour by supporting him for once. He played well, marking Andy Farrell out of the game, and turned up the following day to watch us play down the road. He might have been regretting it afterwards, for ours was a game littered with errors and hesitancy.

Sale is never a great place to go. One of the northern outposts of rugby union, Heywood Road is a small and slightly run-down ground and you do not feel particularly inspired playing there. In the previous couple of seasons, we visited towards the end of the campaign, when we were flying high and they did not have much to play for. We had probably had a slightly easier ride because of that. Now, however, they were up there around the top of the Premiership and the game assumed different proportions for both sides. They wanted to show that their recent form was not a fluke and we desperately needed a win to get ourselves back on track. We started poorly, conceding three penalties before a brilliant Geordan Murphy try and a penalty by Tim Stimpson narrowed the gap to 9–8 at half time. Shortly after the turnaround another Stimmo three-pointer gave us the lead and we had a golden opportunity to extend that when some great combination play between Paddy Howard and Tim found the ball passed out wide to Winston Stanley on the right wing. Winston was home clear and had actually got over the Sale try line but instead of touching down immediately he tried to run round under the posts to make the conversion kick easier. I was watching him, thinking 'Put the ball down, Winston, you're taking a risk here . . . ' Unfortunately, he did not read my mind and Bryan Redpath pressured him into both running over the dead ball line and dropping the ball.

As the game wore on, though, we extended our lead through two more Stimpson penalties, one from the halfway line, and, with 79 minutes gone and the score 9–17, looked certain to win. But after good pressure, Vaughan Going got over in the corner for the home side to narrow the gap. Nicky Little missed the conversion but then banged over a 30-metre injury-time drop goal to help his side share the points from a 17–17 scoreline. It was hugely disappointing and I wondered whether we might end up cursing those missed three points at the end of the season.

Paddy Howard felt his backs were to blame for our failure to win, telling the media: 'I don't know how you blow a game quicker. Once again we made enough breaks to finish the game 10 times over but didn't finish them. Sale looked like scoring twice and scored once. It's really, really frustrating.'

One of the breaks, obviously, had been Stanley's. Winston knew he had screwed up. Sitting in the changing room, he shook his head and said: 'Hell, I've seen guys do it, I never thought I'd do it.' I didn't bollock him. He felt bad enough. Our attitude is that we win together as a team and we lose together, too. If a guy scores a great try to win a match he does not go round saying,

'Hey, that was me folks!' Unless he is Austin . . . Talking of Austin, he was one member of a mini-injury crisis which was taking shape. His hamstring was giving him trouble and both Geordan Murphy and Dorian West were nursing ankle injuries. Austin and Geordie were both crucial members of our back line and Westy, too, was a big loss.

The draw meant the championship had drifted further away, with Saracens now top of the table, having beaten Bath. But I tried to look on the bright side: OK, we had dropped some points but we had played almost half of our away games already and I felt our home record would stand us in good stead. Another factor in our favour was our fitness, which was as good as anyone's and better than most.

The fact that eight Premiership games had been played by the end of September highlighted the fact that the league had started way too early. The league's England contingent had only finished playing the previous June which gave us just four weeks off. Then it was back to training and, before you knew it, the pre-season games. Non-international players had not fared much better.

Rugby is a sport with serious levels of contact and, ideally, players need at least six weeks of absolutely zero rugby to rest and recuperate, then a good period of training before the first game is played.

Towards the end of the season, there would be some very tired bodies and I knew that if we could keep our energy levels up we could cash in. For the time being, though, the domestic agenda was closed. Our European campaign was about to begin.

*

WE HAD a block of four games: Pau at home, Glasgow Caledonians away and both our group-stage games against Pontypridd. Some critics feel this is an odd way to run a calendar, suggesting it makes it hard for players to focus and that it asks too much of us because we have to switch on and off to different competitions. This has led to endless debate about the so-called structured season. Should we switch from Zurich Championship to Heineken Cup to Tetley's Bitter Cup and so on – or should we play each competition to a conclusion and move on to the next? To be honest, I do not think it makes any odds to the players. It certainly does not to me. I approach each game exactly the same, whether it be a big Premiership clash, a run-out against a team of minnows in the Tetley's Bitter Cup, a vital qualifier against Pau in a big European game or a Test match, and I think other guys are pretty much the same. We prepare properly and we look to win.

That said, obviously, Europe is as big as it gets in club terms; it is the championship of the continent and a couple of defeats can mean an early end to your European season, unlike in a league. Additionally, in theory, you are playing better teams than you come up against domestically. Certainly, some of the big French sides present a really tough challenge, as do the likes of Cardiff and Irish provinces like Munster, Leinster and Ulster.

Looking at our group, the danger side was obviously Pau, which meant that the most crucial game of our group stage would be the first: Pau at Welford Road. If home advantage helped us to beat them we would be off to a good start against our main rivals. That was not to discount Ponty or Caley but we felt we had the beating of them. Pontypridd were not the strongest side in Wales and the two Scottish super-districts had yet to really take off north of the border (though Glasgow had beaten us the previous season, of course).

It is crucial to win your group because that gives you a home quarter-final and playing at home in front of your own supporters really does give you a lift. We had played Pau twice before and beaten them once. Most recently, we had lost to them in the quarter-final of the cup in 1997. They were a typical French team. French sides are a 'type', even though the national characteristics that once applied are diminishing in the professional era. People play each other more often, there is more TV and therefore video, and with the extra time for analysis and training players from different countries have been able to absorb some of the good points of other nations' play and also find ways to defend against them. The French have picked up some Anglo Saxon discipline but they do still have that flair, that Gallic sense of drama and daring, which enables them to play out of their skins at times. Look at the World Cup semi-final in 1999, when the national side came back from the dead to shred the All Blacks. Since forever, French sides have had dangerous backs, who run devastating, shocking angles and can rip you apart from nowhere. They are also traditionally extremely strong scrummagers but their forwards have tended to have good ball skills too.

Along with the tough physicality and the flair comes emotion, of course. They can lose it, big time. When we beat Toulouse at home in the European semi-final in 1997, their hooker freaked out and went completely crazy. It was a horrible day for them to come up from the South of France – a freezing cold English January, with the pitch only just playable. We scored from an interception early on and then another try and everything went our way. Towards the end they were beaten and they were getting really upset with the referee. He was probably Welsh but they heard him speaking English to us and they got paranoid about it. This hooker lost his temper, threw the ball down and started stamping around. *Shooting Stars*, with Vic Reeves and Bob Mortimer, was on in those days. On that show, if someone lost their temper, Vic and Bob would mince up to them with imaginary handbags and shake them in their faces going 'Ooooh!' So Austin walked up to the hooker and gave him the 'Ooooh!', much to our amusement. He, however, did not see the funny side.

I love to see them getting emotional, personally. I think it is great that they care so much. Far better than being the other way and not giving a toss.

The French fans, too, are renowned for their passion. Our first game against Pau, down in the Pyrenees, had been a brutal affair. John Wells was gouged, punches were thrown and the supporters were chucking things at us throughout the match. As we came off, having won, we were spat at and – I presume – sworn at by a furious-looking mob. We managed to get out of the stadium alive and headed back to the hotel. Later that night we came back to an official dinner in a marquee at the ground to find the very same supporters there. This time they gave us a really warm reception and we had a great time with them – one of those memorable rugby evenings which will stay with me forever.

All that went into the melting pot as we planned to welcome Pau to Welford Road. We expected a tough game, because they had recently beaten Stade Français at home, but it was, in fact, a fairly easy win. We dominated the first half without actually scoring a try, Stimmo kicking well. Within a minute of the restart, Jamie Hamilton had gone over for our first five-pointer. There was a brief worry when they regrouped and came back at us, scoring twice in quick succession, but we never allowed them near our line again and ran out 46–18 winners. We had scrummaged particularly well, pushing them over their line to create two tries, which is very rare against a French side. It obviously rankled with them because there was a flare-up towards the end and one of their props, who had been under the cosh all afternoon, got himself sent off. I was pleased because I felt an emphatic win like that set us up well, psychologically, for the return trip in January.

Next up was a trip to Glasgow. The Caledonians had beaten us fair and square the previous season, when we were in the depths of our European slump. It had been my last game before my lengthy enforced absence through a heel injury and Darren Garforth was already out with neck trouble, meaning Graham Rowntree had had to play tight head. That is a tough call: tight-head is one of the most difficult positions to play. Technically, it is harder because you are scrummaging against two blokes. That also makes it physically harder too, of course. Wiggy had done a manful job in difficult circumstances but we had still lost, basically playing without any spark and deserving to go down. This year, we wanted to avenge that defeat and we did so, winning more comfortably than the 21–33 scoreline suggests. They seemed to be suffering from playing some fairly low-quality games in the Welsh-Scottish league because we had the edge in pace and organisation on them and I felt from the start we were going to win the game. That can be a dangerous feeling; you must remind yourself you are playing a team with a lot of very good players in it and that you are only beating them because you have played well. If you switch off, they are going to have the majority of the ball and you are going to be defending and, no matter how good your defence is, eventually you either give away penalties or leak tries.

Rugby is a lot easier going forward. You have momentum, they are under pressure. You get the territory, you get the decisions, you get the penalties, you score the points. If you are defending, even with a 20 point lead with 20 minutes to go, it is hard work making all those tackles. If they score seven points, suddenly they are in the game. If they score again, all hell is let loose because they are in with a sniff . . . they are charging at you and your heads are down. It is not like soccer where, with a 3–0 lead, a good team can keep everybody behind the ball, retain possession, pass it around and relax. There is no such thing as keep-ball in rugby; to retain possession you need to work very hard to avoid turning it over. A personal hate of mine is when a team is on top and players *do* get that 'they can't catch us' feeling and they start trying to do things that you do not practice, the flash things, things that are not likely to come off. The million dollar, one-time-in-ten pass is thrown and I just think 'Why the hell did you do that? We got here by playing good solid rugby so let's keep it that way.' It is not so prevalent now because teams are more disciplined but a few years back if you had scored 30 points suddenly guys would be spinning off all over the place trying things they had never even seen before.

Two wins from two games was a good return and we now faced back-to-back matches against Pontypridd. First up, Sardis Road, and a Friday night kick-off. I have a great deal of respect and admiration for Pontypridd and clubs like them. They are not one of the big Welsh outfits, like a Cardiff or a Llanelli, though they were recent champions, and I think they feel somewhat overshadowed by their bigger rivals. They are based in a mining town, up in the country a bit, and the club reflects its home: traditional, honest and hard. There is nothing flash about the place. It has produced some great players over the years – Neil Jenkins is a Ponty lad. They love their rugby in the Valleys and they love beating Englishmen so the atmosphere is always immense – I always get shivers down my back when I play over there. This night was no different. The team and the fans were all really psyched up to turn over the English champions. It was perhaps the biggest night of their rugby year and we knew the crowd, packed into their tight little ground, would be a factor early on. The louder and more passionate they are, the more this spurs the home side on so our plan was to try and dominate from the start and not make any mistakes to excite them. If it works, after 20 minutes you can feel the wind go out of the supporters as they realise it is not going to be their night. It was wet, and we expected a physical slog of a game on a muddy pitch which was the way it turned out. They never really threatened our line and we did not make the most of our opportunities. We did actually score one try – Geordan Murphy was over the line with the ball under him – but the referee did not give it. I do not want to take anything away from Ponty but the ref was frankly out of his depth. The worst incident came when we had their scrum on rails, going backwards near their line. On a slippy pitch, there was no way out for their pack and there was a 90 per cent chance of a Leicester score. Suddenly, their loosehead whacked Garforth.

The referee blew his whistle to stop the game, had a word with this lad and then reset the scrum. We could not get them going back again and the moment was lost. Obviously we would have preferred to have played the advantage and tried to score; by all means caution or card the guy after the play has ended, but don't stop it like that. Apart from all that, why was the guy not binned for punching? The match ended 18–11. Later, I watched it on video and Jonathan Davies, as Welsh as they come, was asked how they had managed to beat us. It was, after all, a shock result. Davies suggested they had had a little help from the official! Ultimately, though, the ref cannot disallow every try, or stop the ball bisecting the posts, so we only really had ourselves to blame. We had not troubled the scorers in the second half and you are unlikely to win a European Cup match with 11 points.

We were pretty down about the loss. If Pau beat Ponty at Sardis Road our return match against the French would be a must-win to enable us to cancel out our loss in Wales. And it is never a good thing to travel across the Channel needing a win. First, though, Pontypridd were coming to Leicester. As well as being a vital game, it also marked the debut of Freddy Tuilagi. And what a debut it was. The Welford Road crowd, many of whom would have been watching him on the TV for St Helens, had piled into the club shop before the kick-off and bought the entire stock of specially-obtained Freddy wigs – horrible, black dreadlocks which mimicked his long, beaded air. A massive cheer greeted the announcement of his name on the PA and an even bigger one when he appeared for the start of the match. I think the fans saw Freddy's acquisition as a bold move by the club and I am sure they were also looking forward to seeing this squat powerhouse in action.

They did not have to wait long. At one of the early line-outs we had called it short. That meant I was standing in midfield waiting to take the ball from the fly half, from where I would set up play. Freddy was on the left – blind side – wing. As the ball came down from the line out and was passed to the scrum half, he bolted off his wing in a blur of legs and beads, grabbing the ball in mid air as it was passed from 9 to 10. He then took it up into the midfield where he made good yards, just bashing through the Welsh defence. The crowd were going ballistic because Freddy had got his hands on the ball so early and was making inroads. I was surprised, but I just thought 'Fair enough, the backs have pulled a shifty one here to get Freddy straight into the game and haven't told the rest of us about it'. Then I saw the blank look in Pat Howard's eyes and realised this was not a planned move! Freddy made one or two other pulsating runs, enough to suggest he was going to have a big impact. He is a big unit and has a lot of power and energy – he is the sort of guy who can bowl people over while standing still.

I had thought before the game that we would win the home leg and we did, 27–19. But I had been expecting to put a few more points on them than that and, to be fair to Ponty, they played a lot better than they had when they had beaten us at their ground. We were glad of the points and felt that, with three wins out of four, our European campaign was back on track.

*

FROM THE heights of Europe it was down to earth with a bump the following weekend, when we played Otley in the fourth round of the Tetley's Bitter Cup. Some people have questioned the worth of the Cup, particularly since the European scene has assumed such importance in recent years. Personally, I love it. I have been lucky enough to be in Tigers' sides which have won it twice and got to two other finals. But the key thing is the romance of it all. The way it allows smaller teams a shot at the big boys, in the same way the FA Cup does in soccer, is fantastic. Two years before, for instance, we had played Barking – Jason Leonard's former club – and it had been a big day out for them, coming up to Welford Road to play Leicester. We beat them fairly soundly but I know from Jase that their guys enjoyed the game tremendously. Without wanting to sound arrogant, it must be great for lower league sides to get the opportunity to play against the likes of Tim Horan or Jason Little, Jason Robinson or Dan Luger. Those sort of memories will stay with guys for life. Of course, in these days of professional rugby, with the increased fitness and skill levels among Premiership sides, they are unlikely to be able to cause an upset, although London Irish were beaten by Thurrock a few years ago. Of course, Otley are not exactly minnows. They were a tough National Division One outfit and I am sure they harboured faint hopes of an upset against us. Unfortunately, those hopes were extinguished pretty quickly and we scored 13 tries to win 83–11, Freddy Tuilagi and Perry Freshwater each grabbing a hat-trick. It was a level up for them and it showed, as it should. Like all amateur or semi-pro players, Otley's guys do not have the time to train for the pace and organisation, in defence and attack, that the modern game requires. Not surprisingly, they also lacked fitness, strength, size and a little ability in comparison with us. I do not want to be patronising. I am sure there are players lower down who, if they gave up their jobs and dedicated themselves to the sport, could slot in to Premiership rugby, but this result just highlighted the gulf that now exists between the various levels of the game.

I sat on the bench, something I hate. It makes me nervous, even for a match like that, so I tried to keep active, up and down, running onto the field, giving the guys their water bottles, even replacing divots in the pitch at one stage – for which I received an ironic cheer. I actually made it on for the last 10 seconds, coming on for one of the backs and immediately bottling the opportunity to make my first and last appearance on the wing. There was a scrum on the far touchline. I could have stood out wide on the Crumbie Stand side but the fear of looking stupid if their winger got the ball and skinned me forced me over to the set-piece where

I packed down on the flank, asking one of the younger back row guys to go to the wing.

We had suffered one or two injuries and those Tetley's Bitter Cup critics immediately latched on to the fact. They suggested, once again, that the competition was an anachronism. They argued that the Cup throws too many extra games into the way of the top teams and should be left to lower clubs. Again, I do not necessarily agree with this: it is only five extra games if you win it . . . surely sides can cope with that?

The Otley game gave us a chance to rest a few senior players and, as for the injuries, you can pick something up reaching for your TV remote control. Ask Leon Lloyd.

The following week, we faced a rather stiffer challenge: Gloucester, away, in the fifth round of the Cup. Kingsholm has always been a tough place to visit. The Gloucester fans are a loud, aggressive bunch who really get stuck into opposing teams, right from warm-up. It can have an intimidating effect on some players but I love a noisy, partisan crowd. It is how supporters should be and it stirs me up and makes me want to play better. Having said that, Leicester have not been too successful down there. A record of 19 wins in 87 visits going into the match marked Kingsholm out as something of a bogey ground for us and we were keen to turn this tide. Surprisingly, Philippe Saint-André chose to rest some of his key men, like Jason Little and Ian Jones. Injury meant a few of our first-choice players, Neil Back and Geordan Murphy, were missing too. Gloucester are a hard side, led by Phil Vickery, and they do not flinch from physical contact. There were a couple of punch-ups in the first five minutes, with Dorian West and Chris Fortey both being binned, and this theme continued throughout the game. Ultimately, we had more stitches than points: Westy needed 15 and had to be subbed, Paul Gustard had 10 and Graham Rowntree four. But the 25 points we did post beat the home side's 13.

It had started badly for us when we collapsed a driving maul and conceded a penalty try, a rarity for a Tigers pack, but we hit back through a dazzling score by the young centre Ollie Smith. Ollie, just 18 and, like Deano, a product of John Cleveland School in Hinckley, was making only his second full appearance for us. He received the ball 30 metres out and stepped two defenders to touch down in the corner, giving us the lead for the first time. As a teenager, to go to a place like Gloucester and score a try like that you have to be something special. He is a powerful young player, he has good pace and he has been compared by some at the club to Paul Dodge. As a guy I do not know him too well – he is a quiet, modest sort of lad who does not have too much to say – but I think he has a great future ahead of him.

Leon Lloyd also scored and by the end it was our magnificent travelling fans who were making all the noise, celebrating our passage to the Cup quarter-final as the Shed fell silent.

England Duty

THE SEASON then split in two. The England internationals – myself, Backy, Austin, Dorian West and Martin Corry – left to join up with Clive Woodward's squad for Tests against Australia, Argentina and South Africa.

Back in Leicester, the boys were preparing for three testing Premiership games: home to Wasps, away at Harlequins and then home to a Gloucester side who would want revenge. It would be tough for them with so many experienced guys away but the other sides were missing players too. Wasps had Lawrence Dallaglio and Phil Greening on international duty, Quins would be without Will Greenwood and Jason Leonard and Gloucester minus Phil Vicks.

It was hard to forecast the results but it was clearly a crucial period for the club: three wins would probably see us on the road to a third Premiership win while anything else might open the door to another side. I felt two wins was probably the best we could hope for.

In the event, the boys did themselves and the club proud. Wasps were beaten 28–13, after we had been down at half-time, which meant we had done the double over a side we had feared at the start of the season. Quins, away on the Friday night, was another tough call, and again the team was down at half-time. Again, they showed the bottle and spirit to battle back and win 13–16, a great win in the circumstances. Best of the lot, though, was the Gloucester match. Licking their wounds after the Cup game, the South Westerners would have wanted to beat us, for pride and for league position, and must have felt they would never have a better chance. They fielded big guns like Ian Jones and Jason Little and put three tries on us. We apparently looked dead and buried but the boys scrapped hard and Freddy scored right at the death to take us to a 31–28 win.

It gave the Tigers maximum points from those three tricky matches when title rivals like Bath and Saracens had not fared as well. Equally important, to the players, was their defence of Welford Road. The place, and our three-year unbeaten record there, means something indefinable to us. The atmosphere at the ground was, I am told, incredible. Caught up in the euphoria, Paddy Howard led the team straight off the pitch and into one of the bars, still in full kit, for a celebratory pint or two.

I was particularly pleased for Richard Cockerill, who captained the side in my absence. Cocker has seen the highs and lows of sport in recent years. When he was in the England side he became something of a cult figure, particularly for his facing-down of the All Black hooker Norm Hewitt when the Kiwis came to Twickenham. The photo of the two of them eyeball to eyeball has been reprinted hundreds of times and speaks volumes about Cocker's competitive spirit. Then he lost his England place to Phil Greening and, shortly afterwards, his Leicester place to Dorian West. He starts more games on the bench for us these days. Some players would lose interest but he has never let his head go down. He has a great attitude, both in training and on match days, and the players respect him enormously for that. He is a very good player still and also a top bloke whom many people misunderstand. They only see the theatrical Cocker, pulling faces, acting about and shouting the odds on the pitch. Behind the scenes, he has a heart of gold, doing a lot with disabled supporters and kids at Leicester, and it is a shame more people do not see that side of him. He has a great sense of fun too. He and Hewitt are currently being lined up for a series of boxing matches which will take place in Walkabout bars all over the country, which should be amusing. Thanks in part to his leadership, we had a Premiership lead which we would not now relinquish.

Spin back a couple of weeks, though, and I was heading down to London for those three Investec Challenge autumn internationals.

I left home late on the Sunday afternoon for the drive to our Pennyhill Park base. We had been meeting up there on most Mondays for weeks in the lead-up to the Australia game. It is tough, particularly if you have played a Sunday game, and you do not get home on the Monday until late on, but it is vital. The idea is to make sure you are not starting from scratch in the week before the match. Modern rugby requires players to absorb and understand a lot of information – line-out, scrum, back row and backs moves, all different to the clubs' – and you could not achieve the necessary levels of sophistication in five or six working days. You then need only to do the minimum amount of work in the final week, keeping everyone fresh for the game. We do not have an easy time of it. Clive and the coaches drive us hard but we do not have people standing around asking what is going on, which would lengthen the sessions considerably. Players hate it if they are out on the park for two-and-a-half hours but only do 90 minutes' proper work.

In structure, pre-international weeks are very similar to a week at the club: we gather on Monday morning and talk through our objective. Then we train that afternoon and twice more on Tuesday and Wednesday. Everything gets looked at: restarts, defence, attack, scrummaging, line-outs, the breakdown. We might spend 20 to 25 minutes on rucking technique drills, for instance, then go into what the coaches call 'rhythms', where we play across the field, getting used to the lines we need to take. Then we will have a full-scale team run, playing phase play out of defence and on attack, playing off set piece defence, set piece attack and so on.

Mostly it is two hours at a time and often, come Wednesday afternoon, when we have finished, the boys are quite tired. That evening is our team meal out of the hotel at a local restaurant, with everyone looking forward to Thursday which is our day off. Friday morning we meet up again. If we are at home, we will head down to Twickenham to train. If we are away we will train elsewhere and then visit the stadium for a look around. Friday afternoon is off.

The constant moan about England has been that we can win against the big names from time to time but not consistently. It has probably been a fair criticism. But we had beaten the South Africans the previous summer – we won one Test and should have won the other – and had rightly received plaudits from the media and fans. Our defence had been outstanding and we had been much the better team against a Southern Hemisphere side, on their turf, over the two games. The question on everybody's lips now was: Can England beat the Wallabies?

Games do not come much bigger than Australia at Twickenham. The World Champions, the side some of us would shortly face for the Lions and a team which had had the beating of England for years.

If we could win, we would show that the South African trip had not been a fluke. If we could not it would be back to the old refrain – 'England cannot beat teams from Down Under regularly'.

Officially, like the Argentina and South Africa fixtures which were to follow, it was a friendly. Forget that idea. There is no such thing in international rugby and certainly no such thing when you are playing the Wallabies. This was to be a full-on game, bigger than any Six Nations match, except perhaps a Grand Slam decider, because of the nature of the opposition. They were, are, the world's best.

My first thought that week was that I would rather have played Argentina first up. No disrespect to the Pumas, a big, aggressive team with some good players, but we would normally expect to beat them and could have used it almost as a warm-up for the two major teams. But it was not to be.

The guys were fairly tense in the changing rooms ahead of kick off. John Eales and his team would be without their two main playmakers, the scrum-half George Gregan and fly-half Stephen Larkham. Clive and the coaches really played on this at team meetings in the week leading up to the game. If you can't beat them now, they told us repeatedly, you never will. The players all felt under enormous pressure to win.

I remember feeling that the first half was following a familiar pattern. We had more possession and more territory than they did, but did not look like scoring. That has often been the story of our matches against the big three. We have had plenty of ball but we have not been able to use it effectively. I did feel, though, that we had the backs to put chances away the longer the match went on, as long as we did not get frustrated.

At half time in the changing room, as the boys took on fluids, we talked about the need to retain the ball and keep the pressure on in the set-piece.

Rod Macqueen had clearly decided tactical changes were needed from his side. From the restart they changed their game, playing more directly with a lot of pick-and-go from Jim Williams and the other forwards.

We started the second half poorly, turning over a couple of balls and before we knew it they had spun the ball wide, Austin Healey had missed Joe Roff and Matt Burke had scored from his pass. That is the hallmark of great backs: give them half a chance and they punish you. It was a tackle Austin should have made and one I know he was very disappointed to miss. In retrospect he says he dived too soon and either bounced, or was pushed, off, when he maybe should have tried to get closer before trying to grab Roff. A few commentators suggested it was a size thing, little Austin against big old Joe. That was nonsense. Defensively Healey is normally as solid as a rock and I would back him to stop Roff 99 times out of 100. On this occasion he used poor technique and we suffered for it. Suddenly, they were on top and I could almost sense the Twickenham crowd sighing. 'Oh well, here we go again,' seemed to be the attitude. Conceding a score like that, after you have put in so much effort for little reward yourselves, can sometimes take the wind out of a team too. But I was very proud of the way we responded. We were right back at them, harrying and chasing, battering and tackling, just keeping the pressure on. We did not make best possible use of our possession and we lacked structure at times, but we showed great spirit and belief. And the Twickenham crowd, so often criticised for their polite applause and seeming inability to get behind England, had sensed our mood and were starting to really roar.

With 20 minutes or so to go, Clive threw on Iain Balshaw for Healey. At just 21, Balsh was something of an unknown quantity to most people outside Bath. I had seen enough of him in training, and in playing against Bath, to know he could do some real damage if he got the opportunity to attack from deep. I remember chatting about him to Will Greenwood at one session. Will just shook his head and said: 'It is all so easy for Balsh with his pace . . . he just terrifies defences.'

I did not expect him to terrify the Australians but he certainly had an immediate impact. On a wet pitch, running at tired players, he created alarm, opening them up a number of times.

But his most important contribution came not through his pace but through his vision and sheer footballing skills. A ruck formed, it was our ball and somehow it got out to Balshaw. It was deep in injury time and there was nothing on. Suddenly, he spotted a gap, accelerated and produced a little chip kick. With my typically astute reading of the game, trapped at the bottom of the ruck and seeing boot hit ball, I lay there groaning 'Oh no,

Balsh, it's all over, why have you kicked it?' I was sure the ball was going dead, and that the game was finished. Then Danny Luger raced by and *looked* to have pounced on the ball as it crossed the Aussie line. Luges and the rest of the boys were leaping around and the crowd had gone absolutely berserk but I honestly did not see properly . . . I was too busy lying on the floor cursing Balsh.

The video ref was called in and we faced what seemed like minutes as the decision was made. I went over to the match official, André Watson, to check the eventualities. If it was a try, great, how long left for play? If not, what was it – a 22 drop-out, a five-metre scrum, what?

He said: 'Martin, it's all over whatever the video shows.'

We stood around waiting while the video was replayed time and again on the big screen. I did not look. I was pretty tired and I just wanted to wait and see what the decision was, not waste energy worrying about it. I knew the crowd would let me know, and they did, raising the roof when the try was given.

As Jonny was lining up the conversion, I went back over to André just to confirm that the game really was finished after the kick. If Jonny potted it, that would make the score 22–19, leaving the Aussies a penalty away from a draw and I have known referees tell me the game is over and then change their minds. 'That's it,' he said, 'it's over.' So I knew that we had won. There was a tremendous feeling of relief.

The rest of the boys had gone back to the half-way line where I joined them.

'Right, guys,' I said. 'André says three minutes left whatever happens.'

I could see all their shoulders sagging. It had been a really hard game on soft ground and their legs were gone. Lawrence and Daws were looking at me going 'You what? You must be joking?' Unfortunately, I can never keep a straight face and I started smirking. 'You bastard, Johnno,' said a relieved Dawson.

I have watched the Luger try on video several times since. It was certainly controversial and it is perhaps the sort of score on which you would be disappointed to lose a match. It was a judgment call for the video ref: Dan got the ball down with his forearm and the question is how much pressure did he apply and for how long? Did he have control? I have seen those decisions go the other way, most recently on our 2000 tour to South Africa, when what I thought was a clear Tim Stimpson score was denied. Stimmo was pulled down in the act of scoring. He either grounded the ball – which I think he did – or he was tackled off the ball to prevent him scoring, in which case it was a penalty try, but the video referee ruled against us. You cannot win them all and it will always come down to opinion, even when it is on a TV screen. As for Dan's try . . . well, I think Tim's was a clearer score.

Another controversial aspect of the Australia game was the time-wasting tactics of the Wallabies towards the end. Guys were going down with cramp and there were lots of little stoppages. At one point, they were messing about behind their own 22, chucking the ball around. André Watson called a halt to that after someone passed the ball directly into Jim Williams' face . . . I think he felt enough was enough. Was the time-wasting irritating? Yes. Do all teams do it if it suits them? Yes, to be honest. You cannot be seen to be doing it deliberately but it happens, especially when teams have guys in the sin bin. They walk slower to the half-way line to kick off, they take their time walking to line-outs. There is no law which says you have to run, after all. It is frustrating if you are trying to get on with the game but it is also something that the crowd, with one eye on the clock, is possibly more aware of than the players.

As the rest of the boys celebrated the win, I followed my usual post-match routine. Immediately I get into the changing room, I always take off my wet shirt, pads, boots and socks. While I was doing this, Woody said a few words to the guys, most of whom were having a laugh or stretching, rehydrating or taking on some food. Nothing dramatic: 'Good win guys, but let's keep our feet on the ground'. As the banter and the jokes were flying around, I put on my track suit and headed outside for interviews – a couple for TV and a couple for radio – before going straight into the press conference.

By the time I got back to the changing room, most of the players had showered, dressed and gone, as is usually the case. It always feels a little lonely and anti-climactic with no-one to talk to or share the victory with. Because of this, I prefer the after-match atmosphere at Leicester games. Even if the game is on TV the media interest is much less so there is time for me to sit there in my shorts with a cup of tea or, if it is a really momentous game, a beer. If we have won we will usually be taking the mickey out of each other, relaxing for an enjoyable 20 minutes or so. We are on our own and the pressure of the game has gone. We have a night off to look forward to and, assuming it is a Saturday game, time to recover and chill out the next day too.

After showering and shaving, I got into my blazer and went up into the Spirit of Rugby. This is a big function room at Twickenham where both sets of players gather with family, friends and RFU people for the speeches and a little buffet after Autumn games. There is no post-match dinner after those matches. When we play at home in the Six Nations we host the opposition for dinner at the Hilton on Park Lane in London. Then we will pile onto the bus and have a bit of *craic* on the way there, a few beers if the mood takes us, sometimes a sing-song. These used to be led by the recently retired team doctor, Terry 'El Tel' Crystal. His favourite was *Delilah*: he knew fewer words each year and had only a vague idea of the tune. Phil Greening is another keen singer, with a wicked Boyzone impression. This evening, though, there was no sing-song and no dinner and everything was all over by about 7pm. With Argentina the following weekend, a lot of us were staying at Pennyhill Park. It is a great hotel with a superb à la carte menu, but I had a craving for fish and chips. I asked around and pretty soon I had an order for 25 portions of fish and chips, one fish cake and chips, two sausage and chips and a chicken and chips. Off I went with a couple of other guys to a chippy just down the road in Bagshot. And that was how we celebrated our win over the Wallabies.

Confrontation

THE WEEK before the Argentina game took on an almost surreal air.

Behind the scenes the England camp had been turbulent for a long time, with players and the RFU locked for months in negotiation over a number of issues.

The main bones of contention were playing fees and player image rights. In both cases, we felt we were getting a raw deal from the RFU.

The fee issue revolved around the RFU's wish to make more of our international earnings dependent on winning. That Australian game proved more eloquently than any words how victory can turn on one moment – a video referee's decision – which is quite out of the players' control. There would have been no difference in our effort or skill level if that try had not been given but there would have been a difference in our incomes. The argument that the players' representatives – myself, Matt Dawson and Lawrence Dallaglio – put forward was that, in the short term, the RFU's income is not changed by winning or losing. Why should ours be?

The other area of conflict was image rights. We were being asked to sign contracts that gave the RFU the right to licence our images. This meant England players could end up seeing their faces on hoardings advertising almost anything and would have no say in the matter. They would also receive no money for the use of their images. This could run into many thousands of pounds, with the licence to use the images of top rugby players becoming more valuable every year as the game becomes bigger and those faces become more familiar.

Some people will question whether the players' priorities are right here. Should we not just concentrate on playing? My response is simple. There are two issues. Firstly, there is the RFU asking you to play rugby for your country and then, secondly, there is the RFU going out to commercial organisations and offering them the right to use Martin Johnson's face to advertise something . . . backs of buses, perhaps. I have signed a contract to play rugby and I am happy to do that. But when the RFU introduces the issue of advertising, and image usage, I expect to have a say in the matter and to be rewarded. Why shouldn't I? They wanted to wrap the two in together, which was fine: the players just felt they should receive some of the monies the union would then earn.

The dispute dated back to before the World Cup but we had not brought it into the open then, hoping that the matter would be resolved. After the tournament we said as a squad that we would take action if we had to, but continued talking. Despite months of to-ing and fro-ing, however, we had been unable to reach agreement with the RFU. Finally, in talks before the Autumn internationals, their negotiating team had just dug its heels in.

'It is not the money,' was their constant refrain. 'It is a matter of principle.'

They seemed happy to let the issue drift on forever. Our only serious card was the withdrawal of labour. If we went along with them and played in the Investec Challenge matches, that card would disappear from our hand for another three months until the Six Nations.

Eventually, as the three games approached, and it became clear we were not going to reach agreement, Lawrence, Matt and myself went back to the squad to take instructions ahead of the Australia fixture. With only one abstention, by a senior player, the result was otherwise unanimous: we would withdraw from all commercial activities before the encounter with the Wallabies.

Clive Woodward, his focus rightly on the match, met us and asked that we delay our stand. He was confident, he said, that the matter would be sorted out with the RFU the following Monday. After a period of reflection, we agreed. We did not want to let anything affect our preparation for the Australia game. We also hoped everything would be agreed the next week. But at that meeting, with the win over Australia under our belts, we found that we were back to square one. Despite Clive's intervention, nothing had changed.

We went back to the players and this time there was no hesitation. We informed the Union that we would not play against Argentina that coming Saturday unless our concerns were addressed.

All hell broke loose in the media. It can leave a nasty taste in the mouth when professional sportsmen start talking about money, particularly because so many people would almost kill to do what we do. The simple approach, which some members of the press took, was to accuse the players of avarice.

'Look at these guys,' was their attitude. 'Most people would play for England for nothing. These guys earn a lot of money for representing their country – they are just greedy.'

Let us analyse that argument.

We, too, would play for England for nothing. Many of us did, remember?

We *are* well-paid – some of us. With my club salary, I comfortably earn a six figure sum each year. But national newspaper editors certainly earn more without risking a busted nose every time they go to work and they can carry on until 65. And some England players are on as little as £10,000 a year with their clubs.

Greedy? The issue is a lot more complex than that and greed does not come into it.

The fact is that the players did not turn rugby professional. We do not set the Twickenham ticket prices at £40 and £50. We do not negotiate multi-million pound TV deals or shirt sponsorship arrangements. We do not run the corporate hospitality boxes, or the merchandising operation, or the restaurants and bars.

These things add up to a massive money-making operation centred on 70,000 people coming to watch 15 guys play rugby. Nothing wrong with that at all – after all, much of the cash filters down to the grass roots to keep the game healthy, something of which we are all in favour. All we expect is a fair share.

I was happy as an amateur, earning an average wage in a bank. But once professionalism was a fact of my life, it was only fair that I was fairly recompensed. Like all the guys, I have a mortgage and bills to pay. Many of them have children to provide for, too.

A sporting career is a fragile thing and few are more so than rugby. You can play for England one week and score the winning try against Australia and the following week you might be injured and never play again. Are the RFU going to be there for you then saying 'How much is left on your mortgage? Can you get by? If not, here's some money that we earned from sponsors and advertisers over the years on the back of your performances.' I very much doubt it.

Rugby is not soccer and most players are not earning the huge amounts people might think they are. Meanwhile, the top guys at the Union are earning large sums. While negotiations were going on I remember walking out of Twickenham one morning and seeing Danny Grewcock's car parked next to that of a senior RFU man. One was a second-hand Ford Mondeo, the other was an Aston Martin Vantage with a personalised number-plate. Guess who drove which?

I was particularly annoyed by suggestions in some quarters that, with Matt and Lawrence, I had somehow forced the younger players into threats of a strike. This is something none of us would ever do and nothing could be further from the truth. The decision was taken by the squad, reluctantly, as a whole behind closed doors. I was very careful to tell the boys: 'This is your decision. Don't let anyone make your minds up for you.' As I have said, one player – I will not name him, but he is an older, senior guy – abstained. The rest voted to strike.

This accusation does not stack up, in any case. It is impossible to calculate the total figures involved if we had accepted the RFU's proposals over both win bonuses and image rights. But I would guess that, across the squad, you would be talking about an increase of £20,000 in our annual income at the most. I do not want to sound blasé about that sum of money but all three of us, and other senior players, could earn that very easily and very quickly by attending a few lunches and carrying out a speaking engagement or two. If we were acting in our own interests, surely we would have tried to influence the squad to agree to the RFU's proposals, sign the deal and then get on with making money outside the game?

As the week wore on we started to get some of these arguments across – I readily concede we had lost the early PR war – and the RFU negotiators called us back in. A compromise deal was eventually reached, in which we met each other halfway, and we climbed down from our threatened strike. Some of the press we had received had been pretty 'anti' us, particularly early in the week, and Clive had been worried that we would be booed as we ran out against the Pumas. It was not something which concerned the players: in our hearts we knew we had been in the right and if the supporters felt differently we would live with it. In the event, however, their response was terrific . . . as Jason Leonard led us out, marking his record 86th appearance as an England forward, we got a tremendous cheer, which may say something for what the average rugby fan thought about the dispute.

Unfortunately, the game did not live up to that. It had been a very wet week, as the whole winter seemed to be, and the pitch was sodden to a point I had never seen before – I would not have been surprised if we had been called off. Rain streamed down throughout and the combination of a mushy surface, a wet ball and a bad training week for England led to a high percentage of handling errors. Ben Cohen, whose father had recently died, was back in the side after missing the Australia game, and he scored under the posts. We were all delighted for Ben. He is a top man, very unassuming, and he had been through a hell of a time in the past week or so. Otherwise, it was a forgettable game and we were all glad to get off the field at full-time, having won 19–0.

*

THERE WAS less pressure on against South Africa. The main challenge had been the Wallabies but in beating them we had proved we could win twice in succession against Southern Hemisphere sides. It was still a huge game and we had a lot of respect for the Springboks but we knew them reasonably well.

They were in a transitional phase. Traditionally, South Africa have had big, very powerful forwards with a lot of their game built around the pack. This is still true to an extent, with the likes of André Venter, Corne Krige and Mark Andrews, whom I rate highly. He is the sort of bloke you would rather not play against. Like Eales for Australia and Ian Jones for the All Blacks, Andrews has been an almost ever-present for the Boks all through the '90s. He is a very good lock, athletic, tough, hard and uncompromising. He is actually two years younger than me but he seems to have been around forever and his baldness makes him look older too.

Now they were trying to play a more fluid game with a lot of handling and unloading in the tackle to keep the ball alive. They had more pace, with Breyton Paulse in particular looking slippery.

Even with this change of style, you always expect a physical game against the Springboks, and so it turned out, with Neil Back and Richard Hill both needing large number of stitches in head wounds. It was a game played at a fast and furious pace, with both sides throwing the ball around. At first, we were too impatient and almost expected to score, which is silly against a solid defence like theirs. When we tightened up and played more directly, we reaped the rewards, Will Greenwood breaching the gain line with a little sleight of hand and stepping the full back to score after 20 minutes or so. They pegged us back with a score by Van Straaten but we eventually took the game 25–17, with Jonny Wilkinson kicking 20 points.

It was a good result and I was pleased by our reaction. Afterwards, in the changing room, there was no triumphalism: we had won, we had played well without being brilliant, and had beaten a Southern Hemisphere team again. Before, it was always a big thing because everyone – press, fans and, to be honest, players – felt we were underdogs. I remember playing South Africa in 1995. The England team was itself then in a transitional phase – Brian Moore, Rob Andrew and Dewi Morris had all gone, Deano did not play – and we walked out at Twickenham to a very flat atmosphere. It was almost as if the crowd had no expectation of victory and, sure enough, we lost. Business as usual, seemed to be the feeling.

Twickenham ought to be an intimidating place for the opposition to play. Unfortunately, it has traditionally been the opposite – all polite applause, jolly well done, and may the best team win. That is all very nice, very English and very sporting but it does not help us. Over those three matches in 2000, however, the crowd got louder and louder and I got the feeling that they, too, had more belief in us than before.

After the match we headed to a hotel in town and went out for a beer as a squad. Adedayo Adebayo was having his 30th birthday party at some trendy bar or other and I ended up sitting cross-legged on a cushion-strewn floor in a darkened room chatting to Martin Corry. It was a strange but enjoyable end to our Autumn fixture list.

Banned!

BACK AT Leicester, we were to face Saracens at home in the quarter-final of the Tetley's Bitter Cup. It was good to be back at the club and nice to have a big game like this to look forward to. The lads had done well to win those three games in the absence of the international players and there was a good buzz about the place.

We started off playing quick and wide, stretching them right across the pitch and playing some very entertaining rugby. You knew almost from the off that it was going to be a high-scoring affair, even though the first half saw no tries, Stimmo and Duncan McRae exchanging penalties to make it 12–3 at the break. In the second half, we gained the ascendancy immediately with a try after two minutes by Adam Balding. Luger replied quickly but a sensational score, with the ball passing very quickly through the hands of Pat Howard, Andy Goode and Tim Stimpson, switching the play from right to left in a matter of seconds, saw Westy dive over. Healey and Back also scored and more Stimpson kicking saw us rack up 41 points to their 24 in what had been perhaps our best performance of the season thus far. To put 40 points on a side like Saracens was impressive; it undid some of the damage from our earlier league loss and I felt the manner of the victory would give us an edge in the championship match which was to come.

One downside was that Sarries had scored three tries of their own in the second half, opening our defence up worryingly easily with Kyran Bracken making darting little runs and putting people through in the midfield. If you are attacking with at the pace with which we were you can end up leaking but we hate to concede and we would spend more time on the following Monday and Tuesday looking at where we had gone wrong defensively than patting ourselves on the back for playing well.

The other negative involved myself and Duncan McRae. As our games often are, it had been a little sparky. Graham Rowntree and Danny Grewcock had scuffled and had both been sin-binned. There had been plenty of aggression and niggle all through the game, some of it involving me, but there was nothing excessive. At one point, I clashed with the fly-half Duncan McRae. In another incident, I punched Julian White – but only because he was stamping on one of our players. He would have done the same to me.

I thought nothing more of either episode until after the game, when rumours started flying around that action was going to be taken. On Monday, official word came. I was cited for two things: use of the knee on Duncan McRae and the punch on Julian White.

The McRae incident was one of those things. Knee contact is quite dangerous and players can be seriously hurt but in a physical game like rugby this sort of thing happens. You get into trouble if you start talking about hurting people but the fact is if you tackle someone hard it hurts them and they do not want to come back and get tackled quite so hard again. It is part of the game.

'Use of the knee' is a very emotive phrase but this was not the worst of cases: I did not 'knee drop' McRae, putting my whole weight on him as he was on the ground. The contact was made in the air. My rucking style involves going in with head and knee first and, unfortunately, he had sustained a broken rib. If I had hit him with my head would it have been a head butt? No. If he had not been hurt I am sure that would have been the end of it but the fact that he was out for a few weeks probably tipped Sarries' hand.

Having decided to cite me, they obviously decided to lob the kitchen sink in my direction and had me for punching White too. That was pathetic, I felt, and would have been an embarrassment to Julian.

We spent the next week preparing our case for the hearing. I wanted it to come round quickly. You hate these things hanging over you and, more importantly, Leicester would be denied my services if I was found guilty and banned. Given how long these things sometimes take – and that it had happened on December 9 – that could also take me dangerously close to the Six Nations. Looking at the video, I felt the McRae aspect could go either way. It was not a particularly nasty incident but he had been injured. The White element, I felt, would probably go away.

It is not ideal to have these things hanging over you but we had a Championship to win. That Saturday, we would face Bath at home. The following weekend we travelled to Rotherham and then, just three days later and on Boxing Day, we had Bath again – this time away. An interesting quirk of the fixture list and one we could have done without. No-one likes travelling at Christmas and Bath is a long way to go. Added to which, we were guaranteed a hard game. There is that little bit of history to our fixtures with the West Country side. For most of the last 15 to 20 years, one or other of the clubs has been No1, with the other not far behind – between us, we have won every league title but three. At that point, they had six league titles to our four, they had also won the European Cup and had dominated the domestic cup throughout the middle 1980s and middle 1990s. They were ahead on points. Our fans love the big games against the likes of Northampton and Saracens but Bath at Welford Road is still the most important game of the season for them: there is often quite a bit of animosity in our crowd towards them, which you do not usually see in a rugby crowd, even though most of the players they loved to hate – Barnes, Guscott, Callard, Hall – have finished playing.

The home fixture was a bruising encounter, with Freddie, Olly Smith and Martin Corry absent. A rare Darren Garforth try, provided when Austin Healey got away from the side of a ruck and handed him the ball, opened our scoring after six minutes and after a brief period where Bath were in front Pat Howard went over in the corner. Healey was sin-binned for dragging a Bath player back off the ball and Gareth Cooper – probably a little over half my size – tried to whack me. Tim Stimpson kicked a stack of penalties to give us an eventual victory 27–19 but it was not much of a spectacle on a very cold day.

This did not bother me too much. When you get to December, it is just about winning the games. We had been playing rugby for four months and there was still another five to go. You are training and playing on grey, miserable days in the sleet and the mud, it is heavy on the legs and tough on the spirit. This is the time when champion teams dig in. If you do win your games at this time of the year it sets you up because others sides can tend to fall away.

Bath often fall victim to this: they will start and finish the season well but can tend to have a down patch in the middle. I was hoping this would hold true for our visit to the Recreation Ground on Boxing Day.

Around this time I learned that my citing hearing would take place on December 28. Quite why it takes 19 days to arrange something like this is a mystery to me. I also think the system is flawed in that it is left to the 'victim's' club to decide whether or not to cite. All sorts of factors influence this sort of decision. For instance, if the guilty player is a real star of a side who will be playing your championship rivals the following week, you may decide not to cite because you want him playing against those rivals and, hopefully, helping to defeat them. The only fair way would be to have citing left to the referee and touch judges, or maybe even to a third official. At least there would be consistency.

The Rotherham game saw us take an unusually high-risk strategy. With the Yorkshire side struggling to establish themselves, and Bath away the following Tuesday, Dean introduced eleven new players and made thirteen positional changes. It was a bold plan; we had had a very tough game with them at home and the coaches were nervous about how the match would unfold. Unusually for an away game we travelled up on the day but, Rotherham is not too far up the M1 and it gave the boys an extra night in their own beds. The ground has a real junior club feel to it, and I think they were fairly proud of the way they had come all the way up from local Yorkshire leagues to the Premier Division. Fair play to them, as well: they had done very well.

One of those making his Tigers debut was Steve Booth, a young winger who had converted from rugby league and who would also take on the kicking duties. He played a blinder, scoring 17 points including a try created by Austin and Winston Stanley. Oz threw a long pass to Winston inside our 22 and he raced through the Rotherham defence, putting Booth in for the score. Earlier, Ollie Smith had also scored and a Cocker try had been disallowed for reasons that I could not understand, so we were well on top. I sealed things myself with my first try of the season, coming from one of my trademark jinking runs from deep . . . if you can describe three metres as deep.

The game ended with a hell of a punch-up in the near-dark – their floodlights were really weak – when I tackled one of their players. A few of their pack decided to run up and down the backs of my legs. By the time I got to my feet it was like a scene from a wild west movie, with haymakers being thrown all over the place but in the gloom the officials could not really see who was doing what to whom so the referee, Ed Morrison, grabbed both captains, gave us a quick telling off and then blew his whistle to end the game as quickly as possible to stop anything else happening.

It was a good win, with guys like Glenn Gelderbloom and Louis Deacon playing really well, though we had failed to get the four-try bonus point. Austin had a penalty kick which I wanted him to put into the corner so we could attempt to drive over but he put in behind the try line for a 22 drop out so the chance had gone.

Despite that, I was happy with the result; a young and largely inexperienced side had won 9–27, a good scoreline in anyone's book, and we could look forward to Christmas Day. Well, sort of. In the old, amateur days we tended to play Barbarians fixtures on the 27th of December and a few clubs had traditional fixtures on Boxing Day, more social games than anything. Professional league rugby is a different story. Boxing Day games are now every bit as important as any other – our trip to Bath was a game that could well decide the league – and guys have to be alert and ready. That obviously takes away from the family Christmas slightly and you cannot really enjoy the day because your mind is always on tomorrow. Home games are not so bad. Obviously, you do not have to be at the ground until 1pm and you can head straight back to the fireside and the TV after playing. Away to Bath, you know you are not going to get home until late.

For away games, our camp is always split between guys who like to travel down the night before – I am one of those – and those, like Austin Healey, who would rather go on the morning. Normally, the club would insist that we all went down the night before but for Boxing Day games, with players reluctant to leave their families on Christmas night, we travel down in the morning. Bath in a coach in a fair old way. We met up at the Hilton Hotel on the M1/M69 junction at Leicester, had a bit of breakfast and were on our way.

It was a good time to go to the Rec. Right next to the river, it has a high water table and, with the winter's rain, the pitch can be a little soft in December. Bath tend to rely on their pace these days and softer ground would negate their quicker men a little. It would do the same to the pacey players we would field, too, but we felt that, mentally, it would affect them more.

It is ironic that, in recent years, Leicester has been known for its forwards. When I was a youngster watching matches at Welford Road, Bath's name was built on a very tough forward pack. They tended to dominate the Tigers up front with guys like Gareth Chilcott, Graham Dawe, Ollie Redman, John Hall and Andy Robinson. Meanwhile, Leicester were chucking it around all over the place through Clive Woodward, Paul Dodge, Rory Underwood, Les Cusworth, Dusty Hare and so on.

These things go in cycles. By the time those guys retired from the Tigers, Bath had Guscott and de Glanville in their centre and they were now running the ball more; I remember one game where that pair had more international caps than our centres had club appearances. Ever likely, in those circumstances, that we decided to keep it tight.

As we arrived at the Rec that morning, we were trying to use the Rotherham game, when the younger guys had stood up to be counted, and the disruption to our Christmas as motivation.

Everyone needed to pull together and get a win. We needed to guard against that tired, switched-off festive feeling. But those are just words and, in the first half, we put no substance behind them. It was all Bath as we committed what felt like dozens of errors. Iain Balshaw had put them ahead with the only try of the half after a quick penalty and Matt Perry was kicking well. All we could manage in reply were two penalties and we went in 16–6 down. To be 10 points down in a close game on a wet pitch is less than ideal and our team-talk in the changing rooms was all about getting the basics right. If we retained possession, recycled well and kept our defence tight, maybe things would look up. And they did. We drove the ball at them better, retained it well, and played some nice inside passes. Backy scored very early on, which got us right back into the game and Goodey hit a monster drop-goal from 50 metres out to give us the lead, 10 minutes before the end. Then it was a case of holding out as they threw everything at us. We defended well but did give away a couple of penalties, both of which they missed, and eventually ran out 16–17 winners. It was a game we could easily have lost and to win, nil-ing Bath in the second half, was an outstanding achievement.

We had gone through the autumn period unbeaten, had just won three games in 10 days and had done the double over Bath. That was a massive boost to us and, for the first time, I started to think in terms of retaining our title.

*

TWO DAYS later, though, there was some bad news when I travelled to Twickenham for the McRae/White hearing. Our case was fairly simple: mine had not been isolated incidents. It had been a niggly game, with Sarries giving as good as they had got, and we produced video evidence to back that up. It cut little ice with the three-man panel. After a very long deliberation, they banned me for 35 days. I had been prepared for a three-week ban and I was surprised by the severity of the ruling. The press, who had been taking a keen interest in the case, noticed that the ban conveniently ended on the Friday before England played Wales in our first Six Nations encounter and there was some suggestion that the RFU had engineered it that way. Who knows? If that game had been four weeks away would they have banned me for 28 days? Would they ban me for the England Wales game, the start of the Six Nations at Cardiff? Impossible to tell with these things, believe me.

The club appealed, looking to have the ban reduced to three weeks. Once an appeal is lodged, you can continue to play until the new hearing.

However, if the ban stood, or was increased, I would definitely be out for at least the Wales game. To avoid this, Leicester agreed to suspend me internally until the outcome.

The hearing, at Coventry's Trusthouse Forte Hotel, failed to produce anything, apart from some amusing press stories. I had parked at the back of the hotel and wandered in through a convenient rear door. In the lobby were a lot of the national newspaper rugby writers and a couple of TV cameramen. They were all poised for me to walk in through the front door and had totally failed to spot me standing behind them. Eventually, they realised I was inside and their stories the next day were full of phrases like 'Johnson avoided the cameras by sneaking in the back door.' I had to laugh. You don't 'sneak' anywhere when you are 6ft 7in and 19st. I just used the back door because that was the nearest one to where I was parked.

I do find the press, and TV news people in particular, amusing at times. Afterwards, I did a few brief interviews and then walked out, again through the back door, to find my car. One of the cameramen, all packed up and wandering to his own vehicle, suddenly saw me, got his camera up and started filming. He was obviously looking for the quick getaway shot – Johnson jumping into his car and roaring straight off. I was tempted to get into the boot and change a wheel . . . anything to avoid being filmed racing away. It felt a little surreal: Martin Johnson, not exactly a household name, standing in a half-empty Coventry car park, on a cold, wet evening, being filmed by someone he has never met. I would like to have been able to think of something amusing to say but the old brain let me down. In the end, I folded my jacket on the back seat, got in slowly and drove away like I was chauffeuring the Queen Mum.

Sale, at home the following Saturday, was postponed because of snow. That was good, although we would be expected to beat the Sharks. It gave the guys a little time off after the Bath game, which had, of course, been a midweeker. My ban really hit home that morning, though. I woke up feeling miserable, angry and under the weather so I stayed in bed all day, sulking. Everyone was telling me it would be nice to have five weeks off.

'It will do you good in the long run,' they would say. 'Give you time to recover from the season so far.' Frankly, it was all 'blah'. All I could think was that we had a Tetley's Bitter Cup semi-final against Quins and three big European games, including, if we qualified, a quarter-final. I was going to miss all of these. I felt I was letting the club and the boys down.

On the Sidelines

THE DOMESTIC semi-final, at The Stoop, was first up the following Saturday. For us, it was almost like just another big game in a big season – though an 11th Cup final would have been fantastic. For Harlequins, who were not playing well in the league, it was a different story. I got the feeling that beating us and getting to Twickenham would make a horrible season seem a lot brighter for them. And they were very committed and up for the match.

We tried to play too much rugby early on and their defence was very quick to come up and hit us hard. Our kicking was poor, we did not look for field position and I suspect playing well and winning had made us over-confident. Wood scored in the first 10 minutes and, although we hit back with tries from Goode and Murphy, they finished the half stronger with a score by Will Greenwood. After we had let Will go the previous season I am sure he was itching to prove something to Deano and he did play really well. From the late 1990s on, Will had become an international-class player at inside centre but he had struggled with injuries. After Pat Howard joined the club, we never really saw the best of Will, week-in, week-out. He did not do himself justice with the Tigers and I was pleased for him that his move had worked out so well. He had outplayed Pat on the day, for sure, taking the ball up very hard and working very hard in defence. In the second half they kept possession very well and we hardly got out of our half and a try for their ex-Wallaby openside David Wilson gave them the cushion they needed to see us off.

I had to watch from the sidelines, which I always find very frustrating. You can have no effect on the game – and it is much easier to play from the stands. You think 'We need to do this, we need to do that' . . . actually doing it in a tough game is another matter. One thing which was clear, though, was that our set piece had been poor. Corry had played in the second row, alongside Ben Kay, and that had affected our line-out options. From then on in, we played Louis Deacon alongside Kay and used Cozza in the back-row and things improved.

The players were pretty down in the changing rooms afterwards. To concede three tries was disappointing for them and they were gutted to have lost a semi-final and played so poorly. That big quarter-final win over Saracens, the tough battle with Gloucester . . . suddenly they felt it was all for nothing. There was nothing I could really say. When you lose a game everyone expects you to win, the losing is tough to take.

I take it particularly badly. We were stuffed by London Irish in the Cup the year before. Again, I had been injured and, again, it was the end of a hard week, with wins over Saracens and Wasps in the previous seven days. After the match I signed a few autographs and then walked across the pitch to go and see the guys. Some gloating Irishman, mobile phone jammed to his ear, ran about 20 yards over, grinning all over his face and shouting 'Hard luck, big fella!' I said, 'Mate, I didn't play and it was nothing to do with luck, you idiot.' He wrote a letter to the club complaining about my bad sportsmanship. Maybe I was overly grumpy. But I hate losing. Don't approach me and expect a laugh and a joke.

As we sat in the Stoop changing room after the Quins defeat, listening to their supporters going mad outside, the only consolation was the fact that Harlequins would have swapped places with us in the blink of an eye. OK, they were at Twickenham. But we still topped the league and we were in Europe.

There was even a bright side to the loss. For one thing, games like that stiffen the resolve. The following week, we had a tough game away at Pau. If we lost there, we could struggle to qualify for Europe. Then the season really would have taken a downward turn. Being beaten by Quins had been a reality check. It also meant one less game to play. Maybe it would keep us stronger for the rest of the season.

We flew over to France on the Friday before the game and I went to the stadium in the late afternoon to do a fitness session with a young guy called Mike Holford. We were taking him over to experience a European weekend playing away. It was early January but there was a spring-like feel to the air down there in the South of France. The pitch was in good shape but the grass was littered with tiny pebbles. They made the ground firmer but would clearly be abrasive in the tackle. It was something I had not seen before.

We were 1–1 with Pau and they had recently beaten Stade Français. We were anticipating a really tough game but we needed to win if we were to get a home draw in the quarter-finals. A lot of the British press were regurgitating all those old theories about Leicester not winning well in France and dragging up our loss the last time we had played Pau, so we felt the pressure on to prove them wrong.

Once again, on match day, I was forced to sit on the bench. We were expecting the usual Pau greeting – a very hostile and aggressive attitude from their fans, objects being thrown, bands playing – but they were having a poor season by their standards and the atmosphere was much more low key. I got the feeling that the supporters did not expect their team to win and their resignation helped us. From having been lovely earlier, the weather had turned dull and slightly wet and the whole afternoon lacked bite and anticipation. We were on top from the start. Early on, we knocked a penalty into the corner to go for the line-out. Ever the master tactician, I immediately turned to Dean and Wellsy and said 'I'd have kicked that at goal.' A few seconds later, we drove over to score and I decided to shut up.

Goodey dropped a couple of goals which kept us ticking over: if you are dominating possession and territory you must keep the board ticking over or else you feel you have missed your opportunity and the opposition starts feeling better about the game. You want to keep building that scoreline to the point where they are going to find it very hard to come back. We ended up winning 3–20, a great win away from home in Europe. Pau would expect to do better than three points so we were well-satisfied.

It was a crucial game as far as the season went: suddenly, a quarter-final home draw looked likely. Our fans are worth a few points at Welford Road and they give us great support away, too. A lot of Leicester fans had travelled to Pau, which was great to see two weeks after Christmas, with all that expense. That night, the team went out for a few celebratory beers to the Black Bear, a bar which had been owned by Robert Paparemborde. As the evening wore on, it filled up with Tigers supporters and turned into one of those great nights out that you will cherish and remember. It is good for the players to mix with the fans though it is more enjoyable if the fans do not want to talk rugby. Usually, the guys are out to enjoy themselves and forget about work. If you want to chat to a player, far better to talk about something completely different. I understand where the supporters are coming from, though. I often go down to watch Leicester City. Sometimes I'll see someone like Steve Walsh afterwards and find myself asking him a question about the game . . . why did so-and-so do such-and-such? I have to stop myself doing it.

Our final European Cup qualifier, the following Saturday, was at home to Glasgow Caledonians. We had beaten them well away and we just needed to get the return won. But at that time of the year, there were some injuries and tired legs about and we had a changed team out. It was a little bit nervy and they started well, camping in our 22 for the first 10 minutes and scoring under the posts. With the conversion and the try, they were soon 3–10 up and I was getting decidedly anxious as I watched. We were over-confident and we were making mistakes and losing concentration. The last thing we needed was to lose this game after winning in Pau. But gradually we fought our way back into it and ended the half 21–16 ahead. In the second half we pulled away a little and the guys ended up doing the job that was needed, winning 41–26.

I was pleased. It did not matter that we had not been all that inspired. A win and no injuries is all I had wanted. We had our home quarter-final, against Swansea. That was going to be a big match. We had had a bad time in Europe the year before, with the media giving us a hard time, and to lose the following week, at home, would have been a disaster. We just had to win.

Of all the games I missed through the ban, this was the worst. I had never played against Swansea and now I may never do so. This was only the third European quarter-final we had played in . . . I had appeared in the last two and did not want to miss out on this one. I felt really sick about being out: it was a huge occasion, with the ground buzzing when I arrived, and I got all the nerves and adrenalin as though I was playing. But instead of getting ready with the boys I had to do the rounds of the corporate boxes and talk to the sponsors. That is fine, but I did not want to be there on a game day.

Faced with the agony of watching, after I had done my corporate duty I got in my car and went down to the nearby David Lloyd's gym to do a session on the rowing machine. I needed to get rid of a bit of adrenalin. Of course, as I walked into the gym the match was on the TV and I could not avoid seeing the score. We had had a good start and were already points up, which relaxed me a little. It was hard to avoid watching it but I found the rower furthest away from the TVs to avoid finding myself having a quick check every few minutes.

Just after half-time, it was clear we were going to win so I finished my session, showered and drove back to the ground to catch the last five minutes. I think Swansea scored a try right at the death but the final score, 41–10, was outstanding. I had expected a tough quarter-final but the boys had killed it off early on against a side containing some good players – a lot of Welsh internationals, like Darren Morris, Scott Gibbs, Colin Charvis, Arwel Thomas and Mark Taylor.

We had played very well and everyone was back on a high with the Harlequins loss out of our system. We had a big night out in Leicester, safe in the knowledge that our European business was taken care of until April.

I had missed playing but there had been a silver lining to the cloud for the club: Louis Deacon had come in in my absence and had played really well in the three games so far, suddenly going from being a good young prospect to a guy who had played a European Cup quarter-final, who had played away against Pau in Europe, and someone who we knew we could rely on in big games. No matter how low I felt, I was delighted for Deacs and pleased, too, for Leicester.

Grand Slam Hunting

ANOTHER SPLIT in the season now, with the international players leaving for Six Nations duty. This time, though, the guys we left behind would be able to relax, since club matches are suspended during the competition.

Once again, we were firm favourites for the Grand Slam. This is not always a good thing. The Celtic nations in particular react well to being told they are underdogs. Look at how Scotland beat Ireland in the re-arranged fixture in September 2001. Everyone was tipping Keith Wood's side to win but they were well-beaten. Or look at Scotland vs England in 2000.

On the other hand, we could hardly have expected anything else. We had won four out of the five fixtures the season before and had come off a summer and autumn in which we had beaten Australia and South Africa. All the critics were raving about this 'confident', 'expansive' new England with the ability to put a lot of pace and width on the ball.

I felt our first game, at the Millennium Stadium, would tell us a lot.

It was, of course, my first game back since the completion of my ban following the McRae incident, the 35 days having flown by. I had not been sure of selection – England have a lot of quality in the second row, with guys like Archer, Shaw and Borthwick to choose from alongside Grewcock – but I was glad to get the call from Clive and to join the boys at Pennyhill Park on the Monday for three days of training. I shot home on Wednesday night to spend Thursday at home with my wife, Kay, pottering around the house the next day and relaxing. It was a nice mental break from rugby. In the team hotel you cannot get away from it, even if you do not talk about the game. About 6pm on the Thursday I set off to drive down to Cardiff. Pulling on to the M42 I hit a lot of traffic so I phoned Dorian West, who I knew was heading down at around the same time, to let him know of the hold-up.

'Where are you, Nobby?' I asked. 'About 10 yards away from you, Chief', he said.

I turned and there he was, grinning at me from his car. We drove down in convoy to our Cardiff base, the dockside St David's Hotel, decorated in an interesting, minimalist style. The following day, we headed for training at a sports centre in town – we had been refused permission to train on the pitch, which has a reputation for cutting up badly – before heading back to the Millennium Stadium for a nose. It was the first Wales vs England game at the new ground and a few journalists seized on this, suggesting it would intimidate us. In fact, we were all looking forward to it. Playing in truly great stadiums is inspiring to players. Although it is huge it is also very personal, with the crowd almost on top of the sides. Also, unlike most other international venues, it is right in the centre of town so as you drive through in the team bus you really get a flavour of the match-day atmosphere.

As we arrived, eight life-size inflatable Martin Johnsons, England kit on, ball in hand, were strapped to car park railings opposite the ground. These 'Rubber Johnnos' had been produced by Tetley's Bitter as a promotional gimmick, and they had deposited 150 of them around Cardiff in the small hours that morning as a PR stunt. It certainly worked – both *The Times* and

The Independent carried a photo of the inflatables on their front pages!

Then we were inside the stadium. From ground level it is even more impressive than from in the stands – I had watched the 1999 World Cup final there. Kicking coach Dave Alred also handles some of our mental preparation work and he told us to go off individually and visualise what it was going to be like playing there with a full crowd. Nobby and I went off and kicked the ball around for a bit. Visualisation is a good thing but I did not want to start focusing too much on the game at that point. It starts me buzzing and rushing with adrenalin and I can go a bit yampy, wanting to get stuck into the opposition there and then. It was only Friday lunchtime and I wanted to relax.

I knew I would be fine for the game, even though I had not played since Boxing Day. I was apprehensive – a five-week break before an international is not ideal – but I had felt good in training.

Before leaving, we went inside. Life-size cut-outs of the Welsh team had been placed in our changing room, which the management leapt on.

'Look at this, look at this.' they were going. 'They're trying to intimidate us!'

We were just laughing – they were obviously there to enhance stadium tours. The first three we saw were Rupert Moon, Peter Rogers and Graham Henry . . . not a Welshman to be seen.

Saturday morning I was up around ten o'clock. Some of the guys can hardly close their eyes the night before but I am a sleeper. I like to be up five hours before the game to get rid of the sleepiness and also to get a couple of meals inside me to help with energy levels. For breakfast I had my usual – Weetabix, some fruit, a yoghurt, and a plate of scrambled egg for protein. I do not touch sausage or bacon. I like greasy food – fish and chips, Chinese food, an English breakfast – as much as the next man but it sits heavily on your stomach for some time. I love a rare steak but I would never eat it within three days of a match.

After breakfast, we killed a bit of time, walking down to a primary school near the hotel to do a few lineout spotters. On our return, at about 11.30am, I forced myself to eat again – this time a little grilled chicken with no skin, for protein, some pasta and a jacket potato. I also took a carbohydrate drink.. It was not easy and it never is; I get a lot of nerves before a game and sometimes throw up. Occasionally, this can even happen on the pitch. Usually it is just a bit of excess fluid coming back up. My nausea is as nothing compared to Richard Cockerill's, however. Cocker has always been a theatrical pre-match puker, with retching sounds echoing out of the toilets, and Jenks, in the 1997 Lions series, was also sick before the games.

Two hours before kick-off and we headed to the ground. There were Welsh fans everywhere, unsurprisingly, and a few of them had already been getting stuck into the beers. We had a few gestures and the odd shout but we all felt good. Woody had said to us: 'There has been a lot of chat from the Welsh about how intimidating the stadium will be, and how loud the singing will be, and so on. If they think that's going to win them the game then they have already lost.' Which I thought was spot-on.

We did not feel their fitness or defensive organisation were up to scratch and the game plan was to attack them with pace right from the off. To that end, Clive Woodward had selected Iain Balshaw at full-back in place of Matt Perry. I felt very sorry for Matt. At 23 or 24, he was already England's most-capped full-back and he had never let us down. He is heroic in defence and solid in attack, and is quick with a great kicking game. But Balsh is quicker still and, to an extent, there is nothing you can do against pace like his. You can organise defences to give yourself the best chance of stopping him but he can capitalise on mistakes in ways slower players cannot. This meant he was seen as being a more dangerous runner from deep and in broken play and that was the way Clive wanted us to play. Typically, Matt took his dropping on the chin and maintained a good attitude.

At game time, the stadium was all I had thought it would be. Walking out onto that pitch was one of the great experiences of my rugby career. The place is massive and there were red shirts everywhere, with pockets of English support drowned out by the Welsh singing. The anthems raised hairs on the back of my neck. As they sang *Land of our Fathers*, Dorian West turned to me and said 'I wish this was our anthem.' I had to suppress a grin – he is from Wrexham.

It must have fired up the Welsh boys because they started well, winning the kick off and putting pressure on us, but after five minutes we had taken control, hitting a purple patch and never really looking like losing. Matt Dawson and Will Greenwood each scored twice in the first half, Will executing a noncey little hop of joy, for which he has paid heavily ever since, as he scored his first, and we ended 8–29 ahead.

The only downside to the first half was a mistake by me which led to a Rob Howley score. We won a lineout just outside our 22 and took it up the middle. A ruck formed and I got my line wrong, allowing Colin Charvis to nick the ball. Rob got his hands on it and raced away from 30 or 40 metres out to score a good try.

That score gave them hope but we killed that off right at the start of the second half with Will passing to Austin Healey and then looping round him to receive the ball back as Austin was tackled, allowing Will to run in for his second try.

After that the game was all but over. We could sense the Welsh players knew there was no way back and the crowd was silenced too. Early on, the fans were very emotional. There was great singing and lots of anticipation and that rose as they started well...you could sense the supporters thinking 'We're in with a chance here.' Then we hit them with quick tries – bang, bang, bang – and it was like letting a balloon down.

I feel sorry for the Welsh. They are great lovers of rugby and I respect them immensely for that. But as a nation I do not think they have ever quite got over the 1970s, when they were a superb team with genius players like JPR Williams and Gareth Edwards. They demand that class of their team, and those thrilling performances, and at the moment they are not there. The players suffer with this expectation. You talk to some of them and they feel terribly pressured because they all live almost on top of each other and they just cannot get away from rugby. The main clubs – Swansea, Cardiff, Llanelli, Neath, Newport, Bridgend . . . they are all very close and every other person on the street is a rugby nut. Lose to England and you do not want to walk out of your house. Wales still have world class players like Rob Howley, Neil Jenkins and Scott Quinnell but the depth is perhaps not there, either in the national side or in their club game. It is a vicious circle because they do not get the competition to help them become a great side. I remember Scott Gibbs saying that even playing some of the weaker English sides was better than playing the Welsh clubs.

The only downside for us had been an injury to poor old Dan Luger. He would not play again until just before the Lions tour.

Leaving the stadium in our coach, we got a taste of the passion of the Welsh fans. One or two of the English boys had had death threats the year before after saying things in various newspaper articles and we were left in no doubt that the traditional enmity some of them feel for us was alive and well. It was about 7.30pm and they had been in the pubs for a few hours after the game. Everyone was on the streets, boozing. At one stage our bus's wing-mirror clipped a Welsh fan who wandered off the pavement and he went down, out cold. We had to wait for the police and ambulance to arrive and were there, marooned in a sea of red, for ten or fifteen minutes. The fans were challenging us to get off the coach and fight them. I was not exactly nervous but I remember thinking to myself 'If this gets any uglier it could be quite bad.' If someone had thrown a pint glass at a window there could have been another 10 following it and things might have become quite interesting. As it was we were eventually on our way again without too much trouble and arrived at the post-match dinner to meet up with the Welsh boys. They are normally a quiet bunch anyway and naturally enough they were even more sombre than usual. I chatted with Rob Howley for a while, talking through the tactics we had used in the game. He was a bit down and was clearly desperate for things to pick up for his side.

*

AFTER THE highs of the Millennium Stadium it was a more down to earth affair on the following Tuesday evening, when Leicester faced Bristol at a wet, windy, Welford Road in the Premiership. The game had been rearranged from its scheduled spot, when we had been unavailable because we were in the Tetley's Bitter Cup semi-final. Leicester were very clever in slotting in these games in February, rather than taking the easy option and leaving them till later. That way we got them out of the way and avoided a fixture pile-up.

We rested a few guys who had played in the Test but still put out a good side. We knew Bristol would really want to beat us to complete a double over us and, with the wind with them in the first half, they scored a try early on after a defensive mix-up between Freddie and Tim. It was a poor display by a much-changed side from the one which had beaten Swansea. I remember warming up and some of the crowd were shouting 'Come on Johnno, sort them out' – though one player is seldom the difference – which indicates how off the pace we were.

In the second half, we managed to score quickly to get ourselves back into the game and then went ahead. I actually came on with about 20 minutes to go. I always find it very difficult to come off the bench because the pace of the game is hard to judge and however warmed-up you are it is always hard to make an impact. I am not used to it and it definitely is an art.

Going into the final minutes, with the scoreline at 17–10 in our favour, it was very tense. A converted score would give them the draw and they are a tough side to keep out, with a big, abrasive pack. I was delighted when the whistle went. No bonus points, and no-one would have gone home saying 'My God, what a great game of rugby', but we had got a tricky midweek game out of the way with a win.

Next up was London Irish. Like Bristol and Sale, this was the sort of game we needed to win if we were to retain our title. You might not have to beat Saracens, Bath or Wasps away to win the league but you do need to beat the teams in the bottom half of the table because your rivals probably will. Irish had played fewer games than us and were unbeaten at home. They had also had a lot of time to prepare for this game. By contrast, coming off a midweek game, we had had scant preparation. By February, when the ground is heavy, you really feel it when you are playing two or three games in a week, believe me. The training had been light but, despite that, the Bristol game was still in our legs.

Normally, the adrenalin will kick in in the changing room and will bring you up for the challenge. This time, that was not happening. The atmosphere was low and quiet and the guys looked tired, just sitting round until warm-up. As I ran onto the field, I felt that fatigue in my legs and I knew other guys were in the same boat. This was confirmed by the flatness of our warm-up. Somehow we needed to get the team fired. It is then that senior players can really earn their money and Garf was the man this time: he butted into the side of our huddle, screaming that we were not ready and that we needed to raise ourselves. He rarely says much so when he does it has an impact. He is a very highly respected and valued member of the side and will be irreplaceable when he finally hangs up his boots; after all, there are not many zoos who will let their prize silverbacks out on a Saturday afternoon these days. I joined him and gradually the guys started to look a little more lively. And we actually went out and played very well, creating a lot of chances in a fast and furious game.

Ezulike managed to beat Geordan on the outside early on but that was the only time they really stretched us and we ran out 9–28 winners. Stu Dickinson, the Australian referee, was in charge and afterwards he spoke to Pat Howard, telling him he thought it was as fast as a Super 12 game. I knew what he meant; I had played in slower Test matches.

A good win, then, and the sort of result, in the dark, dog days of February, that helps win leagues. In our three Championship seasons, we have lost just two games post-Christmas – one away at Bath and the other later this season, when we put a second team out at Gloucester. Teams with the ability to raise themselves, who can play in the mud and the wet and the wind, who can grind out wins with guys away on international duty – they are the teams who will prevail. A great Welsh mate of mine called Dai Griffiths came out to Reading from London for the game and afterwards we went into town to the Jongleurs comedy club in Camden with Kay and some friends for a nice evening out, basking in the glow of three good wins in a week.

Records Tumble

AFTER A week of domestic dog, it was back into the Six Nations. Italy were making their first trip to Twickenham since joining the competition. We were expected to win that game, and win it well, and at pre-match media day a lot of the journalists questioned how we got ourselves up for a game like that. My response was that I was always motivated in an England shirt. More to the point, we had to give Italy some respect. They were in the tournament by right. In some aspects of their game, the Italians are as good as any other team in the tournament. They are physically strong, for instance, and are also very committed and passionate. They work hard in the scrum and they hit you harder than some other sides in the tackle. I was a spectator in Rome in 2000 and the guys told me afterwards that at half-time they did not feel they were ahead because they had taken such a hammering. They also have some excellent individual players, such as Dominguez and Stoica, who would get into most sides, and the excellent young openside Mauro Bergamasco, a player Leicester had tried to sign earlier that season. We might well put 50 points on them but we would have to work hard to do so. It is a cliché, but you do not get any easy games at this level. We could not just turn up and thrash them.

That said, I was surprised and disappointed that we conceded two tries to Denis Dallan and Carlo Checchinato in the first half, actually finding ourselves 0–7 down after three minutes and then 17–20 down after 27. They played well in the first half, with Scanavacca kicking well and their pack proving every bit as physical as we had thought they would. In the second half, though, we pulled away, scoring seven tries and running out 80–23 winners. It was our highest score in the championship, the biggest-ever winning margin and saw a record haul of 35 points for Jonny Wilkinson, beating Ronan O'Gara's previous best of 30. Jason Robinson had made his England debut, coming on in the second half when things had opened up. You almost felt sorry for the Italians. It did not seem fair somehow. He was immediately electric and was on the outside of several tries but because their defence had tired he was not needed and on each occasion the man inside him finished the score but he could easily have gone over three or four times against another side on another day.

I like the fact that Italy are in the Six Nations. I think their future is bright, they are a credit to themselves – they scored more points against us than any other side would in the season – and they also have trendy blue Kappa shirts which you can swap with them. For a small union with limited resources, they have uncovered a lot of naturally talented players, many of whom could play comfortably for England given the right training and back-up. They have formed a Super 12 league with all-professional clubs which should help them keep more of their players at home where the national coaches can work on them more.

How good are they? Would the Leicester side of 2000/01 beat them, for instance? It is an interesting question and I am not sure of the answer. I like to think we would have a good chance. I hope the Tigers would not be beaten by 80 points by England so perhaps there is the answer: Italy are currently somewhere around the standard of a good Premiership side, which is not bad at all.

Back in the Premiership, Saracens were our next club opponents. They would have been looking to do the double on us, having beaten us at Watford at the start of the season, and they started well, getting a couple of tries in the first half. But playing them seems to bring out the best in us at Welford Road and the second half was pretty much one-way traffic. The best try was scored by Geordan Murphy. Andy Goode put through a kick and Geordan ran onto it, catching it as it bobbled up. He was one-on-one with their full-back and he just tapped it round him and ran on to score. The ball always seems to bounce for Geordie but basically he has unbelievable ball skills. When we had beaten them in the Cup they were still there fighting for the game right to the end. This time, a few of their heads dropped – they were not the Saracens we had known in the past. The competitiveness and that abrasive edge had gone and they had lost a little of their fighting spirit somewhere.

It all seemed to be going horribly wrong for them and it would get worse, as they were about to lose a lot of good players at the season's end, guys like Danny Grewcock, Paul Wallace, Tony Diprose and Dan Luger. I was surprised to see players of that quality being allowed to leave. I do not know the reason: maybe it was a salary cap issue, maybe a personality clash. When we first started playing professionally, and Newcastle won the title, I felt Saracens were really the best team out there. Their performance in beating Wasps to win the Tetley's Bitter Cup at Twickenham was perhaps the best domestic club performance I have ever seen. They played very efficient, stylish rugby, with very few mistakes. We looked at them and thought, this is going to be the team to beat for the next couple of years. They were hard-edged and very competitive and you sensed a real team spirit about them, that they were all there in it together. Now, something has changed. They still have some great players, and they have recruited well from abroad – look at Tim Horan – but you cannot lose so many good players and not feel it. One thing they do well is bring through a lot of young guys and maybe they will turn things around.

Whatever, beating them 56–15 was a great result: we came off with everyone on a high. Games like that are what you play for.

Geordan was our man of the match. He is a great fellow. He originally came over from Ireland with a mate, Jimmy Ferris, another good little player who has since gone home. His first big game for the club was a cup tie at Coventry in the days of Bob Dwyer. It was January, we had loads of injuries and a tired squad and he was played at full back. Cool as you like, after 15 minutes, he banged over this drop goal from 45 metres. I knew then he was going to be a special player. A very slim guy, though he is getting bigger through weights work, he is known as 'The Pencil' by the boys – or 'Goofy Bastard'. That said, he knows me as 'Goofy Bastard', too. He has tremendous talent and he has guts, too. You never see him bottle out and you never see him get blown away by bigger players, either.

*

ON THE international scene, England faced Scotland at home the following Saturday.

Pre-match, all the talk in the media was of the game in 2000 when we had been beaten in the driving rain at Murrayfield to deprive us of our Grand Slam. That was on the players' minds too, to an extent. We were not over-focusing on it but we wanted to make amends for the way the team had played on that day.

Conditions at Twickenham were about as far removed as possible from the way they had been in that game the previous year: the pitch was dry and firm, just right for our attacking backs.

But for most of the first half it was pretty tough going. Lawrence scored early on but, with five minutes to half time, we were only 8–3 ahead. Scotland were defending well and were occasionally looking threatening with the ball in hand. Then Hilly got over in the right-hand corner after good work by Phil Vickery and Nobby West and, a few minutes later, Dallaglio had his second. Jonny converted both tries to send us in 22–3 up and suddenly we had a comfortable cushion. The game had been a lot closer than the scoreline suggested, with Budge Pountney and Scott Murray both playing well and the Scots having some territory and making a few breaks, notably through Kenny Logan. In the second half, though, we overwhelmed them with the pace of the game and the pace of some of our players. Balshaw was lethal once again, scoring two tries and looking strong in defence. When Catty went off with a cut head, we were able to move Austin Healey from the wing into the centre and bring on Jason Robinson. Once again, he showed how lethal he can be against tired defenders, opening up their defence a few times and creating a try for Will Greenwood. Seeing a guy like him come on, all fresh and eager, with his pace and his agility, when they were tired, when their defence had been stretched and they were losing, and there were still 25 minutes to go, you could see the Scots thinking 'Oh my God, I don't need to see him.' They have already had to cope with the likes of Balshaw at the back, Cohen and Healey out wide, Catt in the middle and Johnson in the second row, guys with lethal pace, and now they have this to contend with.

Often there are people in rugby who have real top-end speed – who might well be quicker than Jase over 100 metres – but they never get chance to show it. If you take 10 yards to get going in rugby you very rarely do get going before someone stops you. Jason has tremendous acceleration; he is almost into top gear inside a couple of strides. What makes him even more dangerous is that he has the ability to stop at that pace, step inside at right angles and then bounce back off at that pace. He is an awesome sight, with his head bobbing all over the place and his very fast cadence – he does not have the long-legged stride of someone like Iain Balshaw, so his legs move really quickly. He does not have a slow twitch muscle fibre in his body. It is almost unfair bringing him on in those sort of circumstances.

When the final whistle went, with the score at 43–3, we had posted our highest Calcutta Cup total, and Jonny had kicked an English Championship record 18 conversions – four more than previous record-holder Paul Grayson, who had taken five games to reach his number.

At the post-match dinner at the Park Lane Hilton there was plenty of chat and banter but no gloating. A lot of the Scots are good guys and mates; I knew Tom Smith and Gregor Townsend from the 1997 Lions tour, Danny Grewcock played with Scott Murray at Sarries, Lawrence Dallaglio and Kenny Logan were Wasps team-mates, Dawson and Pountney were together at Northampton. It is not a great feeling if you have been stuffed and you do not like to rub it in. I have been in their situation. You know you have been beaten, you tell the other side they played well, they say thanks and that is it. The tendency is not to talk about the game too much, anyway, so we just concentrated on other subjects. Afterwards, we all headed off to Sugar Reef, a bar just off Piccadilly Circus. It is a trendy bar full of celebrities – not really my scene, but they treat us well. Two guys came up to me and shook my hand . . . apparently they were on *Castaway*, but I did not recognise them. About 1am, 10 of us headed back to the Hilton for a few more drinks, some sandwiches and a trawl through the entire Nobby West CD collection . . . The Clash, The Undertones, The Jam and The Stranglers.

Two Championships Retained

WITH THE Six Nations temporarily on the back-burner, the Sale Sharks game Leicester should have played at the end of December had been rearranged for the Tuesday evening after the Scotland game. It was a tough match, played in bad weather against a side who were very physical. Sometimes, you find teams that are lower in the table – as Sale now were – tend to play more physical rugby, almost because they think they have to, whereas, conversely, teams higher up often seem to pride themselves on their skills and are less physical, relying instead on finesse. Jamie Hamilton had to go off after he was injured very early on in a heavy, late tackle and Steve Booth was later sin-binned after he went in to help Austin after he had been hit. The crowd was getting agitated because they thought Sale were playing dirtily and it did feel as though things could turn really nasty at any moment.

I managed to score my second vitally-important try of the season, from an equally impressive distance of three metres. They had a line-out five metres from their line and went for a short line-out option. I defended at the back, playing scrum-half. There is always the chance that if the hooker throws it a little too high and you put pressure on their jumper he will miss the ball. That happened, the ball came straight to me and belly-flopped over the line to score, helping us to a 24–12 victory.

On the down side, Freddie had been badly bruised in the groin and that was the end of his season but I felt we were getting close to tying up the league.

Northampton away followed on the Saturday and it was a reprise of the London Irish game: another tough game on heavy ground a few days after a big midweek match. What resulted was one of the dullest games I have played in in recent years. When I was younger that would not have bothered me: I would have been happy with the win. Now, though, I do like to play to the highest standard. It is more enjoyable and more satisfying and it also keeps the spectators happy; they pay everyone's wages, after all.

Despite our tired legs, we dominated the possession and the territory but we could not put our chances away and it turned into a penalty duel, which ended 9–12 in our favour. Matt Dawson missed a couple at the end, which could have given them the draw or even victory, but I felt justice had just about been done since we had been slightly the better team.

Afterwards, I knew the league was ours – we just needed one more win and other results to go our way. Everyone else had been conceding it to us since January but we knew how close some of our results had been. We seemed to be getting all the breaks, with the opposition missing kickable penalties in Bath and now at Franklin's Gardens. With luck on our side, we were almost unbeatable.

On the way back from Northampton, we stopped at the White Lion pub in North Kilworth for a beer or three. Ian Stafford, a Mail on Sunday journalist who had accompanied us on a pre-season tour to Ulster, had become fascinated with the aura surrounding the back seat of our team coach. It can get pretty violent as guys fight to get back there and Stafford had threatened to come and try to take the back seat after the match. I told him afterwards it was a good job he had not bothered. The boys were pretty yampy after another long week and things got a bit lively after our pub stop. If Stafford had been anywhere near the bus he may well have been murdered and his naked body dumped in the lanes of South Leicestershire. Which, some may say, would not be an entirely bad thing.

*

NEWCASTLE FALCONS at home was a TV game, so we had a 1pm start. I never like playing that early, having to be at the ground at 11am, but once you get going it is OK. Newcastle, with one eye on the play-offs, had brought a weakened team down. Jonny Wilkinson, Inga Tuigamala, George Graham . . . they were all missing from the starting line-up. That sounds great but it can throw your plans out; you have been preparing for one bunch of guys and another set turn up. Playing a second XV, as we almost were, gave us a flat feeling in the dressing room, as though the challenge had gone. Still, we blew them away, going to a 39–7 lead in the first half. They only scored when Leon Lloyd tried to take a quick drop-out and spooned it straight into one of their guy's hands, who then ran straight in. With the match won at half-time, we were able to bring on a few replacements and relax, to an extent. We were still very keen to keep them out, which we did while adding to our own total for a final 51–7 scoreline. This time, I did not hear Rob Andrew whingeing about the refereeing. I think he blamed injuries.

With a 1pm start, the game was finished by 2.30pm and we had a nervous wait to see if Bath beat Wasps, our nearest challengers. At first, the only news we heard was that Wasps were ahead so I was sitting in our clubhouse having lunch and cursing Bath for losing at home. There is something I never thought I would say.

Then it came through that Mike Catt had scored late on to win the game for Bath. We had won the Championship with two games to spare. I could hear the fans in the main bars going berserk. For us, it was a little weird: when we had won in the two preceding years it had been after tough games at Newcastle and Bristol. Now it all felt a little anti-climactic and it took a little time to sink in.

It had been a pretty comprehensive win, helped by an increasingly competitive league. That may sound like Double Dutch but it means that the teams you would expect to be challenging us were being beaten more regularly by sides who, historically, had been weaker. As the standard continues to improve I think whoever wins the Premiership in 2001/2001 could well do so with a record number of losses.

The TV guys wanted to film us being presented with the trophy, so we went out with the supporters who had hung around – around 700 or so, down from the 15,000 who had been at the game – and lifted the trophy up for them.

Lloydy was lucky, by the way: because we had won the league, his drop-out cock-up was glossed over. I shall be bringing it up at some point in the future, though, rest assured . . .

That evening, we all met up in town with the wives and girlfriends for a meal and then a serious number of beers, drinking until the small hours. The feeling of winning three championships on the trot was dawning on me and it felt great. In domestic terms, at least, I think we had laid down our claim to being a truly great club side, even if we had ridden our luck and had our breaks in beating Wasps, Bath and Northampton away.

It had been a squad effort – a cliché, but no less true for that – and the management had played their part, too. Resting eleven guys to play Rotherham away was a big gamble but they had backed their judgment and their faith in the younger players and been proven right on both counts. They had done well, too, to re-organise our postponed games when they had.

That night it was great to relax.

And there was an added bonus: we had no game the following weekend. Unfortunately, as the foot-and-mouth epidemic spread, Ireland vs England had been postponed. While it meant our workload was lighter, the England boys among us were disappointed. We would love to have played Ireland when we were at the top of our form. The epidemic was obviously a disaster for agriculture in the UK and Ireland, a country very reliant on its farming industry, was desperate to keep it out. I accepted that – up to a point – but I did feel rugby was being singled out. The Republic of Ireland soccer side was still playing and goodness knows how many tourists were flying in and out . . . most of the England fans who had planned to fly out to Dublin for the game probably went anyway because often you cannot cancel flights and hotels without paying a charge. If they seriously wanted to keep foot-and-mouth out, why did they not suspend all flights?

I called Keith Wood about some Lions issues and suggested a game of beach rugby in Spain, Ireland vs England, and we would tell everyone the result later. Sadly, he was having none of it.

On the up side, the Tigers' management used the weekend off to take a big squad of players out to Portugal for four days' warm weather training, staying at a hotel between Albufeira and Vilamoura which was popular with athletes. Lars Reidel, the discus world champion, was there at the time. Training in the sun makes you feel better and those injuries seem to heal quicker, too. It is much easier to run round the track, work on sprints or move weights around in the gym when you know that, afterwards, you can go for a dip in the pool or lie in a sunlounger and relax, maybe have a game of cricket in the afternoon.

It must have cost the club a fair bit and I guess it was, in part, a reward for winning the Championship. But there was serious work to be done, too. Ahead of us was the European Cup semi final against Gloucester. We were already putting in ground work on how we wanted to play that game which was a little different;

normally we prepare for a match three or four days away, not three or four weeks.

On our return it was back down to earth with a bump; you don't get much more down to earth than Kingsholm.

With the title in the bag, most of the international players and some of the other front line guys were to be rested for our league clash, which was a luxury we could now afford. With one eye focused on the European match 21 days away, it also meant that we would give less away to them, in terms of tactics and how different players were performing – a feeling you only really get by playing against them – than they would to us.

Despite fielding a largely second string side, with lots of up-and-coming guys, we were still very competitive, which says a lot about our strength in depth. As it had for us when we had faced a weakened Newcastle, maybe it demotivated the Gloucester team. They certainly did not have everything their own way. We played well in some phases, scoring a try, but losing out 22–13.

*

THE POSTPONEMENT of the Irish Six Nations clash had affected the competition as a spectacle, no doubt, but our encounter with France would go ahead as planned and, for the players, believe me, there was no loss of nerves or anticipation ahead of that game because of the deferment.

I always have a tremendous amount of respect for French sides and so do the rest of the England guys. We have all been torn apart by French teams, at international level and club level, through their pace and ability and they have that ability to play utterly out of their skins which few, if any, other sides do.

They have great strength in depth, with a club rugby scene which is probably the strongest around; teams like Pau, Toulouse,

Stade Français and Biarritz can give anyone in the world a run for their money on their day.

Without wishing to show disrespect to the Celtic nations or Italy, in recent years England vs France has usually been the Five or Six Nations decider.

Even if it is not it is always a special game with its own atmosphere and history.

Intoxicated by the rich vein of form England had shown in the Six Nations to date, the media and many of the fans were talking about us putting 50 points on them. This was not talk I wanted to hear; potentially it could fire them up and a fired-up French team is the last thing you want.

They had named a good side, bringing back Abdel Benazzi. He is a world-class player and I rate him highly. Other really talented guys in their line-up included the openside Olivier Magne, Bernat-Salles and the wing Christophe Dominici. Their pack will always cause you problems and we had been forced to go into the game without Danny Grewcock and Phil Vickery, two of our key forwards. I was glad the game was at home; Paris is always a tough place to go and win and the growing atmosphere at Twickenham, louder since our wins in the autumn internationals, would be helpful to us against the men in the blue shirts.

We could have done with a few of the supporters on the pitch in the first half as the French guys got going in real style.

We scored early through Will Greenwood but I felt we were over-confident, turning the ball over out wide too often against a side who counter-attack with frightening pace. As we ran at them we lost possession – nine times in the first 40 minutes, I later learned. Once they have ball in those situations they are very good at using it, keeping it alive well, and they came back at us like lightning, looking lethal and scoring a try of their own through Bernat-Salles. It could have been much worse: Iain Balshaw showed he was not just a razor-sharp finisher, using his pace to bring off two try-saving cover tackles, one on a flying

Dominici. Christophe is quick in the feet and in the brain: he is very good at spotting a shortage in numbers and he had exposed us on the blind side and was away for what looked a certain score.

We went in at the interval at 13–16, battered and bruised. Greening, Borthwick and Leonard had all gone off for stitches and we were pleased to trail by only three points. My main message to the team in the changing rooms was to play a little more directly and to concentrate on the simple things: good passing, good retention, good territory. I felt if we worked at keeping the ball and played in their half we could win.

After the restart, it was almost like no-one had been listening to me: it turned into a very loose game, with the ball flying everywhere and going wide very quickly. With 20 minutes to go, both sets of forwards were almost down on their knees with the running they had done. Richard Hill, one of English rugby's unsung stars, got us back in front with a dynamic run to the line from 30 metres out after Matt Dawson had taken a quick penalty and Balshaw pounced not long after to add another. Suddenly, the French were on the back foot. Greening, replacement Matt Perry and Mike Catt all scored as we racked up 35 second-half points against just three by the opposition. Catt's try, in particular, was a gem; Austin Healey, his back to the French line, kicked the ball over his head for Catty to run on to and score. It was a move Geordan Murphy had tried to put Pat through in the European Cup quarter-final.

They kept coming back at us, and almost scored through Xavier Garbajosa who was brought down by a great cover tackle by Daws. We needed to defend well and we did. Ultimately I think we were fitter and that was perhaps the difference: a 48–19 win, with the weight of our scoring in the second 40, tells its own story. We did not know it yet, but we had retained our Six Nations title.

Afterwards, we had the usual post-international dinner. I cannot say I know the French players too well. A few – Benazzi, Castaignede – are good guys but as a team they can seem a bit standoffish until you get to know them. It may just be the language difference or the fact that they change their team fairly regularly, so you do not get the chance to build friendships.

It was – albeit by default – the end of our England season and I celebrated a successful campaign with a few bottles of beer with Dai and a fashion designer mate of mine, Julian Murray.

True Champions of England . . .

WITH THE internationals – Ireland excepted – out of the way, we welcomed Harlequins to Welford Road. I say 'welcomed': that may not quite be the right word. We wanted to stuff them after they had knocked us out of the Tetley's Bitter Cup.

It was the first time our first team had played together for almost a month, since beating Newcastle Falcons. It was also the week before the European Cup semi-final so it was something of a full dress rehearsal. We also had our three-year record of not losing at Welford Road to protect.

In short, there was no way we were going to lose.

It was the last league game of the season and Quins had nothing to play for in Premiership terms. They, too, had an important European campaign – the Trophy – to finish off and we won comfortably. Austin scored a fantastic try off the back of a scrum, chipping and chasing about 75 yards and Leon Lloyd finished with a good score, beating a number of defenders on the outside to get home.

The 35–5 scoreline was nice and after the game, the trophy was re-presented to us in front of a full house. It was a nice feeling, and it was great for the supporters, but the excitement of winning it, a month previously, had dissipated. We spent an hour or more signing autographs on the pitch but our minds were 100 miles down the M1, at Watford, where, the following Saturday, we would face Gloucester.

Additionally, of course, we still had the Zurich Championship to play for. There had been a lot of controversy earlier in the season, when the governing body had suddenly introduced the suggestion that whoever won this later knockout competition was the champion side. We were, to put it mildly, a bit hacked off at this; if they had said so at the start of the season, fine. I think they were worried that, with a lot of people resigned to us winning the league from January on, the domestic competition would become stale; changing it kept the interest going. I thought it made the game look stupid and badly administered.

That said, I think it is a good way to end the season because it means it will always build to a finale. The previous season, we had played Bath at home on the final day of the season. We were top, they were second and all the pundits were saying they were the better side. There was nothing riding on the match – the Championship was ours – but it gave the game an added interest . . . and made us feel even better when we beat them. In future years, the play-offs will artificially create what the fixture list had thrown up then.

I would take a leaf out of rugby league's book, though. In Super League, the team which finishes top is seeded into the final. They play fewer games to get there than the side which finishes fifth, and they can actually lose and still make it. I think it is a little harsh to win the league by a distance, as we did, only to perhaps have one one-off game and get beaten by a team that had kept itself fresh for three weeks, knowing 8th is good enough to qualify. Seeding would help to solve this.

*

I HAD mixed feelings about the Gloucester game.

The only other European semi-final I had played in had been against Toulouse in 1997. That felt right: we were playing a glamorous French side and you knew it was a special day. The Cherry-and-Whites at Watford somehow does not have the same ring to it. After all, we had already played them three times that season and they were not even near the top of the English Premiership. Everyone expected us to win – the only loss had been with an under-strength Tigers side – and that added to the pressure on us. If we went down it would be far worse than defeat by Stade Français or Munster – or even Bath or Saracens.

At Leicester, we are never complacent; every team demands respect and preparation and Gloucester were certainly no different. We were not foolish enough to think it would be a routine game. A big cup final – the biggest in club rugby – would have more than made their season. They had some excellent big match players, notably Phil Vickery and the All Black legend Ian Jones, and we expected them to come out stronger than they had in our previous encounters.

Again the club gave the players the option of either going down to Watford the night before the game or on the day itself. We are a democracy and the guys chose match day. I felt this was a mistake; it would only take an accident on the M1 and we would be late. As it turned out, there was heavy traffic. We were forced to take some very obscure way into the town off the motorway and we did arrive late. As I have said, I like 90 minutes of preparation time ahead of a game and in the end we got less than 60 minutes. Driving through the middle of Watford on a Saturday afternoon an hour away from the European Cup semi-final is not ideal preparation. In fact, it is ridiculous and I was fuming. It would mean our warm-up was rushed. I like the time to sit down, to go and look at the pitch and the stadium, and to feel the game approaching gently – not rushing at me. We did have a police escort; their idea of escorting us seemed to be sitting in their car, in the traffic, in front of us. Not a fat lot of good.

Everything happened too quick and, before we knew it, we were on the field playing the game. And it was exactly what we had expected: tough, fast, furious. They started very well, putting in some big hits. I was one victim – Junior Paramore smashed into me and knocked the ball about 10 yards out of my grasp, which was not great.

Watford is a good place to play, a tight little ground with a good surface, and the fans were really getting into it. The Gloucester Shed had turned out in numbers and plenty of the Leicester faithful had travelled down, too. It felt like a big crowd, very noisy and a huge atmosphere, though it was actually some way off a sell-out, with a lot of people having reservations about getting to the ground – not the easiest thing in the world to do, as we had found. A venue somewhere more central, between the two clubs, might have been better: perhaps Villa Park in Birmingham.

You could feel the pressure and the tension as the game wore on and the kickers exchanged penalties. The turning point came in the 20th minute when they cleared their lines with a high ball. Tim Stimpson took it well, ran down the blind side and cut back infield before passing to Leon Lloyd who handed off Andy Gomarsall to score under the posts. Tim converted to make it 13–6 and we had a precious lead. More penalties brought the score up to 19–15 in our favour but they had a chance to nick it at the death, when Ian Jones stole our line-out ball near our goal line. But Martin Corry turned it over and we cleared the danger. I had earlier been sin-binned with Paramore – I genuinely do not know what for – but we played our best rugby with me off the field so I was not that unhappy about it in the end.

In the changing room afterwards, I nursed a sore neck, probably from that Paramore challenge and some other big hits in the game, and reflected on a long, hard season. There was little elation – there would have been, I think, if we had beaten someone like Toulouse away – but just a sense of relief to have won. We had gone in as favourites and Gloucester had not been a million miles away from turning us over. We all had ice lollies on the way home, looking forward to a final against Stade Français, that after they had beaten Munster with a controversial decision from a touch judge.

Now that *would* be a big game.

*

IN THE week that followed, the Lions party for Australia was announced. I did not attend the press conference, as I have said. Wednesday is our biggest team session of the week and we like everyone to be there. Normally we concentrate on defence, analysing the opposition and then organising our training around what we think they will do. About 75% of it will be the same every week, in terms of our technique and organisation. The other 25% is specific to the other side; Bath can play very wide, for instance, so we would look at defending out wide. Other teams might need more work around the ruck and maul.

London Irish in our home quarter-final of the play-offs was a big game and I needed to be with the boys.

Having won the Premiership our focus, naturally, was on the European Cup but we wanted to win this new knock-out competition, too – if only to avoid some other side being hailed as the best in England. However, we were prepared to take a few risks with our side. Perry Freshwater started at loosehead instead of Wig and the recently-recruited George Chuter at hooker, to rest Westy and Cocker. Martin Corry was named in the second row alongside me to rest some of the younger lads. It was not our strongest line-up but we backed ourselves to win.

We were slightly surprised by how flat Irish were – they almost looked defeated before the kick-off, when we had expected them to come out and try to knock us over after a tough game the previous weekend. Having said that, some key guys – including their influential full-back Conor O'Shea – were out with injury and I think that, in the circumstances, they lacked a little bit of belief. It was a pretty forgettable game but we were happy with the 24–11 scoreline and no serious injuries to anyone needed for Stade Français.

That took us through to a home semi-final against Northampton Saints. As the defending European champions, Northampton would no doubt have loved to turn over one of the finalists who might succeed them. As our near neighbours, they always want to beat us anyway. Finally, of course, they would have loved a Twickenham final to give their season some meaning. Unfortunately, we completed the treble over them, winning 17–13.

Martin Corry and myself started on the bench but a close-to-first-choice front row was selected, in Graham Rowntree, Darren Garforth and Richard Cockerill, to counter the Saints' scrum. Steve Booth, a player with a great step and good pace, scored an excellent try for us – he had not had many opportunities during the season but was looking like a very promising prospect – and Pat Howard scored a nice try on his farewell appearance at Welford Road. That gave us a cushion at half time but they closed the gap in the second half and we could never get away, leading to a very tense final few minutes. I came on with 12 minutes to go and we had a sticky time of it, getting a little too defensive and handing territory, possession and pressure to them. In the end, we were hanging on and waiting for that whistle. In these situations, in a strange sort of way, it is almost better to have the 13 points than the 17 with a few minutes left; you have only one option, attack, and that makes you less mentally restricted. With a slight lead, you tell yourself to keep playing, to have confidence, but at the back of your mind you know it only takes one mistake – an intercepted pass, a charge-down – and they can score. If you are not careful this can inhibit you and make you more defensive than you want to be and that, in itself, can lead to them getting on top. That said, if you have a good defence you can resist pressure and we did, finishing without the score changing. A Twickenham final, against Bath, beckoned.

We were unbeaten at home the whole season and in two finals, with a treble still on. The play-offs were the least important part of the treble, however. We did not want to lose the games but we were not as ruthless as we would have been had that been all we had to play for. We wanted to win but if you had asked whether we wanted to lose our home record or the European Cup final there would have been only on answer.

As it turned out, we rotated our teams and we got through.

Afterwards, the crowd said a long and emotional farewell to Pat Howard. His influence had increased every year he had been with us and his coaching had helped our back line to play the best I have ever seen it. He was later named Leicester's Supporters' Player of the Season and our Players' Player of the Season and was also the Professional Rugby Players' Player of the Season – all well-deserved accolades.

Paddy does not have a tremendous amount of pace but he is a very clever player and that more than compensates. He passed on a lot of rugby knowledge to guys like Leon Lloyd and Ollie Smith and helped them to become better players, both in defence and attack. He may have been a foreign player but he had played his heart out for the team like he had been born and bred in Leicester and the fans and his team-mates really appreciated him for that. Welford Road is the sort of place where no-one can rest on their laurels or their reputation and that was something Pat never did. It was very emotional saying goodbye to him; we had lost a great mate and a great player.

*

WE HAD eight days to wait before our trip to Twickenham to face Bath the following Sunday. It was a strange build-up; it was a bigger game for Bath than it was for us and our supporters had recognised that. The word was that most of the Tigers fans were saving up for their trip to Paris the next weekend.

We approached it in a fairly low-key way, travelling down to the Shepperton Moat House, the south London hotel we usually stay at before London games.

If we're there in the summer and it is nice, we will have a game of cricket on the big lawn outside the hotel. That May it was warm enough, so we got out into the fresh air. There are some very useful cricketers at the Tigers. Andy Goode and James Grindal are both good, Cozza is a quick bowler, as is Lewis Moody – 'Mad Moodos', as he is known, charging in off a long run, not much accuracy but plenty of pace – and Tim Stimpson is an excellent all-rounder. Backy used to play for Warwickshire schools as a batsman-wicketkeeper and Dorian West is a decent player too. That's the wheat. Then there is the chaff. I fall fairly and squarely into the latter camp, though I did york a bloke last time I played, against a Leicestershire club side. Backy cannot bowl to save his life – he has got a horrible round arm action – and Jamie 'The Baby' Hamilton is a disgrace to cricket. The Baby – so-named because although he is only two months younger than me he looks about 12 – is a sight to behold with willow or leather in hand. He bowls with his chin on his chest and brings both arms over as he delivers the ball. Obviously, we make him bowl as much as possible because it makes us laugh. The first time I saw him in action I literally collapsed to my knees in laughter. He was only slightly worse than Craig Joiner but Jocky had an excuse, being Scottish. He must have practised in secret because by the time he left the club to go back north he had become almost credible. Cricket takes your mind off the job in hand and helps the boys to relax, which is important. And we had a great knockabout. Obviously, I was playing for my average which is now up to about six. We finished around 8pm and I headed to my room to watch TV and relax before getting to sleep.

We were up and off to the ground after breakfast and an early lunch. It was slightly strange: we were at Twickenham but it was not a cup final. It lacked that sense of tradition, being a new thing. But my feelings about the fixture were good, despite the match being played on a warm Sunday – two things I have previously said I am not keen on. There were lots of kids there, a real family atmosphere and I firmly believe the play-off final should and will become a really big event in the future.

Despite it not being a cup final, we were all very 'up' for the game. We did not want to go down to Twickenham and lose, especially to Bath. I have been beaten by them in finals – including 'Backy's match', when he pushed over Steve Lander – and it is a horrible feeling because of the rivalry between the clubs. Deano had played a psychological game in the press all week, talking about the European Cup match and hinting that he might not play some key guys. But everyone wanted to start – no-one wanted to miss a Twickenham match against Bath – and a full-strength side took the field.

It was a high-risk strategy, with the much bigger match the following weekend. We could have lost three or four guys to injury, which would have been a disaster. But I think it was the right thing to do. We needed to win; the season before, Northampton had probably been the best side but their success in all three competitions had worked against them, because it extended their season to unmanageable levels. Everyone said that the Premiership would have been theirs otherwise. This year, although we had finished top of the Premiership, people were saying Bath were the better side. They were certainly in form. We wanted to beat them fair and square to silence the chatter and show everyone who were the governors. A play-off final loss would have left the matter open for debate and taken away our momentum ahead of the European final.

They started off pretty well but we gradually got on top of them and ground them down in the heat. I scored the first try, again from three or four yards out. It was actually a very good decision by the referee: I only got the front end of the ball down on the line but he was in place to see it. Austin scored on a quick tap penalty in the second half and then we grabbed another, really putting them away with about twenty minutes to go and allowing Deano to pull people off to rest them for the European Cup Final the following week.

Towards the end of the match, I made a tackle and took a bang on the top of my head, which sent a strange pain shooting through my shoulder. I was lying on the floor with my feet twitching, wondering what had happened. That is a horrible feeling but gradually I realised I was OK. With the game won, however, I did not want to stay on.

I said to Mark Geeson, the physio: 'We might as well get Louis Deacon on, Geese' and waved to the bench. I could already taste that large port and those cigars.

Cue blank, puzzled looks all round. We had all seven subs on at that point and Deacs had not been among them. He was watching from the sidelines.

Suddenly I realised I was talking gibberish. I was not concussed so much as slightly confused. I had to play the final five minutes with a strange jangly-nerve sensation in my neck and shoulder. Inevitably, almost as soon as I rejoined the action someone came running straight at me and I had to tackle him. I was sore by the end. Afterwards a few critics had a go at Bath, saying we had had it easy. That is not how it felt out there in the heat on that pitch. It was a tough match and Bath were no pushovers.

When we had won the league I had tried to get Daz and Backy to go and lift the trophy – I have been fortunate enough to do so twice and I wanted them to have the opportunity, because they had both been stalwarts of the team, its heart and soul, for a decade. They had been reluctant to put themselves into the limelight and they refused again this time. So I grabbed Paddy Howard – it was his last game for the Tigers in England – and the two of us collected the trophy. We paraded it around the stadium for our fans, laughing and joking. My memory is just of a really good day.

On the way back we called at a pub in Toddington, a traditional stop-off for victorious Tigers' sides, and had a couple of celebratory beers. In the past, those celebrations have occasionally got out of hand and we have been banned from the place before now. This time, though, we were models of restraint: we still had one major part of our jigsaw to complete.

. . . And Europe

I HAD problems with my neck, injured against Gloucester in the semi-final, all week ahead of the Paris game. I was in a lot of discomfort and was very stiff. I hardly trained but there was no doubt about whether I would play. I was not alone: the last team run we had in England featured five replacements for first-choice players who were having to sit out. We flew out on the Wednesday to our base at the Trianon Palace Hotel, right next to the Palace of Versailles in a beautiful setting.

Training was pretty light – at that stage of a long season, it is more about nursing guys through than flogging them – and on the Friday afternoon we took the opportunity to take in a bit of culture, wandering round the old palace. Paris itself was really buzzing with the excitement. A lot of Stade Français fans were in town in their colours and half of Leicester seemed to have made the trip over, flying, sailing, driving . . . getting there by any means they could. We were constantly fielding calls from friends and family telling us what time they were arriving and the anticipation was clear in their voices. If we had been in any doubt beforehand of the size of the match, we were in none now.

Although they are one of France's oldest sides, Stade are relatively new to the top end of French rugby but they have an air of glamour and style about them. They had beaten us easily in Paris the previous year, when we had had a few injuries, and they boasted a lot of quality international players.

There was some controversy about the fact that we were playing in Paris, their home town. We were not bothered. If anything, it gave us a psychological edge; we would be the underdogs away from home, which can help a side. Anyway, we had known from the semi-finals on that if we met them in the final we would play the game in the French capital. Our attitude was: If we have got to go over there to beat them we might as well do it in their own backyard . . . what a day that will be. It was also closer for our fans than the other possible venues, in French rugby's southern heartland . . . fewer Tigers fans, surely, would have been able to travel to, say, Toulouse.

And we would be playing at the old Parc des Princes. It was the ideal venue: 50,000 supporters crammed in right on top of you, creating a fabulous atmosphere. A few of us had played there before internationally, but for an English club to get the opportunity was probably a once-in-a-lifetime thing – much rarer than a Twickenham appearance.

We went down there on that Friday and stood on the turf, taking it all in. There is a certain ambience about the place, a certain aura. It is one of the world's great rugby stadia, no question. As a fan, I had watched England play France there throughout the 1980s, when they had a really special team who generally handed us a hiding, and my mind wandered back to those days: watching the French run out of the glass doors to play, hearing the tremendous roar. There was always something special about France in Paris and we knew this was no different. French sides have a reputation for being stronger at home; they are always capable of performing great deeds in front of their own fans. We knew we were in for the game of our lives.

Personally, I was really up for it. My neck was OK and I could not wait. We play some of the world's biggest names, clubs like

Bath and Saracens, week in, week out, and somehow the familiarity of it all means you lose some of the excitement. Here we were about to step into a European Cup Final – it was just much, much bigger.

The Saturday dawned nice and bright and dry, which was good. We wanted to play a fast game, feeling that a high-tempo style would suit us. We hung around the hotel in the morning until it was time to go: then the French police provided us with their traditional escort to the ground. The motorbike outriders will literally kick cars to get their drivers to move which does help with the Parisian traffic.

It was a warm spring afternoon in Paris. Our injury scares had subsided, and everyone was available. I sat in the changing rooms contemplating the job ahead, thinking back to our loss in the final against Brive, brought about by over-confidence. There would be no repeat of that today. Everyone was ready. It was do or die. As we walked out onto the pitch for our warm-up, Nobby West spotted a huge St George's Cross flag with 'The Boot, Ibstock' written on it: that was one of the pubs in his village and it gave us a laugh and a bit of a buzz. From the noise they made, well over a third of the crowd were from Leicester, strong pockets of them dotted all over the ground. The Stade fans were possibly a little more muted. I suspect most of them were relatively new to their club. They do not have the long history of Racing Club in Paris or Toulouse or Dax and their fan-base is not so well-established. They were playing low grade rugby ten years ago and have only reached their current heights after buying in their team in recent years at a substantial cost.

After warming up, we came back inside to change. We have built up a tradition in the last three years of continuing to wear the shirts that we have been winning in, almost to the point where they are falling to pieces. The club did not want us to be wearing scabby jerseys in a European final and had produced some new kit with 'Heineken Cup 2001' stitched on the front.

However, we were adamant we wanted to wear the shirts we had on when we won the league. A compromise was reached: we changed into the new shirts, went out and had our photographs taken in them and then came back in to put our knackered old kit back on. It gave us all a good feeling. With a few minutes to go, the adrenalin is really starting to build and the nerves show on one or two players. Some, like Oz, Westy and Pat Howard, were chatty; others sat in silence.

The spell was broken by the referee knocking on our door and pointing to his watch. Both teams are supposed to come out together but the Stade players were obviously trying to play a little psychological game with us and they kept us waiting in the tunnel for some time. Some of the guys were saying 'Come on, Johnno, bollocks to them . . . let's just go out'. I said no. I wanted to wait for them, to see them in the tunnel before the game. I wanted us to face them and show them we were not going to be messed around. I also did not want them to run out second and get a bigger cheer: if we go out together, the cheer is for both sides, isn't it?

As the seconds ticked away, we were getting more and more aggressive and pumped up. It was an edgy time. The referee was in a difficult position: they were deliberately disobeying him and I felt he should have gone back into their changing room and said to their skipper: 'You either come out now or I'm sending you off before the game starts.' They were clearly trying to gain an advantage.

Eventually, after what seemed like two or three minutes, I gave in to the guys and we ran out. Stade followed shortly afterwards but in a strange way . . . the only way I can explain it is to say they came out as individuals, not as a team. They were in dribs and drabs, some walked, some trotted. It was odd. And then the attempt to intimidate us continued. They headed to the middle of the pitch and immediately squared up to us, staring over. Our players started walking across to them until, in the end, we were toe to toe, eyeball to eyeball.

It was a hell of a dramatic start to proceedings, very charged, very atmospheric. I remember looking across and my brother, the Schnozz, had this stupid big-nosed grin on his face, he was ready for it, we all were. Everyone was making their intentions quite clear.

You watch it now on video and you think 'Bloody hell, it's all going to go off big time here!' If someone had thrown a punch there would have been mayhem.

But strangely, despite the build-up, there was little niggle in the game itself. We had been determined to play territory against them, not to end up trying to play from deep after being pinned back in our own half by their Argentinian-Italian fly-half Diego Dominguez. They had obviously made the same decision and there was a lot of kicking in the first half, all very cagey, both sides feeling each other out and trying to avoid having to play too much. And they probably won the battle; Dominguez has got a big, accurate kick out of the hand and I felt they probably slightly edged the territory and had us under more pressure. Neither team really broke the other; we made a few breaks and they kept banging it back at us but we were evenly matched.

The only worry for us was Dominguez's place-kicking, which was spot-on. He seemed to be kicking goals from everywhere. It is one thing to concede a penalty and three points when you are under pressure in your own 22. That is fair enough. But when you have been pinged for some obscure technical offence just inside their half and they still get three points out of it you tend to think 'Bloody hell, we've got an uphill struggle here!'

The Schnozz sprained his wrist just before half time and was trying to play on with it. I went over to him and he was in a lot of pain, going: 'My wrist, my wrist . . . I can't bend it.' He desperately did not want to leave the field; he has tended to pick up a few injuries and he does get the piss taken out of him, in a gentle way, about that. But, rather unsympathetically, I said: 'Right, you're off!' and Guzzy came on for him. It was hard – he is my brother, after all – but you just cannot mess around with injuries. It was the right decision: he could not use his wrist for a few weeks afterwards, so it would clearly have affected his play.

The half-time score was 15–9, reflecting the fact that they had slightly had the better of the first 40 minutes. But our defence had been strong and they had made few inroads into our 22, despite having some big runners in the back row – Christophe Juillet particularly – and plenty of gas out wide through the likes of Dominici.

We had a sense that the game had not really got going. It had been quick and tough but we felt we were well in contention. All we needed was a score early on. And we got it 48 seconds after the restart, courtesy of Pat Howard, Geordan Murphy and Leon Lloyd. Pat put a lovely chip kick through, Geordie ran onto it, grubber-kicked ahead and Leon beat the defenders to the ball. Bang! We were right back in the game. It was a big confidence boost: we have scored, they haven't.

Five minutes later, though, I was in the bin. I was defending in the 'guard' position, next to the ruck. It is crucial to keep them out here: if an attacker slips through the middle of your line you are in trouble. Juillet was pulling me back, obstructing me off the ball, to try to open us up. It is a cynical ploy but one which can be very effective. If I was the offender I would have my head down because I would fully expect the guy to turn round and clock me for it. And that is what I did, catching him with an open-handed slap across the throat. He went down like he had been shot, playing it up a bit I felt. The referee saw the blow but had not spotted Juillet's first foul on me – it is often very difficult for referees and touch judges to see this sort of obstruction. I pointed it out but there was only ever going to be one outcome: Johnno off for 10 minutes.

It was an anxious period. They piled on the pressure as much as they could, playing some good momentum rugby. Still, they made few inroads into our 22 but, with Dominguez kicking like a dream from all parts of the pitch, we could not afford too many mistakes. And the 14 guys played brilliantly, conceding just three points while I was off. Mid-winter, on a muddy pitch, that would be par for the course. Mid-May, on a fast track, with their pace and ability, it was a magnificent effort, eyeballs out, balls on the line. It was a crucial period: if we had conceded it might have turned the whole game around.

Almost as soon as I got back on, Backy nipped over and Stimmo, also striking the ball beautifully, kicked the conversion from the touchline to make it 21–21 with 20 minutes to go. A couple more penalties were exchanged, making it 27-all. And it was a very tense time because, with Dominguez kicking the way he was, we knew that the game could be put beyond us at any time through a couple of errors. Jamie Hamilton came on for Andy Goode, with Austin moving to 10 and Jamie to scrum-half. Then what seemed like the hammer blow fell: Dominguez landed a lovely drop goal from 30 metres out to take them ahead. Three minutes of normal time left, though I was not even looking at the clock because I could not affect that: I just knew we had to get back into their half and score some points. With the game slipping away, there was a line-out just outside their half and we won the ball. It went out to Oz, who made a great break, running across the pitch before straightening and using his pace to get through. Just as he was about to be caught he delivered a superb pass to Leon who beat Dominici's tackle and banged the ball down in the corner. The score was 30–32: not good enough, because there was still time for them to restart. Defensively, we would be desperate not to concede a try and if they put enough pressure on us between the 22 and our 10-metre line we might be forced to concede a penalty. Alternatively, they might look to give Dominguez the space to drop another goal. Either would probably win them the match. We needed the conversion.

If I was going to bet my house on someone in that sort of situation, Tim Stimpson would be there or thereabouts. And he did not disappoint, slotting the ball beautifully between the posts. They had a last-gasp break right at the death but we snuffed it out, the whistle went and we were European Champions.

Almost immediately, I forgot most of what had happened during the game. I had taken a bang on the head but that was not the reason. It had just been one of those really fast, frenetic matches where you cannot really remember, even straight afterwards, the sequence of scoring. There was a lot of kicking, with the ball moving so quickly from one end of the field to the other, and we were just trying to counter what they had done . . . it was 'They've scored, we've got to score next', bang . . . bang . . . bang . . . kick . . . kick . . . kick. It was a really special moment: the whole squad, even the guys who were not on the bench, ran straight onto the pitch to celebrate with us. And it was right that they did – the whole season had been a squad effort

To win the treble, to top it all off by winning the European Championship in Paris, was almost perfect. It was certainly the biggest and best day of my club career and it ranks with any I have had in rugby. When we had beaten Bath at home in the last game of the previous season, and been presented with the Premiership trophy, we had spent an hour and a half on the pitch with the fans, chatting and signing autographs. I remember thinking 'How could there be a better day for the club than this?' Well, this was it. Where we go from here, though, I do not know. Winning the Cup again next year and becoming the only Champions to defend successfully – that would be special, too. Here's hoping.

Finally, Backy and Garf decided this was a trophy they *would* go and receive, which was great for them, something they deserved. And we walked it around the pitch, saluting our fantastic supporters.

In the changing room, we soaked up a great sense of satisfaction mingled with relief after the dramatic, last-minute nature of the victory. It was, without doubt, the best day of my club career and one which gave me as much satisfaction as leading the Lions to victory in 1997. No-one felt the need to say anything about the momentous nature of what we had just achieved: we all just knew.

After the game, there were supposed to be two buses – one for us and one for the wives, girlfriends and kids – to take us back to a boat on the Seine where we were going to have a party. Only one of the coaches showed up so the players all walked out of the Parc des Princes, carrying the cup. It is a long, straight road with a bar in the distance and all the supporters in and around the ground could see us stroll out with the trophy and walk all the way up to the bar. It was like a scene from a movie.

We had a beer in there and then found our bus, went to the boat and joined the entire Tigers staff for a celebration. All the office staff at the club had worked tremendously hard for this, too, organising supporters' trips, sorting out ticketing and the general logistics.

Sunday found us back in Leicester, meeting some of the returning fans at Welford Road to display all three trophies. Afterwards, we stayed in Hogan's Bar in Clarendon Park until the small hours. But we did not really get the chance to celebrate as a team. It would have been great to come home, throw a big party and wallow in it all. But it was not to be. Some of the guys had a few weeks of chill-out awaiting them. The rest of us were heading off – either with England or on the Lions tour.

An amazing rugby season had almost – but not quite – come to an end.

Epilogue

THE PAIN in my hand was less than excruciating. I knew I had taken a knock but felt I could carry on.

At half-time, the physio checked me over and gave me his considered opinion: it was a break.

With Ireland vs England a week away – not to mention another tough 40 minutes against Northampton about to start – my heart sank. I watched the second half, cheered up by the way the boys came back to win, and then went off to hospital.

The x-ray confirmed the physio's worst fears: I had a spiral fracture of the index metacarpal in my left hand.

*

SEVEN DAYS later, I sat in the stands in Dublin's Lansdowne Road, watching England go down to a spirited Ireland performance.

It was like Groundhog Day: after Wales and Scotland had snatched Grand Slams from our grasp, now their Celtic cousins had done the same job on us.

We had sought to play our wide, attacking game from the off but failed to finish off our breaks. Ireland, a good side, were committed and, with their astute tactical game, deserved their win.

That night at the Berkeley Court Hotel, as we attended the post-match dinner, we had the same sense of disappointment we had felt in the previous two seasons. Nothing for it but to try again. An English Grand Slam in 2002? I'll be striving for it, if selected.

Match Facts and Figures

Western Australia vs British and Irish Lions
WACA, Perth
June 8, 2001
Result: 10–116

British and Irish Lions:
O'Driscoll, Cohen, Greenwood, M Taylor, Luger, O'Gara, Howley, Morris, Wood (c), Vickery, Grewcock, O'Kelly, Hill, Back, Quinnell

Replacements:
Balshaw, Henderson, Healey, S Taylor, Davidson, Leonard, McBryde

Western Australia:
Shannon Apaapa, Mark Gardiner, Aaron Broughton, Hamish Waldin, Brent Becroft, Todd Feather, Mark Fleet, Tim Stevens, Campbell Duff, Adam New, Nathan Hollis, Trefor Thomas (c), Hamish Grace, Anthony Brain, Richard Coney

Martin Johnson

Replacements:
Duncan McRae, Robbie Barugh, Matt Harrington, Patricio Noriega, Tim Cameron, Greg Plimmer, Rob Kellam

Queensland President's XV vs British and Irish Lions
Dairy Farmers' Stadium, Townsville
June 12, 2001
Result: 6–83

British and Irish Lions
Perry, James, Greenwood, Henderson, Robninson, jenkins, Dawson, Williams, Corry, Charvis, Murray, Davidson, Young (c), McBryde, Smith

Replacements:
Healey, Taylor, Luger, Hill, O'Kelly, Leonard, Bulloch

Queensland President's XV
Nathan Williams, David McCallum, Junior Pelesasa, Jason Ramsamy, Scott Barton, Shane Drahm, Ben Wakley, John Roe, Scott Fava, Tom McMerry, Rudi Vedelago, Mike Mitchell, Fletcher Dyson, Sean Hardman (c), Rick Tyrell

Replacements:
Sean Barry, Andrew Scotney, Michael Tabrett, David Duley, Andrew Farley, Simon Kerr, Tim Tavalea

Queensland Reds vs British and Irish Lions
Ballymore Stadium, Brisbane
June 16, 2001
Result: 8–42

Queensland Reds

Michael Tabrett, Junior Pelesasa, Dabiel Herbert (c), Steve Kefu, David McCallum, Elton Flatley, Sam Cordingley, Matt Cockbain, Toutai Kefu, David Croft, Mark Connors, Nathan Sharpe, Glenn Panoho, Michael Foley, Nick Stiles

Replacements:

Ben Wakley, Andrew Scotney, Jason Ramsamy, John Roe, Mike Mitchell, Simon Kerr, Sean Hardman

British and Irish Lions

Balshaw, James, O'Driscoll, Henderson, Luger, Wilkinson, Howley, Corry, Back, Hill, Grewcock, Johnson (c), Vickery, Wood, Smith

Australia A vs British and Irish Lions
NorthPower Stadium, Gosford
June 19, 2001
Result: 28–25

Australia A

Richard Graham, Mark Bartholomeusz, Scott Staniforth, Nathan Grey, Graeme Bond, Manny Edmonds, Chris Whitaker, Phil Waugh (c), Jim Williams, David Lyons, Justin Harrison, Tom Bowman, Rod Moore, Brendad Cannon, Cameron Blades

Replacements:

Sam Payne, Julian Huxley, James Holbeck, Tom Murphy, Patricio Noriega, Peter Ryan, Jono West

Martin Johnson

British and Irish Lions
Perry, Robinson, Greenwood, Catt, Cohen, Jenkins, Healey, Quinnell, Back, Dallaglio, O'Kelly, Murray, Young (c), McBryde, Leonard

Replacements:
Morris, Bulloch, Davidson, Charvis, Dawson, O'Gara, Taylor

New South Wales Waratahs vs British and Irish Lions
Sydney Football Stadium, Sydney
June 23, 2001
Result: 24–41

New South Wales Waratahs
Duncan MacRae, Francis Cullimore, Luke Inman, Sam Harris, Sikeli Qua Qua, Manny Edmonds, Sam Payne, Phil Waugh (c), Fili Finau, Stu Pinkerton, Tom Bowman, Jono West, Rod Moore, Brendan Cannon, Cameron Blades

Replacements:
Patricio Noriega, Jeff Mutton, Lee Green, Peter Besseling, Drew Hickey, Richard Tombs, Ed Carter

British and Irish Lions
Balshaw, James, O'Driscoll, Greenwood, Robinson, Wilkinson, Dawson, Quinnell, Back, Dallaglio, Grewcock, Johnson (c), Vickery, Wood, Morris

Replacements:
Smith, McBryde, Corry, Hill, Healey, O'Gara, Perry

New South Wales Country Cockatoos vs British and Irish Lions
International Stadium, Coffs Harbour
June 26, 2001
Result: 3–46

New South Wales Country Cockatoos
Nathan Croft, Vuli Talasi, Ryan McDougall, Kieran Shepherd, Warwick Crosby, Chris Doyle, Rod Petty, Bernie Klasen (c), Craig Taylor, Brent Dale, Ben Wright, David Lubans, Matt Bowman, James McCormack, Angus Baldwin

Replacements:
Matt Brown, Matt Ellis, David Banovich, Daryl Thomas, John Vaalotu, Gordon Refshauge, Darren Dimmock

British and Irish Lions
Balshaw, Cohen, Taylor, Gibbs, Howe, Jenkins, Healey, Williams, Corry, Charvis, O'Kelly, Davidson, Young (c), Bulloch, Leonard

Replacements:
Worris, West, Murray, Wallace, Dawson, O'Gara, Perry

Australia vs British and Irish Lions
First Test
The Gabba, Brisbane
June 30, 2001
Result: 13–29

Australia
Chris Latham, Andrew Walker, Daniel Herbert, Nathan Grey, Joe Roff, Stephen Larkham, George Gregan, George Smith,

Martin Johnson

Toutai Kefu, Owen Finegan, John Eales (c), David Giffin, Glenn Panoho, Jeremy Paul, Nick Stiles

Replacements:
Michael Foley, Ben Darwin, Matt Cockbain, David Lyons, Chris Whitaker, Elton Flatley, Matt Burke

British and Irish Lions
Perry, James, O'Driscoll, Henderson, Robinson, Wilkinson, Howley, Quinnell, Hill, Corry, Grewcock, Johnson (c), Vickery, Wood, Smith

Replacements:
Leonard, Bulloch, Charvis, Williams, Dawson, Healey, Balshaw

ACT Brumbies vs British and Irish Lions
Bruce Stadium, Canberra
July 3, 2001
Result: 28–30

ACT Brumbies
Mark Bartholomeusz, Damien McInally, Graeme Bond, James Holbeck, Willie Gordon, Pat Howard, Travis Hall, Des Tuivaii, Jim Williams (c), Peter Ryan, Dan Vickerman, Justin Harrison, Matt Weaver, Adam Freier, Angus Scott

Replacements:
David Palavi, Damien Drew, David Pusey, Radike Samo, Matt Henjak, Julian Huxley, Cameron Pither

British and Irish Lions

Balshaw, Cohen, Taylor, Gibbs, Healey, O'Gara, Dawson, Wallace, Corry, Williams, Murray, Davidson, Young (c), West, Morris

Replacements:

Leonard, Bulloch, Johnson, O'Kelly, Jenkins, James, Howe

Australia vs British and Irish Lions
Second Test
Colonial Stadium, Melbourne
July 7, 2001
Result: 35–14

Australia

Matt Burke, Andrew Walker, Daniel Herbert, Nathan Grey, Joe Roff, Stephen Larkham, George Gregan, George Smith, Toutai Kefu, Owen Finegan, John Eales (c), David Giffin, Rod Moore, Michael Foley, Nick Stiles

Replacements:

Brendan Cannon, Ben Darwin, Matt Cockbain, David Lyons, Chris Whitaker, Elton Flatley, Chris Latham

British and Irish Lions

Perry, James, O'Driscoll, Henderson, Robinson, Wilkinson, Howley, Quinnell, Back, Hill, Grewcock, Johnson (c), Vickery, Wood, Smith

Replacements:

Leonard, West, Corry, Williams, Dawson, Healey, Balshaw

Australia vs British and Irish Lions
Third Test
Olympic Stadium, Sydney
July 14, 2001
Result: 29–23

Australia

Matt Burke, Andrew Walker, Daniel Herbert, Nathan Grey, Joe Roff, Elton Flatley, George Gregan, George Smith, Toutai Kefu, Owen Finegan, John Eales (c), Justin Harrison, Rod Moore, Michael Foley, Nick Stiles

Replacements:

Brendan Cannon, Ben Darwin, Matt Cockbain, David Lyons, Chris Whitaker, James Holbeck, Chris Latham

British and Irish Lions

Perry, James, O'Driscoll, Henderson, Robinson, Wilkinson, Dawson, Quinnell, Back, Corry, Grewcock, Johnson (c), Vickery, Wood, Smith

Replacements:

Morris, West, Charvis, Williams, Nicol, O'Gara, Balshaw

Top points scorers:
72 – Jonny Wilkinson
50 – Jason Robinson
32 – Neil Jenkins
26 – Ronan O'Gara
21 – Matt Dawson

Top try-scorers:
10 – Jason Robinson
4 – Austin Healey, Rob Henderson, Dan Luger, Brian O'Driscoll, Scott Quinnell
3 – Neil Back, Colin Charvis, Dafydd James.

Most appearances (starts):
6 – Martin Corry, Danny Grewcock, Dafydd James, Brian O'Driscoll, Scott Quinnell, Jason Robinson, Phil Vickery, Keith Wood
5 – Neil Back, Rob Henderson, Martin Johnson, Matt Perry, Tom Smith, Jonny Wilkinson,

Most appearances (as substitute):
5 – Jason Leonard
4 – Iain Balshaw, Colin Charvis